Key individuals

"I've never lost a homicide case."
— Retired <u>Detective Lou Smit</u>

"I believe there's evidence of an intruder, and I believe people should still be looking for him. There's a dangerous guy out there."
— *<u>Retired</u> Detective Lou Smit*

Most of the 70+ names mentioned below occur in the continuing narrative, but a few [such as the Ramsey lawyers] do not and are added for reasons of completeness.

Many additional <u>key individuals</u> have been <u>left out</u> of the list [such as the <u>Grand Jury</u> members] for <u>reasons of efficacy</u>.

Family

1. <u>JonBenét Ramsey</u> [<u>deceased 1996, age 6</u>]

2. <u>JonBenét's father</u> <u>John Ramsey</u>, former CEO of <u>ACCESS GRAPHICS</u>[1], engineer, <u>pilot</u>, naval officer, <u>businessman</u>, <u>author</u>

3. <u>JonBenét's mother</u> <u>Patsy Ramsey</u>, former <u>Miss West Virginia</u> [<u>deceased</u> 2006, age 49]

---

1 A computer services company and a subsidiary of Lockheed Martin.

~ 3 ~

4. JonBenét's brother, Burke Ramsey

John Ramsey - Extended Family

5. JonBenét's half-sister - Elizabeth 'Beth' Pasch Ramsey [deceased 1992, age 22]

6. John Ramsey's first wife - Lucinda Pasch

7. JonBenét's older half-sister - Melinda Ramsey, sometimes resided in Ramsey family home.

8. JonBenét's older half-brother – John Andrew, resided in Ramsey family home, when not at college.

9. JonBenét's uncle and John Ramsey's brother – Jeff Ramsey

Patsy Ramsey - Extended Family

10. Patsy's mother – Nedra Paugh [deceased]

11. Patsy's father – Donald Paugh [deceased]

12. Patsy's younger sister – Pamela Paugh, former Miss West Virginia

Friends

13. Fleet Russell White, Jr., identified by John Ramsey as possible suspect

14. Priscilla Brown White, wife of Fleet and identified by John Ramsey as possible suspect

15. Fleet White III , son of Fleet and Priscilla, friend of Burke and identified by John Ramsey as possible suspect

16. Daphne White, daughter of Fleet and Priscilla and friend of JonBenét Ramsey

The Craven
SILENCE

2

By Nick van der Leek and Lisa Wilson

"I think that the grand jurors heard the evidence and came up with that conclusion and I would agree with their conclusion." — Former Boulder Detective <u>Jane Harmer</u>

"I recalled a favorite passage recently, Atticus Finch speaking to his daughter: 'Just remember that one thing does not abide by majority rule, Scout — it's your conscience.'" — Detective Steve Thomas, August 7, 1998 [excerpt from Thomas' <u>letter of resignation</u> to Boulder Police Sheriff Beckner]

Important Note to the Reader:

The #SHAKEDOWN books are unique. Throughout this book, the authors have provided hyperlinks to relevant resources including documents, photographs and videos to enhance your interactivity with the story. It is the authors' intention to take you on a thoughtful journey of discovery; one that not only encompasses the lives of the subject matter, and the insights drawn from them, but also your own.

Writing by Nick van der Leek is in black font.

Sections written by Lisa Wilson are rendered in blue font.

[WARNING: This book contains links to graphic images and content]

TABLE OF CONTENTS

Introduction

In *The Craven Silence* we used broad strokes to interrogate this case. In the final chapter of that narrative we chose to take a dark stairway and pulled on a silver thread that drew us away from the intruder narrative. We found ourselves facing the possibility of not just one of the Ramseys potentially being involved in little JonBenét's Christmas murder, but horrifically – *all*.

But is that plausible? How and why would three people keep secrets for each other, even [in Patsy's case perhaps] taking them to the grave? Without dealing with the merits of the case, this hardly seems likely. But that's not enough – we need to answer this question with confidence.

Before we deal with the Ramseys as bona fide murder suspects we need to do our due diligence – we need to probe the alternative theories thoroughly, and we need to follow the leads of some supposedly sterling investigative work that preceded ours.

In this narrative we will test another thread for its tensile strength. To get there we will investigate in more detail Lou Smit's mission to find justice for JonBenét as well as attempt to explain why he failed to do so.

At the same time, we will weave another thread throughout this narrative – the thread of child psychology – and see whether it leads us to the light of resolution. Please note, weaving a thread is not the same as *finding a thread*. But what we hope to achieve by approaching the narrative in this way is something no one has achieved thus far – we want to introduce a long thread and see if we can tie it to the thread that emerges in the basement by the conclusion of this narrative.

In terms of these narrative threads, what we want to determine is:

Can they be tied together?

Do they hold together?

Will what emerges be a golden thread shining with its own veracity from end to end?

If we are to solve this case we must once again cross our hearts and open our minds to curious things. We must fully experience what it is for a child to die under a Christmas Tree in Colorado if we are to find justice for JonBenét.

17. Glen Stine

18. Susan Stine, wife of Glen and identified as possible suspect

19. Doug Stine, son of Glen and Susan, friend of Burke and identified as possible suspect

20. Mike Archuleta, John Ramsey's pilot and friend

21. Pam Archuleta, [refers to herself as "Pam Barday" in Dateline documentary] Mike's ex-wife and friend of Patsy

22. Stewart Walker, friend of the Ramseys

23. Roxanne Walker, friend of the Ramseys

24. Bill McReynolds, Santa, identified as possible suspect [deceased]

25. Janet McReynolds, Santa's wife and identified as possible suspect

26. Rev. Rolland [Rol] Hoverstock, Episcopal minister in Boulder, Ramsey's pastor

27. Leslie Durgin, Mayor of Boulder

28. Jay "Pasta" Elowsky, John Ramsey's business associate, owner of Pasta Jay's

29. Judith Phillips, family photographer and long-time friend of Patsy [sold portraits of JonBenét after her death to the media without Patsy's consent]

Neighbors

30. Joe Barnhill, took care of JonBenét's dogs

31. Betty Barnhill, wife of Joe [deceased]

32. Glenn Meyer, boarded with the Barnhills

33. Luther and Melody Stanton, neighbors and ear witnesses

34. Diane Brumfitt, neighbor and school counselor
35. Stephen Miles, neighbor who lived 6 blocks away and identified as possible suspect by John Ramsey

Ramsey Case Prosecution

36. Alex Hunter, Boulder District Attorney
37. Andrew "Lou" Smit, Retired detective [deceased 2010]
38. Pete Hofstrom, Assistant District Attorney and alleged Ramsey associate
39. Michael Kane, Deputy Boulder District Attorney
40. Bill Wise, First Assistant District Attorney
41. James Kolar, Investigator for Boulder District Attorney's office [2005-2006], wrote a book about the case and appeared in CBS documentary
42. Judge Robert Lowenbach, allowed release of Grand Jury indictments in October 2013

Boulder Law Enforcement

43. Rick French, Boulder Police Officer and the first policeman to arrive at the scene at approximately 06:00
44. Steve Thomas, Former Boulder Police Department Detective and author
45. Linda Arndt, Former Detective and one of first officers at the scene
46. Mark Beckner, Boulder Police Chief
47. Tom Koby, Retired Boulder Police Chief
48. Tom Wickman, Boulder Police Detective

49. Jane Harmer, Boulder Police Detective

50. Thomas Haney, Boulder Police Detective, conducted June 1998 interrogation of Patsy Ramsey

51. Trip DeMuth, former Boulder prosecutor, conducted June 1998 interrogation of Patsy Ramsey. Left his career at Boulder DA in September 2000 to work for Mike Bynum.

Ramsey Lawyers

52. Mike Bynum, Ramsey defense "architect"

53. Patrick J. Burke

54. Hugh Patrick Furman

55. James K. Jenkins

56. Harold Haddon

57. Grady Bryan Morgan

58. Lin Wood , threatened to sue CBS on 21 September for their allegations against Burke Ramsey in *The Case Of: JonBenét Ramsey*

Miscellaneous

59. David S. Sanderton, a Boulder-based criminal defense and civil rights attorney, Republican candidate for Boulder County District Attorney

60. JonBenét's pediatrician Dr. Francesco Beuf

61. Jay Pettipeace, House painter

62. Mervin Pugh, wife of Linda Hoffman Pugh, Ramsey handyman, alcoholic, and identified as possible suspect

63. Linda Hoffman Pugh, Ramsey housekeeper, Mervin's wife, and

identified by Patsy as possible suspect

64. Linda Wilcox, Ramsey housekeeper

65. Shirley Brady, Ramsey nanny

66. Susan Savage, Ramsey nanny

67. Kristine Griffin, JonBenét's babysitter

68. Pamela Griffin, JonBenét's costume designer

69. Randy Simons, JonBenét's photographer

70. Jeff Merrick, Former Ramsey friend and employee at Access Graphics, and identified as possible suspect

71. Paula Woodward, Emmy-award winning author featured in A&E documentary

72. Jim Clemente, investigator in CBS documentary

73. Laura Richards, investigator in CBS documentary

74. Beth Karas, former New York prosecutor, appeared in Investigation Discovery documentary

75. Diane Dimond, television journalist and reporter, appeared in Investigation Discovery documentary, covered JonBenét Ramsey case from start to finish

76. John Mark Karr, confessed to the crime in August 2006 [False confession]

77. Charlie Brennan, Daily Camera reporter, filed a lawsuit on behalf of the Reporters Committee for Freedom of the Press for the release of Grand Jury Indictments, and won

STREETLAMPS

"Life is not a series of gig lamps symmetrically arranged; <u>life is a luminous halo</u>, a semi-transparent envelope surrounding us from the beginning of consciousness to the end." —Virginia Woolf

Lessons in Child Psychology #1

The Dutch-descended <u>Afrikaners</u> of <u>South Africa</u> have a famous saying: *dis die makste hond wat die seerste byt* and a derivative of that: *eie hond byt die seerste.*

The literal translation for these idioms: <u>*the tamest dog's*</u> *bite is the worst* and *when your own dog bites you, it hurts the most.*

The literal translation doesn't really cut to the bone though. What both of these expressions are chewing on has nothing to do with dogs; rather it's the idea of a shy, understated person tending to be the most dangerous. And further: when someone very close to you hurts you unexpectedly, the pain is infinitely worse because there is real betrayal. Betrayal is a gentle word for treachery and treachery is the antecedent to sedition.

If we are <u>to find a golden strand</u> of glowing <u>psychological tinsel woven through</u> that <u>inexplicable</u> Christmas Tree of 1996, we're going to have to bring out the big guns. <u>If we wish to ascend</u> to <u>the star that illuminates</u> from <u>the top of the Tree</u>, we're going to need the best psychology in the business.

Meet Ernest Becker, a Pulitzer Prize winning <u>anthropologist</u>. Simply put, <u>Becker is superb</u> in the science of human beings. That science extends not only to an understanding of how societies function, but also the units of society, the cogs of family and the child that belongs to all of this.

Can Becker really shed any light on what it was like – at a psychological level – to be Burke on that tragic Christmas Day? Can Becker show us what was going on, in intimate detail, between Burke and JonBenét and between the children and their parents? Is Becker up to this; is his psychology on our side? Is it? Are you on our side, Mr Becker?

*In childhood we see the struggle for self-esteem at its least **disguised**. The child is **unashamed** about what he needs and wants most. His whole organism shouts the claims of his natural **narcissism**. And this claim can make childhood hellish for the adults concerned, especially when there are several children **competing** at once for the prerogatives of limitless self-extension, what we might call "cosmic **significance**."* — Ernest Becker[2]

In this short paragraph five keywords blink out at us like Christmas lights:

- Disguise
- Shame
- Narcissism
- Competition
- Significance

To what degree do these concepts have a bearing on the Ramsey children, or their parents, if any? Mr Becker?

The term ["cosmic significance"] is not to be taken lightly, because that is where our discussion is leading. — Ernest Becker

Here Becker offers us a vital clue. Of the five keywords, only one points the way to our starry destination atop the Christmas Tree. The star at the top of the Tree speaks to us about *Significance*.

---

2 *Denial of Death*, 1973.

We like to speak about "sibling rivalry," as though it were some kind of by-product of growing up, a bit of competitiveness and selfishness of children who have been spoiled, who haven't yet grown into a generous social nature. But it is too all-absorbing and relentless to be an aberration, it expresses the heart of the creature. — Ernest Becker

And that is exactly what we're after.

…the desire to stand out, to be the one in creation. When you combine natural narcissism with the basic need for self-esteem, you create a creature who has to feel himself an object of primary value: first in the universe, representing in himself all of life. — Ernest Becker

It is a curious thing, a Christmas Tree. Isn't it? We are using the Tree as our totem in this narrative, and what is a Tree, especially a Christmas Tree, but an object of primary value. It is around the feet of the shining Tree that Christmas gifts are placed; as a sort of modern iteration, a contemporary reimagining of the Tree of Life, just that the fruits have become metal and mechanical, and wrapped in glittering veneers.

The Tree is the thing that stands out to represent Christmas itself, perhaps even more than Santa Claus. The Tree is Santa's destination, and also the destination for the family and the individual at Christmas. The Christmas Tree is a modern symbol for God, and the birth of the Christian God. But is this symbolism authentic?

And what happens when a creature finds himself suddenly usurped, no longer an object of primary value – that is no longer the chief actor in his own drama – but suddenly and unceremoniously relegated to a secondary character playing a supporting role within his own *mythos*?

This is the reason for the daily and usually excruciating struggle with siblings: the child cannot allow himself to be second-best or devalued, much less left out. — Ernest Becker

Well of course, but what more than this? <u>Where does this lead us</u> up the Tree? And how do we link this cosmic significance stuff to the less esoteric idea of a fawning dog biting the hand that feeds it, or the cloying child suddenly lashing out at his usurper, and worse?

Smit

"I believe when this case first started, it did look like the Ramseys did it." — <u>Detective Lou Smit</u>

Three months after six-year-old JonBenét Ramsey's murder, and only a few weeks shy of his own 62nd birthday, Lou Smit climbed into his camper van and headed to Boulder.

Smit had been summoned by the Boulder District Attorney, <u>Alex Hunter</u>. In Hunter's opinion, Smit was one of Colorado's best detectives, so much so that Hunter selected Smit even though Smit had recently retired.

Sitting behind the wheel, starting another case, Smit must have felt the slippage of time. It didn't seem so long ago when he'd signed up for his first day at Colorado Springs Police Department. That was 1966, just 30 years earlier, 30 years that had trickled away. Even though he'd retired in 1996, the detective wanted to end on a high note, and this was his chance.

Smit, warmed by Hunter's <u>valorizing</u> invitation, followed the I-25 North, a 90 minute 100 mile trek from his home in Colorado Springs. In other words, Smit didn't have to go far.

But in another sense of course, Smit would never complete this journey. On that first bright day on the road, the chilling crime that had overtaken Boulder in the Christmas of 1996 must have seemed easily within reach. Time and tide would prove otherwise, as this rare interview with *CNN's* Larry King proves.

From cnn.com [May 28th, 2001]:

LARRY KING, HOST: *Tonight, it's one of the most sensational unsolved crimes in U.S. history: Who brutally killed JonBenét Ramsey in her own home on Christmas night, 1996? Her parents, John and Patsy Ramsey, remain under what authorities call an umbrella of suspicion. But a renowned detective called in to work the case says the evidence indicates that an intruder committed the terrible deed.*

As the I-25 takes him over Monument Hill mountain pass [7,352 feet/2,241 meters], Smit thinks back to how serendipitously things came to him as a detective.

From Wikipedia:

Having tried various businesses and failing, Smit prayed for a solution and saw as an answer from God a call he received from a cousin who served on the Colorado Springs Department suggesting that he apply to serve.

That's how Smit became a cop. God called him. In March 1997 Hunter called him. We'll deal with Hunter's motives in selecting Smit rather than someone younger, or someone living nearer – for example in Denver – in a forthcoming chapter. We'll also get back to Smit in his own words speaking to Larry. But before we do, we need to sow a seed. We need to see what impact Smit's faith had on his reasoning. Was it positive? Was it negative? Was it something else?

Why was it, a man with such impeccable credentials, failed to solve this crime?

From <u>denverpost.com</u>:

Smit's faith in God has always been a top priority for the detective, who for years sat in the third row at the Cragmor Christian Reform Church listening to his wife play the organ before she died several years ago.

In the 1960s, after his bottled-gas and tree-cutting businesses both failed, Smit got on his knees and prayerfully "gave it all he got," his daughter Cindy Marra said.

A few weeks later, a cousin who worked at the Colorado Springs Police Department called and asked him to apply. He saw that as an answer from God.

By the end of this section we'll resolve the relevance of Smit's Christianity to the unsolved Ramsey case. I want to look at Smit not as some gifted vigilante, but as a man.

In March 1997 he's just one man in a camper driving on a busy highway through the rural and hilly areas east of the Rocky Mountains. From Castle Rock, Smit negotiates the partial beltway into Denver and a toll road skirting Centennial Airport and Denver International Airport. Perhaps airplanes float overhead. Perhaps Smit sees them, perhaps he doesn't. Perhaps on his way to Boulder he prays for JonBenét, prays for guidance.

From <u>denverpost.com</u>:

*"**His faith was the most important thing to him**. It was a quiet thing. He wouldn't beat anybody over the head with it," Marra said. **Prayers were part of his investigative routine.***

*"The very first thing I would ever do is stop about a quarter- block away and say a prayer," he said. "**God answered my prayers**."*

Of the 200-plus cases Smit investigated and turned over to prosecutors for formal charges, all of them led to convictions, he said. "I've never lost a homicide case," Smit said.

*Smit acknowledged that he has been criticized for praying with murder suspects, but he said **the prayers helped him establish a rapport with them**.*

Smit's driving on what's considered part of <u>the unofficial Pan-American Highway</u>, alongside the great sweep of The Rockies on his left. Thawing snow fuels <u>glittering mountain streams</u> – the <u>antecedents to the South Platte</u> – as he makes his way north, further and further, deeper and deeper through the first tapestries of spring.

The gleaming double and triple-lane ribbons of tar skirting the high mountains channel his camper almost in a straight line to an unfathomable destination nestled beneath towering precipices of rock. He's headed to a place called Boulder, but the word itself has another meaning.

Bolder – daring, valiant, unflinching, audacious, intrepid

Was that how Lou Smit saw himself taking this case?

But in a real sense, with each mile Smit went north, he was travelling backwards through time; with each turn of the engine, with every white line passing beneath him, he was undoing his impeccable credentials.

Each mile north was taking him further and further back, unwinding the clockwork of the seasons to colder weather, from crystal clear sunshine to murky darkness, from the warm chocolaty promises of Easter eggs and resurrection – to death. Soon, unexpectedly, Smit would be introduced to a seemingly simple case. Its simplicity was a trap…it lured him into a spur-of-the-moment investigation that would ultimately overwhelm him until his own death did the same.

Smit enters the Arapahoe County line and passes street names like Dry Creek Road and Belleview Avenue, places with names like Aurora and the University of Denver. Then Smit continues up north through

Adams County and the I-76 and I-270 interchanges. And then he turns onto the Denver-Boulder Turnpike. The triangle-shaped interchange is one of America's more complex junctions, and prone to malfunction.

From cnn.com [May 28th, 2001]:

Lou Smit, Colorado homicide cop for more than 30 years, joins us for a compelling hour next on LARRY KING LIVE...he'll be with us for the full hour – Lou Smit, the renowned Colorado detective who has investigated more than 200 homicides in 33 years.

Three months after the 1996 killing of JonBenét, he came out of retirement at the request of the Boulder County DA to help investigate the crime, and then a year-and-a-half later resigned in frustration. **After a long silence, he has gone public with his views. Why have you gone public?**

SMIT: *Well, Larry, it's been almost – it's been a little over four years. It's time that someone came forward and told another side of the story.*

That silence Smit was referring to was 15 years ago. It was a silence that engulfed him when he drove into the preternatural calm of Boulder. Meanwhile, the real world seemed to go on north, following the I-25 through shimmering grassland and fertile farms. The Front Range and a tapestry of lakes opened up, with the belch of backed up trucks jamming the road. If this was the world enveloping Boulder, Boulder itself pretended to be apart from it, a republic with its own laws, its own invisible congestions, its own unseen traffic interchanges. It was into this world that Smit ventured, on a wing and a prayer.

Death of Innocence

*"No, this is not a paid job. I'm doing it mainly
because I do want to seek the truth in this case."*
— Lou Smit, May 28, 2001 Larry King Live

*"Perhaps, the kidnapper is also a sadistic pedophile,
perhaps that was his intent all along. I don't know
what was in the mind of the killer. All I know is
that the killer fantasized making this garrotte in his
mind. He fantasized putting this around JonBenét's
neck. He had to put a handle on this garrotte. He
had to put a noose on this garrotte. He had to put
it around JonBenét's neck, probably while she was
still bound and had duct tape on her mouth. This is
a fantasy in the mind of the killer. Why he did this,
inside the house, I don't know. Perhaps he don't have
a place to take JonBenét. Perhaps he couldn't get her
out of the house."* — Lou Smit, May 28, 2001 Larry
King Live

In part one of the <u>A&E</u> documentary *The Killing of JonBenét – The Truth Uncovered* Lou is introduced as the star of the show at rough-ly the 34-minute mark. Smit, we're told, was chosen over and above more than 80 other candidates. To the untrained mind, this may seem a harmless one-dimensional piece of information – little more than a testament to Smit's CV and Hunter's fastidiousness. What more than that?

Well, we believe there's a *lot* more.

I like Lou Smit. I think he's a good and decent fellow. I think he was a supremely dedicated detective, a hard worker, a man of integrity. But he was not the right man to solve the JonBenét case. Instead, he was perhaps the right man *not* to solve it.

By that I don't mean that Smit didn't sincerely try his level best, or didn't make an honest effort. I'm certain he did on both counts. What I mean is…well, I wonder whether Hunter's choice of Smit was more a *strategic selection* than a compliment to Smit. I wonder whether Hunter chose Smit to suit a particular set of circumstances, and the outcome he was gunning for, rather than gambling that Smit would actually solve the case on its own terms.

I'll explain my reasoning further at the conclusion of this chapter.

Meanwhile, on that bright day in March, Smit likely felt nothing less than the warm glow of Hunter's compliment – *Hunter had chosen him*. Hunter had faith that Smit could work his magic where others had failed.

From <u>cnn.com</u> [May 28th, 2001]:

KING: *But all those years – before we get to that –* **that you stayed silent** *and we (UNINTELLIGIBLE) to you during that time, because people knew that while you quit and you were angry and feeling that* *there was someone else who did it and that the Ramseys were being unfairly accused, **why didn't you come forward sooner?***

SMIT: *Well, Larry, I really wasn't angry when I quit. I was – when I quit, I believed that **the law enforcement agency was going to probably indict John and Patsy Ramsey. That's not the way the case told me to go. I didn't want to be part of perhaps putting an innocent person in jail.***

*Since I left, I had been working the case more or less on my own. There are other people involved in looking at the intruder side of the story. I'm just not doing this myself. **I have worked with the Ramsey investigators** for the past 2 1/2 years.*

KING: *Have you been paid?*

SMIT: *No. No, this is not a paid job. I'm doing it mainly because I do want to seek the truth in this case. I believe that there is evidence pointing toward an intruder, strong, credible evidence. And I believe that if law enforcement and others look carefully at the case, we have a good chance of catching the killer.*

KING: *Is there also, honestly, strong, credible evidence the other way?*

SMIT: *I don't believe there's strong, credible evidence the other way at all. If it's not the Ramseys, then it's an intruder. If there is no intruder, then it has to be the Ramseys.*

I see very little credible evidence that John or Patsy Ramsey murdered their daughter.

Lou Smit has some solid ideas, useful observations and strong insights into this case. But I wonder whether Smit was really the best candidate for the subtleties of this case. For a guy who prayed to be a cop, and bopped his own head to meet a height requirement [more on that below], I don't get a sense of either a professional sleuth or a particularly intelligent one. I do get a sense of a good man, a blue collar guy with a big heart.

I'm afraid this case needed someone with a strong mind to solve, not a big heart. But let's play devil's advocate for the moment, and see where this thinking leads us. Why indeed could it not be the Ramseys who murdered their daughter?

From news.com.au:

For this eminently respectable family to be behind JonBenét's murder requires some mental gymnastics. While Mrs Ramsey's stage mother role struck many people as deeply strange at the time, pageant kids are now a familiar [phenomenon], whatever we may think of them.

The Ramseys appear to have deeply loved their child. They had no history of child abuse or domestic violence, which might be expected if either had really snapped and killed the little girl.

For many lay readers, the above paragraphs are entirely plausible, aren't they? God and the Devil are in the details. As much as parents might love their children and not abuse them, there's a grey area that's neither love nor abuse – neglect. There is clearly some history of trauma or tension in the bedwetting and defecation behaviors of both children, circumstances most journalists making cursory flybys of the case tend to miss. The question is: did Smit miss these red flags too?

From news.com.au:

If they covered up for Burke, they would have had to tie a nylon cord tightly around JonBenét's neck and calmly stage a crime scene in the basement. Mrs Ramsey would have had to painstakingly write a two-and-a-half page Ransom Note in handwriting so different to her own that it has never been definitely matched.

Then they would have had to spend years crying and lying to TV cameras and teaching their child to lie, too. All this when the boy was too young to go to prison in the state anyway.

JonBenét was found with unknown DNA in her underwear and abrasions to the vagina, leading many to conclude she was sexually assaulted. In 2008, then-District Attorney Mary Lacy exonerated the family when their DNA did not match and issued an apology.

I'm not sure how hard it would be to stage a crime scene over the course of 7 hours. And what after all is so hard about tying pieces of nylon on someone's hand? How hard is it to write a note if one has a degree in journalism? Is it really so surprising that a note might be written [and rehearsed] by someone heavily involved in pageants, which are all about rehearsals? And for all the sections of handwriting that don't match, what about those that do?

The sexual assault theory is arguably as borderline as the Ransom Note being in Patsy's handwriting. In my view the sexual assault is overblown and the Ransom Note grossly underestimated. JonBenét was not raped, and sexual injury absolutely pales in comparison to the bludgeoning and strangling. This begs the question – would a paedophile wish to brutally damage JonBenét's head and throat but leave her genitals almost completely untouched? In addition, would a paedophile dress her after the sexual abuse, and then cover her in her favorite blanket? If the paedophile is the Ransom Note writer [apparently if Patsy didn't write it, the intruder did] then why is there nothing in the Ransom Note about paedophilia?

Interestingly, neither the Ramsey parents believe a paedophile is involved [this would make them indirectly culpable, for allowing their daughter to appear in pageants]. John Ramsey's view is that the intruder was a jealous or envious business colleague, someone who had seen how much money he'd made in the local news media.

Burke on the other hand has a fairly offhand view that the intruder might be "some paedophile". It's interesting that father and son can't agree on a theory either, but troubling that Smit seems to think the intruder is a paedophile, yet has zero commentary on the Ransom Note in that context.

Smit has mentioned separately that he doesn't think a murderer would be able to write the note after the act, thus exonerating Patsy. Of course in this assessment Smit seems to fail to take into account other possibilities – such as Burke committing the original act, and Patsy writing the note. Fact is whoever wrote the note took several stabs at it, which confirms Smit's contention that a murderer wouldn't be able to write the note satisfactorily. What's slippery on Smit's part is that I think he thinks Patsy did write the note, but is nevertheless innocent.

When Smit says - *I don't know what was in the mind of the killer.… Why he did this, inside the house, I don't know* – he betrays not only his lack of sophistication, but also a lack of effort to interrogate the psychology. To not know this, to not have a carefully considered theory four years after the fact, is poor investigative form.

From cnn.com [May 28th, 2001]:

KING: *Now, Lou, you know that police department very well.*

SMIT: *Yes.*

KING: *What's taking so long?*

SMIT: *Perhaps they've been going the wrong way for four years. I think early on in the investigation I…told them, are you sure you're going the right way?*

I believe that four years later, with some of the most intense investigation that this country has ever seen, that they still haven't been able to put together a case. This has been looked at by the grand jury for 13 months. It is an extremely intensive investigation into the family.

KING: *Into the family. So when a detective gets a case – just so we understand, then we're going to go through all this – does he start with any perception or does a good detective begin with "I don't know, I want to find out"?*

Great question from Larry. Do you notice Larry is gravitating back to the Ramseys did it, but he's aware this isn't Smit's view at all? Larry's trying to find out whether Smit has some sort of prejudice, some sort of tunnel vision. As we're about to see, I don't think Smit himself is aware of it, but Larry may be onto something…

From cnn.com [May 28th, 2001]:

SMIT: *Yes, that's normally the way that a detective goes into it.*

KING: *And is that what you did?*

SMIT: *Yes, I did. I felt, perhaps at first, **I leaned toward the parents doing it,** only because of what I had read and what I had seen on television. But as I got into the case, **I started seeing red flags,** which started pointing the other way. And I did bring that up to the police department and also to the district attorney's office.*

KING: *And what, Lou, did they say?*

SMIT: *They more or less were focused on the Ramseys.*

KING: *And they told you that?*

SMIT: *Yes. In so many ways they told me that.*

"In so many ways" really colors the sense of fatigue and frustration, doesn't it?

Lou Smit is more diminutive than he appears on television. At 5 foot 9 inches Smit was too short for the Colorado Springs Police Department minimum height [5 foot 10]. His cousin hit him on the top of his head with a stick, the resulting bump allowed Smit to meet the minimum height.

From cnn.com [May 28th, 2001]:

SMIT: *The investigation was focused toward the Ramseys.* **There was no one that was really looking hard at the intruder side of the story.**

Just you Lou. It's a pity Larry didn't press Smit on those "red flags", although we have an idea what they are.

1. Smit saying he saw "no snow" on the photographs of the walkways surrounding the Ramsey residence, ergo the claim of "no footprints in snow" becomes neutralised. In *The Craven Silence* we interrogated just how asinine this argument is, and we'll deal with it again – via Dr Phil's PR on the same topic – in this narrative.

2. The "broken basement window"[3] seemed to Smit a huge banner showing where an intruder gained access.

3. The suitcase below the basement window was another huge banner screaming INTRUDER ALERT to Smit

From cnn.com [May 28th, 2001]:

KING: *Therefore, if you're right and no one is looking for the intruder and the Ramseys didn't do it and they don't have any information that can bring an indictment, this is never going to be solved.*

SMIT: *Well, Larry, I don't* **believe** *that. I* **believe** *that any case can be solved.* **I believe...**

KING: *But you have to be looking, though, don't you?*

SMIT: *Yes, we have to be looking, and I think there are some of us that are looking, and I think that there are others who are willing to look if they can receive the right information. There is evidence out there that points at an intruder.*

---

3 John Ramsey added he'd broken the window himself in August 1996 to gain access.

What we want to know is whether Smit spontaneously stumbled on the intruder theory, or whether Hunter nudged him in that direction. Of course the Ramsey's would be doing their own nudging too, so one can intuit some combination of these factors.

From cnn.com [May 28th, 2001]:

KING: *And we're going to go through this with you, but you said the Ramseys had no motive that you could find.*

SMIT: *There is...*

KING: *What was the intruder's motive?*

SMIT: *The intruder's motive might be just as it seems. I've worked many homicide cases, and* **the crime normally is as it seems**, *Larry. Don't make it complicated. If this is initially portrayed as a kidnapping and a murder, don't try to make it into something else. A Ransom Note was written.* **Somebody** *came into the Ramsey home, and they had with them duct tape.* **They had** *with them a rope.* **They had** *with them a stun gun.* **They had** *intended to do something that night.*

The victim was JonBenét. It could have just as well been Burke. Someone...

KING: *The other -- the son, the brother.*

SMIT: *Yeah, the brother. Someone came into the Ramsey house with a purpose in mind and left behind a Ransom Note.*

This is bizarre from Smit, quite frankly. Smit seems to see a crime "portrayed" as a kidnapping and a murder as exactly that. Again, I can't help wondering whether Smit – for all his gifts as a detective – was simply too unsophisticated for the subtleties of this case.

It's also odd how he changes tack from a single intruder [somebody] to numerous intruders [they].

From cnn.com [May 28th, 2001]:

KING: *Why would a kidnapper kill the person they're going to kidnap at the scene while writing a Ransom Note? You're not going to get any money that way.*

SMIT: *That's true.* **I don't know what happened** *during the evening to change this person's mind.*

For someone who dedicated four years to this case, there's really no excuse for not having a hypothesis to back your theory. Notice Smit goes into too little or no detail about the Ransom Note – either who wrote it, or when it was written or even discussion around the contents of the note. The fact that Smit can't explain how it was a botched kidnapping is devastating to his case. Instead, he offers the following defense.

From cnn.com [May 28th, 2001]:

SMIT: *But the opposite is also true. If people believe that the Ramseys for some reason inadvertently killed JonBenét, staged this massive cover-up to make it look like a kidnapping, wrote a 2 1/2 page Ransom Note, brutally garrotted their daughter, and then did not bring her body out of the house,* **<u>no one can answer</u> that question either**.

Well <u>I'm not sure that's true Lou</u>.

For the detective who'd "never lost" a homicide case, the JonBenét Ramsey case was Lou Smit's Titanic. Lou Smit turned the case of the murdered six year old girl into his life's work. Even after Smit's interview with Larry King [timed to coincide with release of the <u>Ramsey's first book</u>], Smit continued to work at solving the case independently. Had he solved it, Lou would have ended his career with a case to crown his legacy in glory. The thing is, <u>he didn't</u>.

Boulder's Finest

"The person I see doing this is a very vicious, brutal criminal, perhaps a sadistic pedophile."[4] — <u>Lou Smit</u> to CNN, May 28th, 2001

By outsourcing Smit, Hunter pulled off a major coup. First of all, he had a detective who – since he was retired – had little stake in the Boulder Police Department, and thus was free to second guess their investigation in order to distinguish himself. How surprising would it be if Hunter called Smit into his office on his first day on the job and told him, "Lou, we got a problem here. The guys are on the wrong track. We need you to set 'em straight…"

Once Smit figured out the cops were investigating the Ramseys, it was up to him – it was kind've his mandate, wasn't it? – to come up with a better theory. And of course when you're looking for an alternative explanation, when that's your only option, you tend to find one. But, as with so much in the JonBenét case, there's more to it than that. Smit's beliefs for starters.

---

4 <u>Bob Whitson echoed Smit's profile of</u> the intruder as a "sadistic paedophile". Whitson was also the detective in charge of the crime scene on the morning of December 26th, who then left the scene in the hands of the inexperienced liaison officer Linda Arndt. Arndt was subsequently permitted to interview the Ramsey's at length on the 27th. No further interviews with the police were conducted until the end of April the following year.

From <u>cnn.com</u> [May 28th, 2001]:

KING: *Give us your theory. Take us through. What do you think happened?*

SMIT: *I believe that sometime during December 25th, 1996.*

KING: *Christmas night.*

SMIT: *Christmas night –* **someone** *got into the house of John and Patsy Ramsey. I believe there is some evidence to suggest strongly that they may have come in <u>through a basement window</u>.*

Again there's the mixing up of a singular intruder with more than one. This might just be Smit's way of talking, but it may also show a guy who's far from sure of his own case.

From <u>cnn.com</u> [May 28th, 2001]:

KING: *A window. Was that <u>window open</u> when they investigated it?*

SMIT: *Yes. When John Ramsey had first seen the window...Now, later on, I believe that it was noted that this window may have been opened even by John Ramsey and Fleet White. But what that window did show us, when we first seen it, was that entry could have been made there. There was <u>a scuff mark</u> down the wall. There was leaves and debris on the floor, directly below that open window.*

Here Lou seems to be embellishing a tad. Leaves and debris on the floor? Really? <u>Where?</u>

From <u>cnn.com</u> [May 28th, 2001]:

SMIT: *And when we looked at photographs of the <u>window well that leads into that window</u>, we've also seen evidence of recent disturbance. There is also <u>foliage under the grate</u>...which would indicate that someone may have opened and shut the grate. There is also disturbance on <u>the windowsill of the middle window</u> only....*

KING: *Lou, if it is, though, a cover-up, couldn't Mr. Ramsey or someone have gone out and done all those things?*

Larry King isn't convinced; neither are we. Compare all of this wishy-washyness to the useful detail we get from the Ransom Note. That's the criminal's calling card, providing insight into the personality and identity of the criminal, but Smit is more interested in photographs of leaves. How does he respond to Larry's query on whether John is involved in a cover-up?

From cnn.com [May 28th, 2001]:

SMIT: *Sure, anything is possible. But he would have had to go out, and lift the grate, go through window well; he would have had to open the window, leaving perhaps finger marks on the window itself. There is also another window that leads into that basement where it also shows recent disturbance, as if someone may have tried to get in that window.*

KING: *No prints on the window?*

SMIT: *No prints that we know of on the window.*

I'm not sure how Smit's argument here makes sense. Someone involved in a cover up wouldn't leave prints, especially not when they have the run of their own home for hours to make sure no evidence is left behind.

I also don't follow Smit's contention that John would have to go outside to lift the grate. The grate may have been opened; it may also have been opened by the police. Or it may not have been opened at all.

The single speck of glass may have been dislodged when the staging occurred, by the simple act of opening an already broken window. Taking this further, that there are not more pieces of glass scattered inside and outside [remember the intruder went in and out – supposedly – the same way], or blood or DNA on the jagged shards of glass, beggars belief. Instead there are old spider webs wafting in the corner of the broken window.

Something else Smit doesn't address is who would know about the broken basement window, and be able to see it, and navigate through it at night?

From cnn.com [May 28th, 2001]:

KING: *All right, then we leave – all right, so that leads us to one thing, the intruder comes in through the window. Then, I remember you are telling me about a suitcase.*

SMIT: *Yes, and that is why it strongly suggests that this was very recent. That suitcase.*

KING: *There, we see it.*

SMIT: *According to John Ramsey, that suitcase – and also according to the housekeeper – was not underneath that window prior to that night. **John Ramsey said that that is not where suitcases are normally kept.***

No shit Sherlock. Even Smit has to concede the broken window could have been broken, and even open, for weeks, and if not, then possibly staged. Suddenly the addition of the suitcase renders this hypothesis moot to Smit. While the suitcase gives a real kick to the imagination, especially the idea of smuggling a child within it, this creative license breaks down when one considers that the suitcase is left behind, and also, it's not empty. Also, how could someone entering the house from the outside have left the suitcase below the window, to allow ease of entry? Besides all this, how could someone using the suitcase as a step on the way out, then be able to retrieve it at an extreme downward angle with someone in it?

And yet for Smit the suitcase is virtually a smoking gun. No, it's not.

From cnn.com [May 28th, 2001]:

SMIT: *The position of that suitcase when it was first observed there, by Fleet White, was that it was directly against the wall, directly underneath that open window. There is evidence on top of that suitcase, **a very small tiny pea-sized piece of glass** which could have come off the shoe of the intruder.*

*There is also what appears to be a disturbance on the top of that suitcase, as if someone may have stood on it at some particular point. **That suitcase is very significant**, because it does allow easier egress from that basement through that window.*

KING: *So, your theory is, the intruder brought the suitcase? Opened the window and put suitcase down to step on it?*

SMIT: **The suitcase was in the house. It does belong to John Andrew.**

But even on this obvious point, Smit has to concede, the suitcase – like literally everything in the crime scene – comes from inside the house. Literally nothing, except arguably the possible manufacturing process DNA [found on JonBenét's underpants], has come from outside the house. Yet Smit sees an intruder lurking around every corner supposedly.

From thefederalist.com:

Every item involved in killing JonBenét was found inside the house, including the pad and pen used to write the "Ransom Note," the broken paintbrush, duct tape, rope and ligature used to pose the girl (police had evidence that Patsy probably purchased the latter two items from a hardware store earlier that month) and the flashlight (the likely murder weapon).

This was a pivotal fact. The question investigators kept asking was: What kind of sophisticated, highly motivated sexual predator and would-be kidnapper breaks into a house planning an abduction and rape of a young girl without bringing a single tool of the trade with him?

Then again, what kind of highly motivated sexual predator and would-be kidnapper would feel comfortable hanging around a house long enough to write a three-page Ransom Note after he'd just murdered a screaming child (neighbors told police they heard a scream, but no one in the house did, allegedly)? If the perpetrator had enough time to write a note at the home, he had enough time to move JonBenét's body somewhere else.

It seems when Smit came up against these psychological dead-ends he merely shrugged and felt he couldn't pretend to understand the criminal mind. Sorry but that's a cop-out. And it's for this reason that the allegations around the Ramseys held substance, because Smit's counter-narrative was so poorly conceived, and virtually indefensible.

From thefederalist.com:

*Even more importantly, why would [the intruder] stick around to write a Ransom Note when the prospect of deriving any money from the crime had already been lost? The only reasonable conclusion, according to an FBI report—and **almost everyone [besides Smit] agreed the Ransom Note was written after the murder**; the perpetrator could have brought one along if he had planned a kidnapping—was that the note had been left behind in an attempt to hide the killer's identity and motive.*

Meanwhile, Larry's playing along with Lou's version of events.

From cnn.com [May 28th, 2001]:

KING: *So, the intruder had to jump in through the window?*

SMIT: *The intruder had to come in through the window.*

KING: *He used the suitcase to get out.*

SMIT: *Yes. It would make it much easier to get out of that basement.*

KING: *Conversely, the Ramseys could have put the suitcase there.*

SMIT: *Absolutely. That could be.*

See how Larry keeps second-guessing Lou? Now note the long drawn out answer Smit gives to validate his expert opinion.

From cnn.com [May 28th, 2001]:

SMIT: *One thing, though, Larry, that I think that should be borne in mind here, the Ramseys have no history whatsoever of any type of criminal activity. They have – there is nothing to even suggest that they would entertain those thoughts, as far as being able to elaborately stage a crime like this.*

This narrative will lay part of the ground work to show that there is a history not only of criminal negligence, but also abuse. Abuse is not such a rare or scandalous thing, rather it's disturbingly common.

Is there a reason Smit was unable to fathom any history of either abuse or neglect in the Ramsey's behavior? Was something blinding him despite his apparently sincere searching through the shadows for clues? And if there was a blindness, did it infect his entire investigation, from top to toe to the detriment of many, none more so than JonBenét herself?

Smit on the Ransom Note

"Whoever killed JonBenét is a criminal who knows these things. There is nothing in the background of the Ramseys to indicate any type of psychological problems, any type of anger that would be directed toward their daughter. There is just no background which suggests that the Ramseys would even know how to do these things." — Lou Smit, May 28th, 2001

If Smit fucked up on the Ramsey case and fucked up badly, then Steve Thomas came through with flying colors. Thomas was investigating the same case at the same time. The difference was Thomas was working with the Boulder Police Department, whereas Smit was more directly employed by the District Attorney's office. Both came up with entirely separate narratives, and both quit the investigation in disgust.

If Smit was a veteran detective with a track record, Thomas was something of a new kid on the block, a rookie. What both detectives shared, however, was an almost obsessive dedication to the JonBenét case. Whatever the results of their respective investigations, it's difficult to fault either detective for their sincerity, though as we dig deeper, it's not always easy to understand whether Smit had made honest mistakes or whether he was a willing cog in Hunter's clockwork of puppets.

Let's dig into the Ransom Note now, specifically Smit's take on it. I'm with Steve Thomas when he describes the Ransom Note as "the most significant evidence in this case." Further, I believe the Ransom Note alone was – and should have been – sufficient to indict Patsy Ramsey during the Grand Jury phase. Alex Hunter's contention that there wasn't enough evidence to proceed seems to be based on the Ransom Note suddenly disappearing into Boulder's thin, Christmassy air.

Let's have a look at Steve Thomas' take on it, followed by his arch rival, Smit's.

From cnn.com [May 28th, 2001]:

THOMAS: *Well, I think the most significant evidence in this case was the pen the pad, the Ransom Note, and the handwriting, and when we finished an investigation after 18 months, and presented our case to the district attorney's office presumably for them to move it forward, one statistic that was cited in that presentation was that **out of 73 people, whose handwriting was examined in this case, there was only one whose handwriting showed evidence to suggest authorship** who was in the home that night who couldn't be eliminated as the author and that was Patsy Ramsey.*

KING: *Lou, tell us why you disagree there is the note.*

SMIT: ***I disagree on the Ransom Note that Patsy is the only one that has not been eliminated.*** *I'm sure that they took handwriting examples from many people. Some of the people they took handwriting examples from is just original writing which is just very minimal in content. Full samples weren't taken of all of those people that Steve is talking about.*

Also, those full samples were only shown to one examiner. I'm sure that there were six examiners that inspected Patsy Ramsey's handwriting, sure those same 50, 60 people he is talking about – those handwriting examples with these other examiners and see what other kind of results that you get.

Frankly this is very disappointing analysis, or lack of from Smit. Rather than providing an examination of the merits of the handwriting, or the content, Smit simply plays a numbers game citing the technical aspects lacking from other samples.

From cnn.com [May 28th, 2001]:

KING: *Did you question the Ramseys?*

SMIT: *Yes. I questioned John Ramsey officially in June of 1998. And since I've left the investigation, I've talked with John and Patsy Ramsey on numerous occasions.*

KING: *Have there ever been moments when you felt: "Maybe I'm wrong"?*

SMIT: *Larry, I have talked to these people in depth.* ***I do not feel at any time when I was talking to them that they did this.***

That's an interesting comment. When John and Patsy went on CNN on January 1st, 1997, the day after JonBenét's funeral, many Americans as well as the media, felt suspicious of the Ramseys. Many wondered, where were the unrehearsed tears? Many wondered, where's the outrage, why they weren't breaking down the police's door to track down their daughter's killer? Many wondered, why instead of co-operating with law enforcement, they'd hired an army of lawyers and PR people.

My sense of Smit and his relationship with the Ramseys is fundamentally through three dimensions.

Smit was <u>charmed, awed and perhaps manipulated</u> by the Ramsey's wealth, sophistication and guile.

Smit's own <u>Christianity made him an easy target</u>, and a gullible victim of – in our opinion – the Ramsey's [and especially Patsy's] Christianity.

<u>Smit's wife Barbara – like Patsy – was fighting serious illness</u>, and would succumb on Feb. 29, 2004, two years before Patsy died of cancer.

From <u>cnn.com</u> [May 28th, 2001]:

SMIT: *I have talked to a lot of people that have also talked with the Ramseys, including very professional people. They don't think they did this. Sure, you can visualize anything. Like I say, you never can close a door completely. But in this case, it's not likely at all that the Ramseys did this. I think there's a very high probability that they did not.*

KING: *If they had acted – the police and the rest – had acted on your concept, right away, assume intruder, do you think more evidence would have been gathered? Do you think possibly someone would have been caught?*

SMIT: *Larry, I think that if they would have put as much effort into going down the intruder path as they went down the Ramsey path, that we would have had a very good chance of catching an our guy. The Ramsey path has been worn out. After four years, there has been so much investigation into that path that **I don't think there's anything else that they can find.***

KING: *Would you agree, Lou, with Henry Lee, who said this was a very damaged crime scene?*

SMIT: *Yes, there were a lot of mistakes made on this crime scene.*

KING: *And what about the fact that Mr. Ramsey moved the body?*

Larry returns again and again to the culpability of the Ramseys, interestingly, for all Smit's dodges, he's not really out there naming any suspects. Instead of the Ramseys, could it be someone else? Well, can Smit name anyone? We will deal with the suspect John Ramsey directly identified to Smit [in his 1998 interrogation] and where that leads later in this narrative.

From cnn.com [May 28th, 2001]:

SMIT: *Mr. Ramsey did move the body, but I think that Henry Lee and other profilers will be willing to say that normally the person who does the killing does not even want to find the body. The fact that John Ramsey found the body, and he did move the body, shows me more that he did not do this.*

Let me explain.

KING: *Please.*

SMIT: *If John Ramsey was involved in the killing of JonBenét, and he went through all of this rigmarole to have the garrotte and to put the wrist ligatures on, and to put the duct tape on her mouth and to put her in the basement, why is it that the first thing he did when he went downstairs is to take off the duct tape, which he had just staged to put on there? Why would he take off the wrist ligature, which he had just put on there to make it look like she was bound, and then why would he take her upstairs after they put her in this cellar to be found by the police? It doesn't make sense.* **Why would you unstage something that you just staged?**

At face value, this is fairly good reasoning from Smit. But he doesn't answer his own question. If you have staged a crime, and have the opportunity to "Stage" the discovery of it, then this is further opportunity to contaminate the crime scene as far as possible. Is there DNA on the duct tape, well of course there is, John removed it. Is John's

DNA on the blanket or on the ligatures – by "rescuing" JonBenét's body, her father has the opportunity to place his DNA all over her, thereby rendering moot any DNA that may have been deposited during the original staging. That Smit seems to be unaware of this, or unwilling to consider this, is yet another symptom – in our view – of the case being oversimplified by him.

From cnn.com [May 28th, 2001]:

KING: *Why do you think, then, as another thing that doesn't make sense – why do you think the kidnaper didn't kidnap her?*

SMIT: *Again, I don't know the answer to that question.*

Do you see how weak this is? A Ransom Note with no ransom. A kidnapping with no actual kidnapping. A murder with an invisible cause of death and invisible murder weapon, and an obvious cause of death, and obvious murder weapon. Isn't the purpose of the garrotte to absolutely misdirect attention away from the damning bludgeoning? Because no criminal in their right mind murders someone and then stages another murder scene. A murderer at most would simply minimize or sanitize their original act, not cover up the underlying act with a sort of crime scene make-up.

From cnn.com [May 28th, 2001]:

SMIT: *Whoever wrote that Ransom Note...*

KING: *Obviously wrote it before he killed her.*

SMIT: *Absolutely.*

KING: *No sense writing it after you kill her.*

SMIT: *Right, you wouldn't have the presence of mind to do this. Take a real close look at that Ransom Note. That Ransom Note is full of violence. It tells exactly what this person's going to do to JonBenét if everything doesn't go exactly right. Many references to death and dying.*

She'll be "beheaded." She'll "not see 1997." Her remains will "be denied you for her burial."

All violent references to the death of JonBenét. The person who killed JonBenét had it in his mind that if anything went wrong, he was going to kill her, and he did.

Well, so much for beheading her, or disposing of her remains. Instead the murderer covered her up in a blanket. Did he have a change of heart? We also know John Ramsey requested that JonBenét be covered in the lounge, and went so far as to cover her without getting permission from Linda Arndt.

KING: *What do you think went wrong?*

SMIT: *I believe that the killer had started out with a kidnapping in mind. Now, this again is my hypothesis. … Perhaps he got into the window and couldn't pull the suitcase out after him.*

So, **I don't know why he suddenly went to that basement room, fashioned a garrotte from something that was right there in plain sight and brutally murdered JonBenet.** *Perhaps she knew him. Perhaps she screamed. Something triggered* <u>this man</u> *to kill JonBenet in a very brutal fashion.*

KING: *Had to be a man?*

SMIT: *I believe it is a man and I say that for a couple of reasons: No. 1, this person did* **sexually assault** *JonBenet. She was sexually assaulted that night.* **She did bleed,** *which means that it was done before she died. She was brutally struck on the head, a very, very violent blow – very coordinated in order to do that with one shot. I believe that – and the garrotte was very deeply embedded in JonBenét's neck. There is male foreign DNA. I think it suggests strongly that it was a man, but* **I will not rule out the probability that it could be a man and a woman or even two men.**

Again, Smit is relying on fairly flimsy evidence. There was blood, but less than a teaspoon and a half, and most contained inside JonBenét's skull. There was zero blood spatter. The sexual assault isn't absolutely certain, which again calls into question the true "brutality" of the "man" who murdered her.

From cnn.com [May 28th, 2001]:

KING: *Wouldn't there be history…*

SMIT: *I would say that the person who did this to JonBenét with the violence and the brutality that he exhibited, that he has done this before, and I believe he will do it again. **This type of a personality cannot stop.***

I think there is some merit in this point, but not in the way Smit means it. Smit is referring to some depraved child sex fiend, whereas it's also plausible that Burke could have struck his sister repeatedly in the past. That's a sort of violence that may have passed under Smit's radar.

Exactly how frequent or damaging this lashing out was is difficult to know. But besides it being plausible, the oddball personality persisting after the crime also plays into a particular personality type.

From cnn.com [May 28th, 2001]:

KING: *Back to the Ransom Note. Weren't there some things in the Ransom Note that were taken right out of the movies?*

SMIT: *When I first seen it, and Alex Hunter first showed it to me – I wasn't hired at the time…*

KING: *The D.A.*

SMIT: *The D.A. And I told him at that time that, Alex, **I think this note was written before the murder.** It was written in a very calm, precise manner.*

How does stack up to the facts though? The note was written on Patsy's notepad, with a pen from the kitchen. There were also "practise notes". That's a helluva thing, to have a criminal arrive at the scene of a crime without writing materials, yet eager to secure – in precise detail – a particular sum of money according to precise instructions.

When Smit suggests the note was written before the murder, one assumes it was written elsewhere, not in the Ramsey's kitchen. Of course as soon as the note is written in the kitchen, on Patsy's pad, with a kitchen pen, and Patsy's handwriting can't be excluded, and the murder weapons are fashioned in the house, and the escape route is used with a suitcase sourced inside the house, the umbrella of suspicion tilts towards Patsy.

But there's more…

From cnn.com [May 28th, 2001]:

SMIT: *There was references to different types of ransom movies in that Ransom Note. The movie "Ransom" itself was playing in Boulder, and it just opened, just the end of the prior month, in November. There are direct quotes almost from, two or three, of the techno, ransom-type movies, from "Speed" and "Dirty Harry" and "Nick of Time."*

Fargo was another movie released in 1996 [also a ransom movie] and Primal Fear about an altar boy accused of brutally murdering the archbishop of Chicago. While Smit doesn't mention either of these films, he neglects to highlight the Ramsey's movie fetish – the walls in their home, especially in the basement, are festooned with framed movie posters

When Larry asks Smit about the significance of the direct movie quotes, Smit gives a bizarre answer.

KING: *What does that [the direct movie quotes] tell you?*

SMIT: *It just tells me that this person who wrote the note **fantasizes about these things**. It's part of his fantasy.*

He [or is it an entire political faction?] fantasizing about kidnapping someone, only…to not kidnap them? For Smit the murder makes sense but perhaps only because Smit has investigated 200 homicides that involved particular motives. And that kind of programming wasn't helpful for deciphering the JonBenét Ramsey case.

Smit's repartee is less than convincing, and thus Larry is prompted to ask an important question at an opportune time. It's one of those things that slips through the cracks, but Larry nails Smit on it.

From cnn.com [May 28th, 2001]:

KING: **What about those who say that you have bonded with the Ramseys;** *that you have become so wrapped in this that you aren't going to not listen to whatever the other side presents?*

CHRISTIANS R US

"It is sick. It is sick, sick, sick!" — Patsy Ramsey <u>on 48 Hours</u>, her response to accusations of child abuse

"The police always look at the parents first. We learned that. And we accepted that. And [we] just assumed [the police] would complete that cycle and move on, which of course, they did not." — John Ramsey

"God has surely blessed me with energy and the ability to return to raising a family. I thank Him every morning when I wake up and see the sunrise reflecting on the Flatirons over Boulder." — Patsy Ramsey's <u>Christmas newsletter, 1995</u>

"Shoes, shoes, the victim's shoes, who will stand in the victim's shoes?" — Excerpt from Detective <u>Lou Smit's letter of resignation</u> to Alex Hunter in September 1998

"Patsy...if you did do this thing, I would be cautious about invoking the name of God, because [you're] right....He does know." — Devon Lambert,
June 2000

W e're not done with Smit. In order to fully address Smit's religious convictions and how they relate to the Ramseys, we need to remind ourselves how right the Ramseys were with the Almighty in 1996, and subsequently. From there we can determine what sort of impact Christianity – specifically Smit's Christianity – likely had on the outcome of this case.

Worth playing for?

When we skip along to the 26 minute mark of the NBC's Dateline Documentary *Who Killed JonBenét*[5] we come across an elderly blonde woman in a turquoise blouse, identifying herself as "Pam Barday".[6] Interestingly while Dateline use titles to introduce other interviewees, they don't identify Barday with an onscreen subtext, there's just one brief introduction providing her name and that she was a close friend of Patsy's. Barday – well, whoever she is – provides an astonishing insight into Patsy's Christianity:

PAM: [describing the funeral service in Boulder at the St. John's Episcopal Church[7] *"Patsy stood up; raised both of her hands straight*

---

5 Dateline's Who Killed JonBenét premiered on September 9th, 2016

6 Pam Barday is Pamela Archeluta, author of the self-published ebook Patsy Ramsey: What the Pilot's Wife Knew. Archuleta shouldn't be confused with the 911 call operator who took Patsy's emergency call – Kim Archuleta.

7 The Ramseys held two services, a memorial service in Boulder of December 29, and a funeral service at Peachtree Presbyterian Church in Atlanta on 31st December 1996. JonBenét was laid to rest at St. James Episcopal Cemetery in Marietta, Atlanta beside her 22 year-old half-sister Beth, John Ramsey's

up [gesturing], turned around and walked down the aisle…didn't look at anybody. Not us, not anybody, just <u>straight ahead</u>. And I thought [<u>gesturing with raised hands</u>], to me, it looked like [<u>Patsy</u>] was giving JonBenét to God."

Is this sincerity, pageantry or a little bit of both? Because this was no isolated, once-off. In fact this exaggerated "performance" was classic Patsy. At the end of April 1997, Patsy provided the same out-of-a-movie drama to a room chock-full of reporters and a breathless television audience.

From <u>eonline.com</u>:

Neither Patsy nor John sat down for a formal interview with investigators until April 30, 1997, and right afterward they tried to explain to reporters why it had taken so long to sit down with the police….Toward the end of the press conference, John [spoke directly to] the camera "We'll find you [John said]. We will find you. I have that as a sole mission for the rest of my life." "Likewise," Patsy agreed. "The police and investigators have assured us that this is a case that can be solved. You may be eluding the authorities for a time, but God knows who you are and <u>we will find you</u>."

During another interview years later <u>Patsy's still swinging</u>: *"We didn't do it. I don't know what happened. God knows, [<u>hands flapping</u>] and he's not tellin'".*

Besides descriptions of prayers in their own narrative describing the circumstances surrounding the Christmas murder of their daughter, there's also an interview fielded by The Today Show's <u>Katie Couric</u> [March 20, 2000] via <u>acandyrose.com</u>:

---

daughter from his first marriage. The date of her death, as engraved on JonBenét's gravestone, read December 25th, 1996.

PATSY: *JonBenét had fallen asleep. She had fallen asleep in the back of the car by the time we got home.*

COURIC: *Did she ever wake up? Tell me what happened once you got her home.*

PATSY: *We put her to – John carried her up to bed, and then I, you know, kind of got her undressed and pulled her pyjama pants on. They were kind of long underwear pants that were in her pyjama drawer. She was sound asleep. Tucked her in bed, kissed her good night, said the prayers, and...*

COURIC: *You said your prayers.*

Even Katie Couric snags on this part. But the other extraneous stuff is equally weird. If the description of the weird oversized underwear-pants[8] seems unnecessary and out of place, the flowery addition of kisses good night, tucked into bed and prayed over, you know, all the perfect family, perfect town sort of stuff...well, it's classic Patsy isn't it? Why? It's a tad over the top.

More likely – we think – JonBenét *never* went to bed that night, was <u>*never* tucked in</u> and nor for that matter did Patsy go to bed that night. Of course for good sounding PR it's important to run through the motions of what would normally take place, the risk is simply that John and Patsy might stumble over one another's flowery descriptions.

Oh did you tuck her in, I thought I did?

Did I say a prayer and kiss her good night? No you did.

Yes, there's plenty of meticulously and lovingly crafted audio versions of the Ramseys putting their daughter to bed, with both parents apparently involved in a relay to get JonBenét [who is completely

---

8 JonBenét's corpse was dressed in brand new size <u>12 bloomers</u>.

comatose she's so tired] undressed, safe and asleep. That this happens when JonBenét's alive, and happens in her bedroom [as opposed to dead and in the basement]…apparently goes without saying.

From acandyrose.com:

PATSY: *I said my prayers over her and tucked her in bed.*

No doubt Patsy, no doubt. We'll move forward now, leaving the matter of how ominous that description sounds, almost like someone praying over the remains of someone, as one does at a funeral…and gather further reinforcements.

If there remains any doubt about Patsy's erratic behaviour underlying and undermining her overt Christianity, two further examples ought to be sufficient to plant the necessary seeds.

Example #1 The Seamstress as Savior

From 21stcenturywire.com:

On December 27th, it was reported that Patsy's friend Pam Griffin [not to be confused with Pam Barday], the seamstress that designed JonBenét's pageant costumes went to comfort Patsy, who was grieving at the Fernie residence [John Fernie is in some instances grouped with John Ramsey and Fleet White in the discovery of JonBenét's body at 13:00 on December 26th]. Here's a passage describing that encounter in a Newsweek report three years after the murder of JonBenét:

*"At the Boulder home of John and Barbara Fernie, friends of the Ramseys', Pam, a former registered nurse, touched Patsy's skin and realized she was dehydrated. She brought Patsy some water and made her drink it. "You need to brush your hair," Pam told her. "You need to lie down a little bit." But **Patsy stood up to greet each new person** who arrived to offer condolences, and as she did, tears streamed down her face. Hours later, Patsy finally took Pam's advice and lay down in the bedroom."*

It's important to stress that Patsy is severely compromised both physically and emotionally on December the 27th. But we can see just how important social currency is to Patsy.

If the 26th was about dealing with the police, the 27th was the first, and perhaps worst day dealing with the full bore of grief that JonBenét's sudden death had unleashed. We believe this grief was raw and real, especially for Patsy. But raw and real as it was, would her grief, could it inveigle something truly authentic out of Patsy?

From 21stcenturywire.com:

"Patsy reached up and touched Pam's face." **"Couldn't you fix this for me?"** *she asked.* **Pam thought she was delirious. It was as if Patsy were asking her to fix a ripped seam**. *"Patsy said something like, 'We didn't mean for that to happen',"* *Pam would say later. Pam couldn't say why, but she remembered feeling as if Patsy knew who killed JonBenét but was afraid to say."*

A feeling is not much to go on is it? Isn't this the Griffin version of Arndt seeing murder in John Ramsey's eyes, after he placed JonBenét's cadaver at her feet? The important takeout though is not the feeling, it's Patsy's psychology, even when she's emotionally compromised.

Patsy's psychology seems rooted in a kind of denial. Patsy's psychology appears to be rooted in artifice. Artifice, of course, is a poor toolbox to attempt repairs when death has torn through the psychological fabric. And yet artifice had served Patsy well for years – so why not now?

From 21stcenturywire.com:

Back in the spring of 1996, Griffin put local dance instructor, Kit Andre in touch with Patsy to help teach JonBenét a routine for the pageant circuit. Andre would later be quoted by media, stating the following:

"She was a fabulous child," I told Patsy at JonBenét's memorial service in Boulder. "She was a star."[But] I never saw JonBenét in a pageant. Never saw her do the routine I taught her until I saw that pageant video on TV. I've looked at that video several times. They [Patsy, her sister Pam and her mother Nedra] **made JonBenét look like a clown.** *Someone else taught her those* **pseudo-adult movements**, *the provocative walk, the poses, all of it."*

The pageantry is a huge part of this case, not so much how it affected JonBenét, though it did, or how JonBenét being in pageants affected outsiders [or would-be intruders], though it did. The psychology behind the pageantry in how it affected Patsy and Burke primarily is of value here, and even to an extent how John took upon the same psychology after his daughter's death – the posing in public, the PR, the "pseudo-adult movements".

From 21stcenturywire.com:

The Daily Mail described the [Ramsey] family preoccupation with the child beauty pageant circuit. Adding to that, family visitors noted that JonBenét's room was <u>filled with pageant trophies</u> rather than toys:

"Patsy later insisted that while JonBenét loved taking part in pageants, it was just a little hobby. Experts immediately pointed to the coaching, dancing, singing, music and beauty sessions — along with the outrageous cost of outfits — that made it an almost full-time occupation.

Of course even Burke described his mother to a child psychologist in 1999 as a "working mom", though he didn't specify what that work was exactly, or which child Patsy's work tended to revolve around. If Burke stopped short, is there anything stopping us from digging into precisely this area?

Example #2 The Doting Mom MIA

We're not done dealing with the "Christian" persona of the Ramseys, and Patsy's brand of dogmatism in particular. In order to provide a complete sketch, we need to address the *anathema* as well. Well, here it is.

From websleuths.com:

In the [May 2004] edition of the National Examiner, with JonBenét's picture on the front cover, Pam Archuleta [aka Pam Barday] says that during the [December 6], 1996 Parade of Lights in Boulder she saw the man who could have killed JonBenét. From the article:

"JonBenét was sitting up high on the back seat of a Christmas-red convertible with two other pageant contestants, waving to the crowd while the song Jingle Bell Rock was played from the car. A plastic sign on the side of the convertible identified her by name and revealed that she was a child beauty queen. Family friend Pam Archuleta held JonBenét's ankle to keep her from falling.

Nothing abhorrent about that is there? What's important to note here is the date – this was three weeks prior to her murder.

From websleuths.com:

"As they went past one of the town's leading banks, a strange man walked from the crowd toward the BMW. Archuleta says he looked "creepy" and had "a face full of anger and hatred" that she will never forget. She had the impression that the man had seen JonBenét before and recognized her.

"Well-dressed in a tweed jacket and jeans, the man was in his 40's, tall and thin with graying hair. He stared at JonBenét and walked to within two feet of the car. For Archuleta, the staring man's behavior marred what until then had seemed an innocent Christmas event that could have taken place in any town in America."

The crazy part of this story isn't the parade or the creepy guy. Nor is the pertinent part that a 40-year-old man would look angry or have feelings of hatred towards a six-year-old. I'm not sure how any of that links to a pedophile. What is crucial to note in this story isn't what's in it, but what's missing. Not what – *who*. And given the subject matter, some "wrath-filled" random dude, a shadow for the mysterious, anonymous "intruder", that absence is even more telling.

From websleuths.com:

The article in the National Examiner didn't mention that on December 6, 1996 John and Patsy Ramsey weren't even in Boulder that night as JonBenét rode in the parade. They were in New York City with Glen and Susan Stine. Burke and JonBenét were being watched by Patsy's mother, Nedra Paugh, and apparently by the Stine's college student live-in caregiver for Doug Stine, Nathan Inouye.

We will address these individuals – the Stine family and the mysterious Nathan Inouye – in due course. The crucial titbit here is the Ramsey parents' jet setting lifestyle. Three weeks before Christmas, they're in New York with their pals. The Stines, three weeks later, would be the last family to see JonBenét alive other than the Ramseys. Curiously, the next morning when the Ramseys called "all their friends" for an unscheduled DNA deposit, they didn't call the Stines. Again, what we tend to miss isn't the presence of something, but the absence.

Which brings us to John's personal brand of Christianity. My opinion is that prior to JonBenét's death there doesn't seem much evidence of John being dogmatic about his faith, certainly nowhere near the sort of commitment Patsy was showing. But let's get this straight from the horse's mouth, shall we?

From 1.cbn.com:

...I [John] was born in a Christian home and that's what you did on Sundays and I didn't really get it, didn't really understand it....Some good friends came alongside me. One in particular, took me aside and said, 'John, I've been praying for you. I want to spend time with you.' He taught me how to study the Bible. So my faith had really grown."

John's a little vague on when he learned to study the bible, and when his faith really got on the right track. One assumes from the interview it's after the death of his oldest daughter Beth, in 1992.

From 1.cbn.com:

SCOTT: *"What do you understand now about God and Jesus that you didn't know back then?"*

JOHN: *"Jesus is real. He's who He said He was. I firmly believe that. I can communicate with him through prayer. He's in our life. He's real."*

It's quite an admission. In 1992 when his oldest daughter died his initial reaction was – John says – confirmation that there was no God, and John screaming that there was no God. When his second daughter dies, this time not from a freak car accident but in murderous fashion, John would have us believe his initial reaction is…faith?

The other thing to note is how John frames the change in how he sees God. God has suddenly become real, and not just real, authentic.

He's who He said He was

And of course, so is John. Despite accusations of either murdering, abusing or covering up criminal activities relating to his youngest daughter in his own home, John – time again, through television appearances, through books, through Dr Phil – expects us to accept that John is who he *says* he was in 1996. Christianity obviously plays a leading role in that narrative.

From 1.cbn.com:

JOHN: *"So when JonBenét was murdered, I had faith. It wasn't just a logical exercise. It had gone from my head to my heart. So **I knew JonBenét was okay and with God, and I didn't question God, as to 'Why did this happen?'"***

Not?

From 1.cbn.com:

[But] John's suffering continued. Patsy had been healed of stage IV ovarian cancer in 1994. But, eight years later, it was back.

SCOTT: *"2002, Patsy's cancer returns."*

JOHN: *"She had, I think, three remissions over the next three or four years."*

Cancer is a damnable thing, but just as a resurgence in faith seems questionable, so does a resurgence of a disease in circumstances like these. Not to be insensitive, but the cancer was erratic too – beaten back again and again only to inveigle itself back into Patsy's body.

From 1.cbn.com:

*"The point came where **I just wanted God to take her home** because she was suffering so much. It was like, 'God, just please take her home. It's time. **It's time to end this suffering** and-and struggle.'"*

We highlighted this statement in *The Craven Silence* but it's worth touching on again. We do so to stimulate open-minded discussion around the concept of euthanasia. JonBenét, it has been suggested, was critically wounded by a head wound, a bludgeoning but the little girl may have died a slow death. It's unclear whether the strangling was staged or whether it was *necessary.* John describing Patsy's death as "going home" and "an end to a struggle" comes perilously close to the psychology we're testing – of a family covering up.

From 1.cbn.com:

JOHN: *"Death became both a sorrow and a relief for me in a strange way. I mean, we knew we'd miss her terribly, but I was grateful that she was not suffering anymore."*

John…you are talking about Patsy here, right?

Meanwhile, the new love of John's life is the daughter of a missionary, someone John describes as a "real solid believer" and "a blessing for me". John's of the view that the "best days of my life are still ahead of me." So how does he sum up the aftermath after JonBenét's murder – a period littered with lawsuits, investigations, indictments and high profile interviews?

From 1.cbn.com:

JOHN: *"People just reached out to u…. It really was an uplifting experience for us…I've learned that everybody, pretty much everybody suffers at some point in their life. Life's not necessarily easy. …That was a kind of an eye-opener for me. And that it has a beginning and an end, and that's kinda what the book was to-to encourage people about. There is an end to suffering. It's not forever."*

Well, for JonBenét when she died somewhere in that 15-roomed house, there was not only an end to her suffering, but also a beginning. There was clearly an end to every Christmas and every other good thing she would have enjoyed as part of the gift of life. Death is perhaps the least "uplifting" experience of all, especially when the person dying is you.

Curiously, when John and Patsy's future was on the chopping block, their response was uniform.

From dailycamera.com:

It was Oct. 13, and **John and Patsy Ramsey were kneeling in front of the television** *at the Lafayette home of close friends Mike and Pam Archuleta. It was the final day a Boulder County grand jury investigating their daughter's death would meet.*

The Ramseys, the focus of the police and grand jury investigations, returned to Colorado in the event they would be indicted. They avoided the press by meeting their friend and pilot Mike Archuleta in Chattanooga, Tenn., and from there flew into an airport in Erie.

"They were ready for whatever was decided," Pam Archuleta recalled Thursday, on the eve of the release of the Ramsey's book, "the Death of Innocence."

Seems they were also ready to release a book. I'm going to play the cynic here and disagree with Pam. I don't think it was a case that the Ramseys were ready for "whatever was decided", I think they were ready for what had been decided all along. I presume Hunter had been hedging for this outcome all along and perhaps kept the Ramseys in the loop all along. Thus his announcement not to indict the Ramseys – even though the Grand Jury explicitly voted to do so – was likely not a surprise to the Ramseys.

If this is the case, and this is merely a hypothesis, then the prayer-filled pageantry at the Archuleto's can hardly be considered sincere. If it was pageantry for the benefit of a small audience, who could then relay the anecdote [with the Ramsey's permission of course, to the media – and subsequently they did] then it was also contrivance. And if it was contrivance who is to say the whole Christian-thing wasn't an act too?

Smit + Ghost Hunters

"I found that one of the best traits of a good detective is compassion." — Lou Smit to Larry King, May 28th, 2001

In March 2012 John Ramsey published *The Other Side of Suffering.* Chapters included:

- *Struck by Evil*
- *Messages from Heaven*
- *Angels*
- *God and Healing*
- *Trusting God*
- *Forgiveness: A Gift to Ourselves*
- *Getting Close to God*
- *Touches from God*

In April 2006 John and Patsy Ramsey gave a TV interview on "Connecting Point" with a Christian pastor in Hawaii [dealt with in detail in *The Craven Silence*]. Three months later Patsy was dead.

And so we finally circle back to Lou Smit. Let's get his take on his faith and the Ramseys, and get a handle on whether the beliefs of these folks factored into the outcome of this unsolved murder mystery.

From cnn.com:

KING: *What about those who say that* **you have bonded with the Ramseys**; *that you have become so wrapped in this that you aren't going to not listen to whatever the other side presents?*

SMIT: *You know, Larry, I know that that's out there. And that just definitely is not true.* **Yes, I do show compassion to the Ramseys. Yes, I do talk to the Ramseys....**I *found out as a detective,* **you do not build walls between you and the person that even you are looking at.** *I have never done that. I don't know where you have to interrogate even a suspect every time that you meet him, or meet them. I do believe, again, in showing compassion toward the family, but* **I have not bonded with the Ramseys.** *I rarely talk to them even now.*

Well that's good to hear because it won't do to have a detective becoming friends with the folks he's investigating, would it? And that didn't happen here, did it?

From cnn.com:

KING: *Weren't there a story that you prayed with them?*

SMIT: *I did. That's a true story. It's part of my...*

KING: *You mean, that's good cop/bad cop theory? You are still a cop then?*

SMIT: *You're still a cop. I found that one of the best traits of a good detective is compassion, and I believe* **the whole thing is being able to communicate with the people that you are even suspecting.** *Don't turn away people without talking to them. Talk to them as long as you can, learn about them.*

Lou Lou Lou – dude. There's an enormous difference between "communicating with" a murder suspect and "praying with" a murder suspect. There's a degree of intimacy and trust involved – mutual mind you – when people pray together. Praying together, whether it's strangers or friends, whether around a dinner table or at a revival, is a massive statement of solidarity.

Here you have a detective employed to investigate the cold hard facts, and he's coming into the case armed with compassion. If I was Alex Hunter and if I suspected the Ramseys were culpable and complicit in JonBenét's murder, and if it was my job to get some credible detective in who would win the public's trust *and* make it seem like I was making a real effort to solve the case too, wouldn't Lou be a great candidate? What if I wanted to seem like I was working on the case but what I really wanted was to screw up the case so the Ramseys would get off, wouldn't go to jail, would escape prosecution of any kind, wouldn't ever see the inside of a courtroom?

If this was my plan, wasn't the perfect candidate to be suckered into it, someone who'd be wowed by the Ramsey's charm and buttered up by a Christian façade, someone who'd be awed by the Ramsey's wealth and graciousness, someone who wouldn't take much convincing to pursue an *alternate theory*?

What if Alex Hunter had called Smit into his office on day one said, "Lou, dude, we're in a big mess here, that's why I've called for outside help, that's why I've called the best, that's why you're here. You're going to meet some people, good people, people who're in a really bad way. My heart goes out to them because…our people are making a mess, Lou. The guys working on this thing have dropped the ball. They're lost, and they're embarrassing us. They suspect an affluent family is involved in the death of their own child, can you believe it? I want you to do what you do, but I want you to look carefully into this other theory Lou – that's what I want you to do, that's why you're here. If the evidence points to something else fine, but I'm telling you, these idiots are on the wrong track, and you're here to set them right. Do you think you can do that Lou?"

From cnn.com:

KING: *Do you like them?*

SMIT: *That what I say.* **I do like them, but I don't love them,** *as far as that type of a thing where I bonded that closely.*

That's some crazy-assed shit right there: I like 'em but I don't love 'em. I guess the obvious question is how much "like" are we talking about? Larry, incisive as ever, cuts through the bullshit.

From cnn.com:

KING: *Can you learn a lot from talking to the son?*

SMIT: *You know, I have never really had a long, in-depth interview with the son.*

Good old Lou, investigating a murder but…well, not <u>really</u> investigating all of it, is he?

From cnn.com:

KING: *[Burke] might have [a] temper, he might have known other people who may have been prowling around, right? I mean,* **wouldn't he be someone to talk to?**

SMIT: *I think that it's very necessary to talk to the son. Burke Ramsey was a 9-year-old boy at the time that this happened. He was interviewed exclusively shortly after the murder. He came in for I believe two or three days and talked to Dan Schuler, another detective. They got almost every bit of information out of him that they could during those interviews.*

I **believe** *that Burke Ramsey has told them the truth. I* **believe** *that he is not involved in this in any way.*

KING: *But, I mean, he would be helpful in talking about temperament of his parents.*

Yes Larry, we're on the same page, but Lou stubbornly is not. Isn't it because he's sort of been asked to look at the intruder theory, to not look at the Ramseys, to follow the evidence leading away from them? I mean, seek and ye shall find and Lou has found…and also in a sense *not found*. Looking for something where there's not necessarily something often creates a sort of confirmation bias – you see what you wish to see, don't you, you don't see what you don't wish to see.

From cnn.com:

KING: *Does the Boulder police deserve the rap they are getting?*

SMIT: *Personally, I have never badmouthed the Boulder police department, other than saying that **I believe they are going in the wrong direction**.*

Of course, for Boulder Police Department, the feeling is mutual, and not without merit. Larry cuts to the chase.

From cnn.com:

KING: *A couple other things…the charges that **the Ramseys didn't cooperate with the police**, didn't go down, didn't volunteer. Some have said, if it was my kid, I would be at that door everyday, knocking the door in, saying, find the killer.*

SMIT: *I know, Larry, **that has been one of the highest criticisms of the Ramseys**, but Larry, what happened in this case the Ramseys did talk to the police for the first two days. There was a police officer that was with them 24 hours a day for the next three days. The Ramseys should have been interviewed right away. That was a mistake. One of the biggest mistakes that was made. They should have been brought down to the police station right away. It was not their decision not to do that…*

Oh Lou, this is disingenuous, isn't it? It's hard to believe good ol' Lou has an insincere bone in his body, and perhaps he doesn't. Perhaps Lou was fed this information, and innocently consumed it and had regurgitated it verbatim ever since. Or perhaps Lou was feeding the media information in a certain way… It's hard to say for sure, but either way, it's incorrect [see timeline below].

From cnn.com:

KING: …*why were [the Ramseys] asked a week later?*

This is an unfortunately phrased question; it's vague. Larry should have been more specific: when exactly were the Ramsey's interrogated? Who was interrogated, who wasn't? When did they "lawyer up" and what effect did that have on the police investigation?

From cnn.com:

SMIT: *The Ramseys a week later were burying their daughter also at the time being advised by lawyers. John Ramsey had talked to Mike,[9] one of their friends. Mike suggested the lawyers. From what I have been able to see, since I have been in this case, even from the outside, is* **the lawyers advised them not to do anything**. *The lawyers were trying to keep the Ramseys out of jail. The focus was on the Ramseys right from the beginning.*

This is an interesting dodge from Lou. First of all, Lou sees the lawyers as the culprits. In the third episode of Dr. Phil covering Burke Ramsey "breaking his 20 year silence" Dr Phil's lawyer – yes you read that right – Lin Wood [who was only hired by John Ramsey in 1999] reinforced

---

9 It's interesting to note the informal manner in which Lou Smit refers to Ramsey lawyer Mike Bynum, a former Deputy District Attorney who worked for District Attorney Alex Hunter. There is the impression Smit and "Mike" knew each other well, and spoke to one another often, thus developing a less formal relationship than lawyer and detective.

the notion that the Ramseys were right to hire lawyers immediately after Christmas in 1996 rather than co-operate with police. Secondly, Lou's offhand remark that "the focus was on the Ramseys right from the beginning" is not only correct, but right. Of course the focus was on the Ramseys. Somehow Lou's been led to believe the focus shouldn't be, and not because of lawyering…because…well, *it just shouldn't be.* The Ramseys are good Christian people, no track record etc. etc.

Actually here's the abridged timeline Lou, and I think it's worth being <u>very clear</u> on it, don't you?

From pbworks.com:

~6:03 AM Whites arrived.

~6:06 AM Fleet White searched basement.

After 6:06 AM Fleet White searched wine cellar room. "Mr. White also opened the door to the wine cellar room, but he could not see anything inside because it was dark and he could not find the light switch. (White Deposition)." [The Carnes Order, 2003].

Between 6:10 and 6:20 AM John Fernie arrived…His wife Barbara, came "later". [Schiller].

*Before 6:45 AM **John Ramsey calls pilot.***

6:45 AM Weiss, Barcklow and Reichenbach arrive.

6:45 AM Victim advocates Mary Lou Jedamus and Grace Morelock arrive. [Glick].

~7:00 AM Burke Ramsey is awakened and dressed [Schiller].

After 7:00 AM Rev. Hoverstock arrived.

*After 7:00 AM **Burke Ramsey taken to Whites.***

Time Unstated Advocates brought food.

Time Unstated Arndt instructed John Ramsey.

Time Unstated Advocates cleaned Kitchen.[10]

~9:30 AM Sergeant Whitson arrived.

1:05 PM JonBenet Ramsey's body found.

~1:05 PM Fleet White calls for ambulance.

1:05 PM Byfield notified.

After 1:05 PM Arndt requested backup.

After 1:05 PM Officers Weiss and Everett arrive.

*~1:30 PM **John calls pilot.***

1:45 PM Ramseys leave for Fernie's.

1:50 PM House secured.

Approximately 2:00 PM John and Melinda arrived… [However the] AngelFire timeline does not have them arriving until 7:55 PM.

2:30 PM Det. Arndt visits the Ramseys at the Fernie's house [Schiller].

*~2:30 PM **Burke interviewed by Boulder Police Department.** "At approximately the same time" Detective Patterson talked to Burke Ramsey at the White's house; Burke reportedly had "slept through the events of the previous night…"[11] [Schiller].*

*Time Unspecified **John Ramsey hired attorney Mike Bynum.** "Michael Bynum, John Ramsey's close friend and corporate attorney… arrived at the Fernie's house. As he walked in, **the family was kneeling in the living room praying** with Rev. Hoverstock. [There is then a description of John's going for a walk with John Fernie in the hills] "When*

---

10 From pbworks.com: "After using the kitchen, the advocates began tidying it up, a law-enforcement official told NEWSWEEK. One friend helped clean the kitchen, wiping down the counters with a spray cleaner--and possibly wiping away important evidence." (Glick et al. 1998).

11 It would later emerge in interviews with Burke Ramsey that Burke was awake at various times in the night, and the following morning.

they returned a half hour later, Ramsey asked Bynum to represent him."[Schiller].[12]

*Time Unspecified **Dr. Beuf arrives [JonBenét's paediatrician].***

7:25-7:40 PM John Ramsey walks with John Fernie and Dr. Beuf. [Steve Thomas].

~8:00 PM Pathologist [Meyer] arrived.

~8:20 PM Meyer entered house.

8:20 PM First Search Warrant Executed. Police obtain search warrant for Ramsey premises and vehicles in Boulder; search conducted 8:20 PM (Byfield 1997:3).

~8:20-8:30 Meyer examined body.

~8:30 PM Meyer left.[13]

9:15 PM John Ramsey left for Denver International Airport to pick up his brother Jeff, who had flown in from Atlanta. [Steve Thomas].

*10:25 PM Patsy got up and asked where John was and where Burke was. She then sobbed. **"Why did they do this? Why did they do this?"** She asked for a Valium. [Steve Thomas].*

10:45 PM Body Removed.

10:48 PM Patsy's sisters and brother-in-law arrive at the Fernie home. [Steve Thomas].

11:44 PM Detective Arndt left… Arndt was last to leave the house.

12-27-96 Autopsy.

---

12 It remains unclear how Mike Bynum was alerted, who informed him about JonBenét, or when. When John Ramsey was questioned on these details, he was instructed not to answer.

13 Incredibly, the coroner spent little more than ten minutes examining JonBenét's body at the scene.

12-27-96 Second Boulder search warrant.

12-27-96 Arndt interviewed the Ramseys.

12-28-96 Ramseys Provided Forensic Samples. Ramsey family goes to Boulder police station to answer questions and give samples of hair, blood and handwriting (CNN timeline). These include John Ramsey, John Andrew Ramsey and Burke Ramsey; **"Patsy Ramsey was too distraught to submit to the evidence collection,** *authorities said" (Daily Times-Call.)*

12-28-96 **Ramseys Hired Criminal Attorneys.** *"Shortly after noon that Saturday, without consulting John or Patsy,* **Bynum told Detective Arndt that the Ramseys would not give any more testimonial evidence without a criminal attorney present, and they would no longer share privileged information with the police.** *Since he was no longer a criminal attorney, Bynum called Bryan Morgan of Haddon, Morgan and Foreman in Denver, one of Colorado's top firms. By Saturday evening the Ramseys had retained Morgan." [Schiller].*

12-28-96 The Ramseys met with attorneys Bryan Morgan and Patrick Burke.

12-29-96 Third Boulder search warrant.

12-29-96 Memorial Service in Boulder.

12-29-96 Ramseys flew to Marietta, GA.

12-30-96 Visitation at funeral home.

12-30-96 John Ramsey hired a prominent criminal attorney, Bryan Morgan, and Patsy hired his partner, Patrick Burke. Patrick Korten … became the **Ramsey family official spokesperson** *(AngelFire timeline).*

12-31-96 JonBenét Ramsey's funeral.

1-1-97 CNN Interview

What we get from the above is an almost immediate lack of co-operation from the Ramseys, especially Patsy. We also see subtleties like John calling his pilot twice but not thinking to call the ambulance or take the police into his confidence. The moment the "lawyering up" happens is also critical – it occurs right after Burke is interrogated. John goes on a mysterious walk with a friend, and when he returns, perhaps on Fernie's advice, the lawyering up occurs. A family spokesman is also nominated, which provides an important clue that the Ramseys anticipated a long campaign, and one in which they would try to try to insulate themselves as far as possible. Talk to the media yes, but on their own terms. Co-operate with the police, but under strict conditions.

This hardly corresponds to Lou's assessment of the police "focussing" on the Ramseys, does it? Isn't it fairer to suggest the Ramseys, even then, were *controlling the narrative*?

From cnn.com:

KING: *But if they knew they didn't do it – you don't have to listen to what your lawyers say.*

SMIT: *And that's exactly what happened. The Ramseys are the only suspects I have ever been in contact with that has been interrogated as a suspect for six days. John and Patsy Ramsey have been interrogated more than anybody I have ever seen.*

Wow. And Larry seems to feel the same way.

From cnn.com:

KING: *Where do we go from here?*

SMIT: *I believe that what should be done, even at this time, they have worn the Ramsey path out, I believe that perhaps they should get in fresh minds and fresh eyes, experienced people that can take a **look at this case with an unbiased view point**. That means getting rid of perhaps even* the detectives that are working on it now. Getting rid of Lou Smit. Let somebody else in there that can objectively take a look at that case.

KING: *Who would make that decision?*

SMIT: *The decision would be made **by the people that are in charge of this case**. All I know is that the case if it's left the way it is now, will sit on that shelf, the Ramseys will be held hostage under this umbrella of suspicion for as long as they live, unless somebody gets out there and looks for this guy. If the Ramseys didn't do that, how long will they be held hostage, Larry? Is that just part of our judicial system that we allow that to separate?*

KING: *What do you think will happen, Lou?*

SMIT: *I'm hoping that other people will take a very close look at this case. I'm hoping that John and Patsy Ramsey, if they can do this, try to help as much as they can in order to facilitate finding the killer.*

KING: *Like, more ransom money?*

SMIT: *No, maybe more ransom money, perhaps even **going in and talking with the people who are investigating this**.*

Ya think? Lou concludes by saying "there is a very dangerous killer out there in my mind. I see this person. He will do this again."

Larry still has a final order of business to attend to. First, he addresses Steve Thomas[14] and then he throws out a final cursory remark which fucking changes everything. Are you ready for it?

From cnn.com:

KING: *A final editorial note: we asked officials from the Boulder Police Department to comment on Lou Smit's theories, and they referred us to a statement issued by Chief Mark Beckner on April 30. He says,*

---

14 The complete version of Thomas' interview with Larry King is analysed in *The Craven Silence 3.*

"The department believes it would be improper for it to debate the merits of the Ramsey case evidence in the public arena."

The statement also says that Lou Smit has not been involved in the official investigation of JonBenét's killing for the past two and a half years. And adds – quoting here, "The case and development of evidence has changed significantly over that period of time."

According to the Boulder police, they formerly interviewed more than 600 people in this case. Investigated about 140 potential suspects. Logged about 1400 items of evidence. And built a file approximately 40,000 pages long.

[Smits] revelations coincide with publication of the Ramseys' book, "Death of Innocence," which will be released Friday.

So there was a silver lining to Smit's arrival on the scene. It had not been made manifest just then, but Smit's investigation would eventually form the essential narrative of both Ramsey parents' book. Smit had wandered quite literally into their story, and what's more, his efforts wrote entire chapters of the Ramsey narrative. That is the extent to which his narratives not only controlled the narrative, but had it sewn up.

If Smit didn't love the Ramseys he sure did them big favors, didn't he? Not talking to the press for years and then "coming out" on *CNN* to talk about a crime he investigated at a time coinciding with the publication of a book written by the same former murder suspects Smit had been tasked with investigating. It beggars belief, doesn't it? Believe it or not, it gets <u>even shakier than that</u>.

In 2008, two years before his own death, <u>Smit associated himself with a television show specialising in psychic investigations</u>. It was called <u>*Haunting Evidence*</u> and featured psychic detective <u>Carla Baron</u>, medium John J. Oliver and Patrick Burns, a paranormal investigator.

Smit made a cameo in this circus probably because it perpetuated his pet theories when few others would.

From topix.com:

MakeTheArrest: *[Smit]... killed all credibility [by] associating himself with such complete and total frauds! If he can be duped by these clowns, then it makes his opinion on the Ramseys futile.*

Did the intruder narrative *ever* have any merit? Was Lou Smit *ever* going to deliver the goods? Was it, Lou? Were you?

On that bright March day when Lou was driving to Boulder, things looked *so* promising didn't they? Like JonBenét's little life, like the pageants, so much seemed shiny and possible, didn't it?

Ultimately Smit would wander the basement of that tall Tudor mansion first-hand and meet Death in all its shitty guises. He'd search for JonBenét in leaves and drifts of snow and wind.

But the stink of blood and shit and dysfunction would soon become his final inheritance on Earth. Patsy would die, and Smit drove up to Michigan to visit her. Then his own wife died. And when it was Smit's turn to meet Death in the face, John was there.

John, whom Smit didn't love – merely liked, merely prayed with – was there. Yes, John Ramsey came to pray at Lou's bedside shortly before his death. The former murder suspect had a chance to turn the tables on the detective; this time it would be John praying for Lou as the great white light beckoned. It would be John praying for Lou as the giant black maw closed over his detective friend.

LIGHTHOUSE

"Where there is darkness, there once was light."
— Saim Cheeda

Lessons in Child Psychology #2

In the Ramsey household we have <u>a snapshot of the American family</u>, but there is a steaming archetype buried in the basement, smeared on the walls of that five bedroom, more than 11 000 square foot home. The prototypical millionaire businessman father and glamorous homemaking beauty queen mother is juxtaposed against a brother and sister who are also – supposedly – idioms of the American Dream. <u>Or are they</u>?

We will deal more thoroughly with Patsy Ramsey's Christmas newsletters [1996 and 1995] and the remaining Ransom Note idiosyncrasies in *The Craven Silence 3*. For now we'll stick to a few highlights and then apply them to the pertinent child psychology.

Let's start with Patsy's <u>1996 Christmas newsletter</u>, addressed to friends and family.

From <u>datalounge.com</u>:

...It's been another busy year at the Ramsey household...Melinda graduated from Medical College...John Andrew is a Sophomore at the University of Colorado....<u>Burke is a busy fourth grader</u> where <u>he really shines</u> in math and spelling...and is currently <u>on a basketball binge</u>! His little league team was #1....JonBenét is enjoying her first year in 'real school.' Kindergarten... is fast paced and five full days a week. She has already been moved ahead to first grade math. She continues to <u>enjoy participating in talent and modelling pageants</u>...Her teacher says she is

so outgoing...<u>*John is always on the go travelling hither and yon*</u>*. Access recently celebrated its one billion $$ mark in sales...He and his crew [sailed the] Port Huron to Mackinac Island yacht race in July...On a recent trip to NYC, my friend and I appeared amid the throng of fans on the TODAY show. We are all enjoying continued good health and look forward to seeing you in 1997! One final note ... thank you to...my dear husband for surprising me with the biggest, most outrageous 40th birthday bash I've ever had! We'll be spending my actual birthday on the Disney Big Red Boat over the new year!*

It may not be clear from the extract above, but Patsy's effusiveness about her family really centers on JonBenét. In terms of sheer volume, <u>more text is devoted to JonBenét</u> than anyone else. The same is true of <u>the 1995 newsletter</u>. But there's something a lot more obvious going on – it's the use [or rather overuse] of exclamation marks. Patsy is a really emphatic person, we see this over and over in her arm waving interviews, in her <u>extravagant countering</u> when interrogated and we see the same verbal and behavioral pattern reinforced in these written newsletters.

But what pattern is this exactly and what does it mean, and what does it have to do with child psychology? Let's burrow down into the details and see if we can find a bone worth chewing on.

Running across both newsletters are a surfeit of exclamation marks – the 533 word 1995 version has 16 exclamation marks, roughly 1 exclamation for every 33 words. The 1996 version has 9 exclamation marks scattered across 407 words, roughly one exclamation in 45 words. Five of the seven paragraphs in Patsy's 1996 newsletter end in exclamation marks including the first and last. We see the same convention in the 1995 newsletter *and the Ransom Note.*

The <u>Ransom Note</u> begins and ends <u>with exclamation marks</u>, but only has a total of three, suggesting that <u>if Patsy wrote the note</u>

its contents were dictated, causing Patsy's "natural emphasis and effusiveness" to fall through the cracks. That would also explain this almost inexplicable slip:

We do[n't] respect your business, but not the country it serves.

So we're seeing exclamation marks – but what do they mean?

From statementanalysis.com:

Exclamation points are used to add emphasis to the statement; "Listen carefully! In talking about killing JonBenét, the writer does not use any exclamation points. Four times the writer wrote "she dies." We would expect this to be a point of emphasis; "If you alert bank authorities, she dies!" We know the writer likes to use exclamation points, but chose not to use them when talking about killing JonBenét. This too indicates that JonBenét was already dead when this note was written.

This contrasts to Lou Smit's contention that whoever wrote the Ransom Note did so before murdering JonBenét, because no murderer could compose him or herself in such a long letter afterwards, even less so an overwrought mother. And this brings us to the child psychology.

In lesson #1 we alluded to this idea of those closest to us being the most dangerous and hurtful. This is particularly true of children, and even more so when it comes to siblings. But even within the sibling rivalry construct what is often missed is **we are our own worst enemy**, our sensitivities, rather than the perceived depredations of the sibling.

*"You gave him the biggest piece of candy!" "You gave him more juice!" "Here's a little more, then." "Now **she's got more** juice than me!" "You let her light the fire in the fireplace and not me." "Okay, you light a piece of paper." "But this piece of paper is **smaller** than the one she lit."…An animal who gets his feelings of self-worth symbolically has to minutely compare himself to those around him, to make sure he doesn't come off second-*

best. Sibling rivalry is a critical problem that reflects the basic human condition: it is not that children are vicious, selfish, or domineering. It is that they <u>so openly express man's tragic destiny</u>: **he must desperately justify himself** *as an object of primary value....he must stand out... [He must] show he counts more than anything or anyone else...*— <u>Ernest Becker</u>

Note this excerpt is also liberally sprinkled with appropriate emphasis[15] <u>to represent the genuine indignation</u> of children towards each other, and to their parents.

In the context of a Ransom Note, and in our view a Bogus Ransom Note, we have the same sense of an effusive [but not sincere] effort to write a Christmas newsletter. It's certainly newsy! But there's also <u>a desperate edge to it</u>, which we get from the torn "practise note", the length of it, and <u>the many movie-make believe moments hewn into it</u> – the "gentlemen" watching over JonBenét, <u>the idea of beheading and a proper burial</u>, the notion of good southern common sense and so on.

That same <u>movie-make believe infests the newsletters</u>, except the newsletters are an effort to <u>talk up the Ramsey family</u> as a sort of modern fairy tale. And who is caught up in this childish pursuit? All of the Ramseys are acting out the same fairy tale, even John and Burke today. In 1996 the living and the dead <u>JonBenét was too</u>.

---

15 The original extract includes three exclamation marks and two italicised words spanning 7 sentences.

Linda Hoffman-Pugh

"If I were speaking to Patsy Ramsey right now, this is what I would say to her: 'You were spent and exhausted, weren't you? The holidays do that to people. At the party on December twenty-third you appeared a little out of sorts, perhaps because there were twenty people in the house with another twenty on the way. It was five in the afternoon, and I was on my way out the door, leaving you without help. So it's okay if you dipped deeply into the Beringer Chardonnay, your favorite wine that you kept in the walk-in refrigerator, just off the kitchen." — someoneisgettingawaywithmurder.com, Chapter One, Linda Hoffman-Pugh's unpublished book.

Linda Hoffman-Pugh was the first name to roll off Patsy's tongue. After all, she had a key, she knew the house, she knew the kids, and she needed money. She'd been a fixture in their home for the past fourteen months. If JonBenét had been kidnapped, then it had to be Linda.

But was Linda part of a foreign faction? Did Linda have a problem with the U.S. government?

While Linda was the first on a long list of suspects, she was also the first to cast a shadow on the Ramsey's fairy tale parade.

From denverpost.com:

The night JonBenét's body was found, Detectives Fred Patterson and Greg Idler knocked on the door of the Ramsey's housekeeper, Linda Hoffmann-Pugh. Patsy had told police her housekeeper had a key to the house and major money problems. When told the girl had been murdered, Hoffmann-Pugh screamed and couldn't stop shaking.

*After she settled down, she was asked to print some words on a sheet of paper – **Mr. Ramsey, attaché, beheaded** and the number **$118,000** (unknown to her, all phrases in the Ransom Note) – but Linda was too upset to write, assuming JonBenét had been beheaded.*

There's an interesting parallel here to statements made by Detective Lou Smit and Ollie Gray – that after witnessing the death of JonBenét, a relative would be unable to compose themselves. That psychology then swung the pendulum towards some psychopathic monster – like Linda the housekeeper? Just how hardcore was Hoffman-Pugh?

From denverpost.com:

Police talked to the Pughs for three hours, according to the [Lawrence Schiller] book. "Had Linda ever witnessed any signs of sexual abuse in the Ramsey household? Had JonBenét ever wet the bed? Had Linda seen semen, blood or anything unusual on the child's bed? On anyone else's bed? Hoffmann-Pugh would know for sure she was a suspect when the police returned the next day to search her house and fingerprint her. At a local doctor's office, she cried as the police yanked strands of hair from her head and she gave blood samples."

Although Linda shared with the police the numerous and stressful issues with bed-wetting and soiling, Linda also [initially] supported the Ramseys publicly. She described Patsy as "warm and nice, just a sweet person" when reporters asked. Linda even said she loved Patsy like a daughter.

But over time, Linda's tune changed.

From rense.com, the Denver Post:

"I think she [Patsy] had multiple personalities. She'd be in a good mood and then she'd be cranky. She got into arguments with JonBenét about wearing a dress or about a friend coming over. I had never seen Patsy so upset."

Quite a contrast, isn't it? The public questioned the credibility of Linda because her opinions of Patsy seemed to evolve over time. One minute Patsy was a saint; the next Patsy was off her rocker. Which was it? Were the criticisms of Patsy simply vengeance once she found out the Ramseys viewed her as a suspect? If it was a case of spitefulness, it would be somewhat understandable.

But I get a sense that Linda was sincere in her outrage towards Patsy, beyond being accused. To me, it seemed like she was deeply distressed and saddened by coming to terms with the true colors of her friend.

In 2001, Linda filed a defamation suit against the Ramseys. But she was no match for their high-powered legal machine. Her case was ultimately dismissed by a judge in 2002.

From dailycamera.com:

Linda Hoffmann-Pugh, who worked in the Ramseys' Boulder home, said she was "shunned, hated, ridiculed and held in contempt by members of her community" because of the allegations in the Ramseys' book, The Death of Innocence. Although Hoffman-Pugh, a resident of Platteville, was questioned in the case, she is not under suspicion in JonBenét's death, Boulder Police Chief Mark Beckner said Thursday. John and Patsy Ramsey, however, remain under "an umbrella of suspicion."

The Ramsey's attorney, Lin Wood, said in a statement that Hoffman-Pugh turned on the Ramseys to make money from paid interviews with tabloids and a possible book deal.

"Ms. Hoffmann-Pugh is not worthy of belief as a witness, and her lawsuit is a frivolous publicity stunt," the statement said.

Wood cited a statement Hoffman-Pugh made on national television in 1997: "Patsy's just the most wonderful person I've ever met in my life."

Wood said later public comments show that her motivation for trashing the Ramseys was greed.

In many ways, Linda was an easy target. She wasn't the most educated person on the block, having dropped out of high school and getting married at the age of fifteen. She also didn't do herself any favors when she started to cash in. The TV show the *American Journal* reportedly paid her $15,000 for her appearance. She also reportedly received $20,000 from the *National Enquirer*, amongst other free perks.

Steve Thomas was infuriated by the money-grubbing that was infecting the case. He commented in his book "Linda Hoffman-Pugh was riding around in a limousine paid for by the tabloids." And she was. The same thing happened in the O.J. Simpson case. One of the more critical witnesses, Jill Shively, who saw O.J. in his Bronco on the night Nicole was killed, was also struggling financially. When offered, she accepted a $5,000 payment in return for her appearance on TV. She was subsequently denied the opportunity to take the stand and admitted later on that she regretted it.

Should making money in these situations automatically discount a witness? While I'll admit, it does put them under a different level of scrutiny, I'm also of the belief each individual deserves to be vetted on their full merits.

Let's not forget, in both this case and in the O.J. case, almost every major player, including the Ramseys, and including O.J. [although, the Goldmans prevented him from collecting money], wrote a book. People making money in high-profile cases is nothing new.

Was Linda greedy? She made $72 a day from her housecleaning job with the Ramseys. Between her and her second husband, Mervin, the Pughs had eleven children. Hell yea, money was an issue. But, in a sense, all of this was a smokescreen too. It was convenient for Patsy to tarnish the reputation of a woman who had insider knowledge of their family. Who would the public believe when push came to shove - the frumpy maid or the belle of the ball?

Unlike the neighbors who only saw the dressed-up version of the Ramseys and who gushed at what a lovely bunch of people they all were, Linda saw the Ramseys in their most intimate moments. By intimate, I mean the every-day, uglier stuff like John's evasiveness, Patsy's entitled, pissy moods, the kids' tantrums, the dirty rooms, the soiled sheets...

From <u>acandyrose</u>:

I spent half my time picking up after her [JonBenét.] She and her brother would just leave everything on the floor – their socks, their shoes, toys, books, just everything. They were never trained to put things away properly.

I always came in the side door, and I'd walk right into the kitchen and not know where to start. Dishes all over. If they had Ovaltine, the jar would still be open. I always had to wipe the peanut butter off the counter. "I think we ought to get a hamper," I told Patsy. "Yeah, that sounds good," she answered. But we never got one.

I think the problem with the children was they didn't have any responsibility. They were spoiled.

Sure, all of us to some extent are more relaxed, and less "put together" in our own homes. But for a family obsessed with their perfect, public appearance, and with a lot riding on that appearance, surely the last thing they wanted was their dirty laundry to be aired. Wouldn't it be better to tarnish Linda before she could tarnish them?

From acandyrose:

"Just go away and leave me alone," JonBenét said when I tried to help her with her boots. Sometimes she acted like a spoiled brat.

"No, don't you answer the door," she'd [JonBenet would] say when someone went to open it at a luncheon Patsy gave. "I'm answering the door."

[On December 23] At one o'clock she went to play with some friends and was back by four o'clock. Late that afternoon she didn't want to wear a dress for their Christmas party. Patsy got a little agitated. Finally, JonBenét put on a velvet one with short sleeves.

We also heard how Patsy wanted to dress JonBenét to be her twin on Christmas Day but JonBenét refused, instead wearing the white shirt with the sequin star. Steve Thomas revealed in his book that Patsy wasn't the only target of JonBenét's defiance:

…sometimes JonBenét had to be given a "time-out" for doing things such as stomping on Burke's Lego creations.

Linda makes no bones about it. She believes that Patsy did it. She told the same to the Grand Jury in 1999.

From rense.com, The Denver Post:

*"At first, **I didn't want to believe** that Patsy could do such a thing," said the 57-year-old Platteville resident, who now delivers newspapers.*

"I loved her. But as time went on, things came to me that made me think she did it. I want Patsy Ramsey tomorrow to look in the mirror and say to herself, "I killed JonBenét."

It's pretty damn significant when somebody who's been a part of your life and family for over a year accuses you of killing your child. Whether you believe it was Patsy who did it, or somebody else in the family, I think it's certainly an indicator of the level of stress in that home.

Before we move on from Linda, there's one other matter to address. Was Linda ever truly a reasonable suspect in this case? Yes, she was cash-strapped and had asked the Ramseys for money. She also had a creepy, alcoholic husband who internet posters dubbed, _Merv the Perv_. Were they a wolf in sheep's clothing; a sinister pair?

From acandyrose:

*[After the Ramsey's Christmas party on December 23] I was supposed to come back the next day, December 24, and clean up. I called Patsy and said I couldn't. I told her I had a fight with my sister and needed some money to pay the rent. **I asked Patsy for a $2,000 loan.** I told her I would pay it back $50 each week. **She didn't hesitate. "Sure."** She said she'd leave it for me on the kitchen counter for my next regular visit on December 27."*

Let's get a grip here. If Bill McReynolds, a.k.a. Santa, who was in his late sixties and had heart failure, was unlikely, physically, to pull off this crime, the same could be said for the Pughs. How exactly did Linda maneuver in and out of the narrow basement window? Or, did drunken Merv the Perv do the deed? Are either one of these individuals, in their 50s, and not exactly in the best health or shape, really capable of stealthily snatching a kid while her family slept?

The other half of the argument is that Patsy had quite easily agreed to loan Linda money. So, why bite the hand that feeds you?

From someoneisgettingawaywithmurder.blogspot.com, Chapter One, Linda Hoffman Pugh's unpublished book:

I had worked for you [Patsy] for nearly a year and I didn't even know that room existed until you had me get those trees out of there. An intruder wouldn't have found that place. Not in a million years. Only you, or John, would know its location.

Stun Gun?

*"As we left [the store] the clerk gave me a…
[catalogue] to take home. When I returned to
Boulder, I threw it into a drawer and completely
forgot about the tape. I <u>surmise</u> that as the police
went through everything in our house, they found
the [catalogue], which apparently turned out to have
an advertisement for....you got it....stun guns! Not
too long after that the police reported to the media
that they had found a stun gun "instructional video"
in the Ramsey house. So on the one hand they were
supporting the stun gun theory, but on the other
hand they were <u>not indirectly</u> saying that I had
used this weapon on my daughter. Of course, for a
period of time [it] created a significant uproar and
cast further suspicion on me. Later we got a copy
of the [catalogue] from the store in Coral Gables,
and found it was recorded in Spanish! Not only*

had I never reviewed the tape; if I had I wouldn't have understood it." — <u>John Ramsey</u> describing aftermath to spy store visit because of electronic bugging concerns at Access Graphics

"Sometimes, MacLeod, the sharpest blade is not enough." – Ramirez in <u>Highlander</u>

[WARNING: Some links to graphic autopsy images]

There's so much <u>smoke and mirrors</u> in this case sometimes it's difficult to know where the misdirection begins and where it ends. How does one navigate through blind space? How do ships find their way through endless chimney sweeps of impenetrable fog?

A <u>compass</u> is one way of finding our way through the murk. And in the JonBenét case, as in all true crime scenarios, psychological patterns are the magnetic forces that we must draw upon to find our golden thread, our true North.

<u>The stun gun</u> – as far as I'm concerned – is a false flag bedevilling this case. The "<u>sexual assault</u>" is another example, the bedwetting yet another, <u>the flashlight</u> another and on and on. And Lisa's take on the stun gun?

I've never believed a stun gun was used on JonBenét. First, <u>stun guns aren't silent</u>. An intruder trying to grab a child out of their bed in the middle of the night with family sleeping close by would be conscious of noise. Second, stun guns aren't typically used to render somebody "unconscious"... they're intended to make you immobile.

But the problem with that is the victim can very likely become agitated and mobile and besides these: vocal. The investigators involved in the *CBS* special did a demo...

Interestingly *CBS has since removed that demo* from their official YouTube Channel probably as part of comprehensive "damage control" in the face of a threatened lawsuit from the Ramsey's lawyer Lin Wood. We'll deal with the merits of that demo in due course, but first let's address whether the stun gun conversation as a whole is worth having in the first place.

Students of this case may rightly argue that all details, even minor details, are vital to building the mosaic. While that's true, if the mosaic ultimately reveals *smoke and mirrors*, we have not progressed at all, but instead fallen foul to the traps laid out by the elaborate inventiveness and pageantry of the criminal [but more likely *criminals*] involved.

So before we even deal with the stun gun, let's remind ourselves of three things:

1. JonBenét was murdered *twice* – the first murder was a massive bludgeoning to the little girl's head.[16]

2. The second murder was a *make-believe* murder.[17]

3. The stun gun [if it was even used] had nothing to do with JonBenét's murder, rather it is [if it was even used] associated with the flowery periphery of the crime, just as the Ransom Note is.

If the Ramseys are involved in covering up the murder of their daughter, the Ransom Note logically can be assumed to be part of

---

16 It should be noted that thus far we have not explicitly stated that the strangling [using the garrotte] was the second murder. Our reasons for this will be made clear in *The Craven Silence 3*.

17 "The second murder" was determined by the coroner.

some very strategic misdirection. Is the stun gun also part of material misdirection *by the Ramseys*? The fact that it is considered at all is really due to one man above all, Lou Smit.

From cnn.com:

KING: *What about stun gun?*

SMIT: *I think that the stun gun is* one of the best clues *left behind by the killer, as far as a clue, not only into a possible way we can find him, because someone would probably have seen him with a stun gun, but it also may explain why JonBenét did not cry out when she was first abducted. There has been a lot of theories on the stun gun.* **I am convinced that a stun gun was used.** *I am not positive that it is an Air Taser stun gun.*

It's these sorts of statements by Smit that tarnish his shining record as far as we are concerned. Smit feels the stun gun is one of the best clues, yet no stun gun was even found at the scene, or indeed inside or outside the Ramsey home. Despite all the other evidence present – the flashlight, the note, the garrotte – Smit fixates on what's *not* there. So what are we talking about? Is it smoke and mirror stuff or just a vapid fog?

1. Evidence For Stun Gun

I must admit I was initially taken in by Smit's contention that it was a stun gun. Part of the reason it made some sense was Smit's suggestion of an injury pattern [in the evenly spaced dark spots on the six year old's neck/face and back]. Was this contention reinforced by what appeared to be a faint blue line connecting the dark spots? Analogous to the bright blue lightning bolt of a Taser, right?

Smit took his super sleuthing even further, suggesting an intruder sneaking into JonBenét's bedroom would need to immobilize her in bed if he wanted to successfully [and quietly] abduct her. The stun gun was instrumental in Smit's mind in getting JonBenét out of the Ramsey residence *quietly*. Makes sense, right?

From cnn.com:

KING: *Meaning?*

SMIT: *Meaning that **the Air Taser stun gun is as close as we've been able to find to the marks on JonBenét**. Myself and Dr. Doberson, from Littleton, the coroner, have conducted experiments on pigs. **We have replicated the marks on JonBenét by using it on pigs**. Stun-gun marks are very distinctive, Larry. Stun gun marks have no cuts, they're not bleeding, **there's no bruising**, there's no swelling, there's no blistering. JonBenét's marks on her body – two sets of marks, one on her back and one on her face – show all of those characteristics. Those same characteristics are shown on other stun gun cases that we've been able to uncover.*

At face value, Smit's contentions carry some weight; all the more so because of Smit's reputation as Colorado's very own virtuous and incorruptible Dark Knight. Unfortunately Smit's reputation precedes the man himself, or rather, some of the conclusions the man drew particular to the Ramsey case. As for Dobersen, well, he's pretty convincing on this issue one moment, but then the next he isn't.

From gemart.8m.com:

Arapahoe County Coroner, Michael Dobersen... In the new UK crockumentary he had this to say:

DOBERSEN: *"My experiments, and the observations that we made and all the work that's been done, I feel that I can testify to a reasonably degree of medical certainty that these are stun gun injuries."*

Sounds impressive right? But then there are glaring contradictions like this.

From gemart.8m.com/Boulder Daily Camera - January, 1998:

DOBERSEN: *"They came over and **showed me some pictures from the (Ramsey) autopsy and asked for my opinion**, whether they could be stun gun injuries...I told them that they could be; that was a possibility..."*

Dobersen told Boulder investigators ...to measure the distance between the wounds and compare that to stun guns.

DOBERSEN: *"Besides...the only definitive way to tell if electrocution was involved in JonBenét's death is to re-examine her body and look for very characteristic changes in skin tissue....[But] **you really can't tell from a photo."***

Jim Clemente and Laura Richards did a commendable job demonstrating the use of a stun gun on a ~~pig~~ person. While not perfectly scientific, what their demonstration did illustrate was that the size and color of the bruising on a living person is radically different. It seems to leave a sort of red blemish, like a welt.

My initial response was that JonBenét was dead when stun gunned; this being make-believe torture/damage of her corpse after the fact. As such the bruising would be more concentrated and darker and thus couldn't be compared to stun gunning a person who would leap out of range once zapped.

Of course this sort of convenient reasoning seems *too convenient* doesn't it, and it feels we have crossed some sort of boundary between verifiable evidence and the twilight zone.

The reason for this is even if the stun gun is accepted as the likely cause of the patterned bruising we still don't have a proper psychology to base even the use of a stun gun on. Was the stun gun used for a stealthy abduction? Was it used to immobilize? Was it used at all?

Just what is the psychology of our phantom intruder who now carries:

a bludgeoning weapon,

a garrotte,

notepad and pen [and perhaps the three page Ransom Note],

parachute cord for tying JonBenét's arms above her head…

…and now a stun gun as well.

If our phantom intruder arrived carrying a sack full of dangerous intent, perhaps he decided to leave with something more suited to travelling with a load [which would include JonBenét]. Like a blue Samsonite suitcase?

Let's consider one psychological long shot, and see how well the stun gun theory fits into it.

From Yerkey's version:

[JonBenét] knows that Santa [Bill McReynold's] will soon be here, what she doesn't know is that his elf is a pervert and not a giving soul. When Santa eventually arrives the large felt bag that he is carrying, surprises her, almost as much as his ability to unlock the door to the house.

At this point Santa places a finger to his mouth and whispers to her… when he has her attention he zaps her with the stun gun. **She screams or perhaps she doesn't** *(the neighbor is uncertain). Santa's helper if he had one is now on the scene. Santa then leads his assistant, who is carrying the unconscious JonBenét to the basement (or perhaps he is doing it himself and is alone).*

Yerkey seems pretty sure about the stun gun doesn't he? Only problem is he is unsure of almost everything else – how Santa got in, if he was alone, whether JonBenét screams when Tasered or not, and who in the team of two does what, where, how and why. That's an awful lot of unknowns, but it doesn't seem to bother Yerkey.

Let's see how Colorado's Dark Knight responds to this question of a Taser being used specifically to achieve a stealthy abduction in a house full of people.

SIGHTS AND SOUNDS

From cnn.com:

KING: *And a kidnapper uses a stun gun to prevent noise, right?*

SMIT: *To prevent noise? Well,* **I'm not saying to prevent noise,** *because this particular stun gun is rather loud, unless it's pressed against the skin. Then it's very quiet.*

Yes Lou, that was what I was thinking – pressed against the skin… The only thing wrong is in Lou Smit's version [and Yerkey's] the stun gun is presented as a device to subdue JonBenét *while she is alive.* But to create those concentrated burns [or is abrasions] it means little JonBenét likely had to be held down while in bed, which – when applying shocking electrical force through a conducting body – is tricky.

Getting to that bedroom would be tricky too. Getting inside the second floor bedroom without waking her [or being seen by anyone else] would also be tricky. Carrying her like a sack of potatoes down two flights of stairs in the dark…very fiddly indeed.

The other thing is a neighbour, Melody Stanton, *did* hear a child's scream close to midnight on Christmas Night, and quite a long one [3-5 seconds]. The problem with the entire *spiel* is if the intruder is able to sneak up on JonBenét and get close enough to subdue her *while Tasering her,* and closing her mouth so she couldn't scream, then why would an intruder need a Taser in the first place? He could simply put his knee on her chest and cover her mouth with duct tape. None of this holds together with JonBenét being bludgeoned and strangled as well.

Of course none of it holds together in that she also clearly did scream. Nothing makes sense except that it's an important theory to hold onto if you're the Ramseys, because the debate then concentrates on non-Ramseys.

But there are more problems with the intruder narrative prancing around quietly in the silent night through the Ramsey residence with a stun gun – maybe silent/maybe not – as his secret weapon.

<u>Bludgeoning</u> – hard enough to crack her skull the way poor little JonBenét's head was cracked – involves a heavy blow, something very risky in a house filled with sleeping people.

The bludgeoning did not involve a flashlight in our assessment either. Think about an intruder bludgeoning JonBenét either in her bedroom or the basement using his only source of light as the murder weapon?

If we discount light as a counterargument, there's also sound. A slight miss or deflection from <u>a massive blow</u>[18] could make a loud THWACK on a cement floor, wall or piece of furniture, besides the meaty <u>melon-snapping noise of the blow</u> itself. And having dispatched the poor little girl, why on earth would there be any point in strangling her as well afterwards [and theoretically, in the dark]?

---

18 The Ramsey's contend in their book *Death of Innocence* that "only a man" could muster the strength necessary to strike the sort of blow that fractured the six year old's skull. In the CBS documentary *The Case of: JonBenét Ramsey* <u>Jim Clemente and crew demonstrate that a ten year old boy</u> could handily replicate the same devastating injury.

We might as well be clear right now that we also differ with the coroner's report that shows JonBenét died of asphyxiation. In our view the bludgeoning killed JonBenét. We agree with John E. Meyer that JonBenét didn't die immediately from the blow. We'll deal with these assertions in more detail in *The Craven Silence 3*. We should draw attention to the trauma to JonBenét's brain that was not only devastating but would have rendered her unconscious. Thus certainly for the purposes of an abduction, the bludgeon blow duplicates the purpose of the stun gun [to stun = to immobilize], and what's more renders the need to silence the child with duct tape, restrain her with cord and strangle her with a garrotte completely unnecessary. The overlapping methods in which JonBenét appears to have been murdered is a match with the two and a half page Ransom Note – it's excessive. It's two pages too much.

It may seem cheeky our rejection of Meyer's autopsy findings, but actually there's more to it than that. We won't deal with it here but it's nevertheless important to sow the seed while we're rooting out misdirections.

Briefly, we're baffled by Meyer's findings not merely because the mortal damage to the little girl's brain is patently obvious, but for other possibly sinister reasons as well. Briefly, these are:

1. In Meyer's autopsy report he fails to provide perhaps the most crucial estimate – time of death.

2. Meyer's work is used by the Boulder District Attorney's office… which never seems to prosecute these crimes…

3. We're wondering whether Meyer sort of plays a supporting role [behind-the-scenes] in fudging the data for the chummy system run by the Boulder D.A.

4. In the *CBS* documentary The Case of: JonBenét Ramsey veteran coroner Werner Spitz points out that JonBenét died of brain death.[19]

Does this seem farfetched? Then consider another case that involved bludgeoning with a mysterious blunt object inside a Boulder home, an early morning 911 call, aspersions of an intruder with no evidence, the Boulder Police suspecting the husband, Meyer as coroner, <u>Alex Hunter as the District Attorney in charge</u>, lawyers to the rescue and surprise, surprise, no prosecution for the man suspected of the murder, a railway worker called Mike Grainger.

From <u>westword.com</u>:

*Boulder County Coroner John Meyer has ruled that while the "manner of death" in the case was homicide, the actual cause of death was "morbid obesity." The coroner based that uncommon finding on his belief that...**the blow to Sonia's head was not a lethal one...***

...according to Boulder police...in February 1995...Grainger hit Sonia over the head with a blunt object while she slept in their Boulder town home, killing her. He now stands charged with second-degree murder.

*There are **no signs that anyone other than Mike was in the home the night of Sonia's death**. But any evidence linking him to her death was, and is, circumstantial. The weapon that allegedly delivered the blow has never been found. **The case is further complicated by another of Meyer's findings**: Even without the blow to the head, the coroner said, Sonia was in such poor physical condition that she may well have died from natural causes within a few days.*

---

19 Spitz also theorised in the same *CBS* documentary that the torch was the murder weapon because it was an exact fit; we don't believe it is.

Let's go through that again. Even though Sonia has been violently bludgeoned, the coroner seems to insist that she would likely have died later any-fucking-way, even days later, from other causes!

From westword.com:

*The Boulder District Attorney's Office cited **insufficient evidence** when it **declined to file charges against Grainger** in 1995...the deputy district attorney assigned to prosecute the case, refuses to comment on the reason for the delay. But given the laborious and so far inconclusive investigation into the Ramsey murder, some have suggested that the Boulder police and the DA's office are using Grainger as a scapegoat...*

"I just don't know if it's political," says Grainger's attorney, Peter Schild. "I have no proof of anything. The DA says they have more evidence, but I don't think they do."

"You can draw your own conclusions," says Neal S. Cohen, a former attorney of Grainger's. "One has to wonder what took them so long."

But the cops aren't the only ones who've accused Grainger of causing Sonia's death. In 1996, before any criminal charges were filed against him, Tonia Kucera, Sonia's daughter from a previous marriage, filed a wrongful-death suit in Boulder District Court accusing Mike of killing her mother.

Oh and one more thing, the Graingers were inordinately wealthy due to a previous insurance settlement.

From westword.com:

*Sonia [while alive] sued the railroad. Though the terms of the 1992 settlement are sealed, Rachetts says the couple received $2.4 million. The bulk of the money went to an annuity that eventually became worth $4 million. According to Rachetts, **$150,000 of the settlement went directly to Sonia**, who was named conservator of the settlement trust.*

After Sonia's murder, thanks to Boulder's legal gymnasts, Mike Grainger received a settlement worth hundreds of thousands of dollars which naturally enough he split with his devoted crack legal team based in Boulder.

Now let's deal with this stun gun shenanigan. The stun gun is important because it allows the narrative to spin off in the broad direction of stun guns. In the chapter Super Predators, we'll deal with exactly how that happened, and with whom. Of course the entire premise behind the stun gun is very, very shaky.

2. Evidence Against Stun Gun

The injuries on JonBenét's back and neck/head are bruises,[20] not the sort of singe/burns typical of stun gun injuries. The autopsy report describes these marks as "abrasions".

Although pattern injuries, the spacing between abrasions do not match Taser prong spacing.

While colorfully imaginative, Smit's contention that the blue arc caused the "corresponding" thin blue line underneath is ludicrous.

From gemart.8m.com:

Apparently Mr. Smit failed his high school electronics class, or he would have known that the color of an electrical arc has nothing to do with the burn you get from it. The arc from an Air Taser stun gun could no more leave a blue line than a [lightning] bolt could turn a person blue if they were struck by it. Welders who expose their skin to the intense blue arc produced by arc welding get a typical red sunburn, they don't turn

---

20 Former investigator Tom Wickman concurs that the marks on JonBenét's body are not from a stun gun. According to the dailycamera.com: *Wickman was sworn in as the grand jury's investigator in 1998 and present at nearly every grand jury session, aiding prosecutor Michael Kane. The grand jury investigated for 13 months without indicting anyone.*

into blue smurfs – nor would their finger turn blue if they were stupid enough to touch the arc. (And where are the blue lines on your pig tests, Lou?)

And then there's this:

"The stun gun theory has been around for some time. I know for a fact that this was submitted to various experts in stun guns and manufacturers, criminalists, forensic pathologists, law enforcement people, they all rejected it.[21] I also know for a fact that Mr. Smit, pursuant to his own request, presented this to one of the top-flight forensic scientists, who along with another top-flight forensic scientist of a different subspecialty, rejected it." – Dr. Cyril Wecht, forensic pathologist, Court TV - The Crier Report, 05/01/01

Air Taser, the company/product identified by Colorado's Dark Knight as the one used by the invisible bogey man, also disputes the claim.

From pbworks.com:

Air Taser, the manufacturer of the stun gun that would have left markings most similar to those found on JonBenét Ramsey's body, was [sceptical] that any stun gun could have been used without either creating much noise or causing JonBenét Ramsey to scream in pain. An extensive interview with an Air Taser representative…aired on MSNBC in July 2001.

On the 18th of July 2003 Michael Kane, the special prosecutor tasked with the Ramsey case, commented for the first time in public [on *MSNBC*] about the stun gun myth:

From gemart.8m.com:

---

21 A small and informal Websleuths poll in November 2014 showed 59% of forum users didn't believe a stun gun was used. The remaining votes were evenly split between "Undecided" and that a stun gun was "definitely" used.

KANE: *"There was one person who was qualified who actually looked at that little girl's body on the autopsy table and that was Dr. Meyer, who's a forensic pathologist. He looked at those very marks and said that they were abrasions. It is a quantum leap – you can take a stun gun and put it up against somebody's body...and it's going to leave a burn. It doesn't leave an abrasion. So all these other opinions that have come out that said that this was a stun gun, there is absolutely no way they would ever get into evidence because there is no evidence that these were burns."*

Dang Dr. Meyer, why did you have to go and call abrasions "abrasions"? It would have been much easier if you'd simply called them...I dunno...injuries.

From pbworks.com:

*DocG writes: The "stun gun" is a perfect example of the lengths to which Ramsey supporters must go when constructing their mystery intruder. Since there is **no real evidence of any such person**, it has been necessary **to concoct evidence** out of thin air. Anyone can take some marks from a photograph, shop around for something that seems to fit those marks, and then assert that the marks "must have been" made by that object. If Smit hadn't found a stun gun with the necessary measurements he'd have found some other object that filled the bill, something the Ramseys were unlikely to possess, such as a plumber's tool...*

Anything that might prove useful in concocting a reasonable doubt defense. All the stun gun theory proves is that Lou Smit is NOT operating as an objective investigator but, on the contrary, a Ramsey advocate. What's most troubling about this whole issue is the way so many reasonable people have taken this absurd theory seriously...

Indeed. So the reader is entitled to ask – why waste a whole chapter on bunkum? Well, if we are going to establish that two sets of patterned abrasions were not caused by a stun gun, then we have yet to answer:

1. **What did cause these abrasions?**

Lou Smit may have lost a few marbles on this case, but he's right about one thing – whatever made both those sets of marks, they were made *while JonBenét was alive*.[22]

2. **Now why would someone jab [whatever it was] at JonBenét – not once but *twice*?**

And finally:

3. **Could the object that caused these injuries give us any insight into where in that five bedroomed mansion the murder took place?**

---

22 The position of this narrative is that the abrasion marks were inflicted while JonBenét was still alive. The current position is that they were inflicted *post mortem*. Since JonBenét likely died on her stomach, and the fact that at least two abrasions were made on her back tend to reinforce this position.

SPOTLIGHT

"Anybody in the spotlight can get lost in that if they are not careful." — Lisa Marie Presley

Lessons in Child Psychology #3

I n this section we begin to narrow our focus somewhat. Let's get to it.

From empoweringparents.com:

*If one of your children bullies his siblings and has to be the boss and control others to the point of getting physical, it indicates some underlying self-doubt and **serious errors in thinking**. He is somehow justifying being hurtful to others in order to make himself feel better. In these cases, you have to **hold all of your kids responsible** when there is an argument, but you have to hold the bully responsible for any aggression over and above the bickering. **Give consequences** to every child who was involved, but if there's a bullying situation, **you have to take a stand**. And I don't mean take sides as if you don't love both of your kids. You have to say "There's going to be no bullying here. There's going to be no cursing at each other. There are **serious consequences** for that behavior."*

In the JonBenét Ramsey case there were serious errors in thinking, there were people [especially lawyers] taking a stand [on television and miscellaneous podiums, just not in court] and there were serious consequences – lawsuits for example, if anyone dared suggest the Ramsey parents or anyone else in the family were involved.

Right now, serious consequences have been threatened against *CBS* for daring to suggest Burke Ramsey may have been involved in the murder of his baby sister. And *CBS* have withdrawn somewhat into their shell, deleting their own content related to this crime off YouTube and allowing their own documentary to contract and then an entire episode to evaporate. 90 minutes of airtime – poof. Because there could be serious consequences to #BreakingtheSilence.

What are we to do about this craven impasse? Well, perhaps an expert in human behavioral psychology, and a Pulitzer prize-winner, can help us out. Mr Becker, if you please.

All power is in essence...the power to deny mortality. Either that or it is not real power at all, not ultimate power, not the power that mankind is really obsessed with. — Ernest Becker[23]

If all power is in essence the power to deny mortality, I'm guessing that means different strokes for different folks. For the individual, denying mortality means denying fallibility, error, guilt, debt etc. So the individual's justification of himself as a hero to the world is one form of power trip. But there's also another. There's denying mortality *in terms of others.* In true crime this literally means denying that you acted [or even had certain thoughts] that rather than heroic, were in fact diabolical.

There is also the denial of life to others – either where people are trampled on, their dreams and desires frustrated towards our own benefit, or their lives are literally sacrificed, so that we may expand ourselves, so that we can walk a red carpet bathed in their blood. When Becker talks about "denying mortality" it can seem mostly harmless. It's not.

Power means power to increase oneself, to change one's natural situation from one of smallness, helplessness, finitude, to one of bigness, control, durability, importance. — Ernest Becker

---

23 *Escape From Evil* by Ernest Becker.

What if one already has that power? What if one is already larger than life, important, in control? Well, if Becker is right the same psychology applies:

Power means power to increase oneself...

And thus, if one is already increased, then power means the power to mitigate the diminishment of self. In the case of John Ramsey, say, this might mean an effort to resist losses. In the case of Patsy Ramsey within this context, this might mean an effort to resist losses – but the losses suffered by John and Patsy would be quite different.

And Burke? What sort of loss could he suffer? Or is the equation entirely different with Burke. Is Burke's equation about surfing a wave of expansion – where in 1997 he suddenly finds himself bigger, back in control, durable, secure and important once more?

The real question we need Becker to address are the mechanisms of power father and son, and also "the mother" are employing in this *schema*. Once we understand the mechanisms perhaps we can pontificate on the possibilities of guilt and/or culpability.

Let's start with the father. Mr Becker, what was John Ramsey's principal mechanism of power?

In its power to manipulate physical and social reality money in some ways secures one against contingency and accident.; it buys body-guards, bullet-proof glass, and better medical care... — Ernest Becker

Yes, and lawyers. And PR people. What else?

...[money] radiates its powers...giving one a semblance of immortality...In short, money is the human mode par excellence [for] coolly denying animal boundness [and] the determinism of nature...

Determinism is: the belief that all events are caused by things that happened before them and that people have no real ability to make choices or control what happens. In the context of True Crime, especially where a criminal attempts to escape his fate, we see contrivances employed to manufacture choices, to conjure opportunities and escape clauses out of the ether. Society pretends to control the outcome of individuals and the agents of this control is law, but the most powerful individuals manipulate these laws, and the strings of that guitar are strung by money. John Ramsey had lots of it, and so, unsurprisingly, he has been able to control – mostly – the narrative as it portends to him across the span of decades.

Of course during this period Ramsey has seen his wealth decimated, along with other prospects. At the same time, the agencies involved in maintaining John's social security have blossomed as treasure has flowed into their pockets. This is the reward for funnelling court cases away from court, by Boulder's courtroom champions. And the reward is mountains of treasure.

What then is the lesson behind money, and what the hell does it have to do with child psychology? Everything actually.

Psychoanalysts [equate] money with feces – it [seems] crass and unreal. We cannot imagine pure pleasure in playing with feces; even to children feces are ambivalent and to some degree distasteful. If as tiny infants they play with feces, it is at a time when feces can have no precise meaning to them; if later they play with feces, this is already a different kind of play, a play of mastery of anxiety, a dealing with a very ambivalent area of experience. — Ernest Becker

And so we must turn this damning indictment where we wish it least. We have to ponder where the Burke we see as a nine-year-old, and the Burke we see as a twenty-nine-year-old, shows any obvious symptoms of anxiety? They must stand out from the norm because smearing shit through your home as a nine-year-old is not the norm. And it is not the norm because for whatever reason, the anxiety this boy is infected with is not the norm either.

This may seem enough for now, but we must bear an even more terrible truth while we teeter here.

Also, it has always seemed simplistic to say that money equals feces, because money has been so supercharged with the yearning of ambition and hope; it could not be merely infantile smearing, not simple self-indulgence? — Ernest Becker

Well…what…more than that? Are you… sure you want to hear this?

*…money does not equal feces at all, does not represent them at all: rather, it represents the **denial** of feces, of physicalness, of animality, of decay, [of smallness] and death…To rise above the body is to equate the body with excrement. In the last analysis, the peculiar fascination with excrement is **the peculiar fascination with death**.* — Ernest Becker

Patsy's Twilight Zone

"I wish I had been, and then we would have had a free and fair trial. And you would have met your Waterloo, Mr. Thomas." — Patsy Ramsey

"For the safety of all of the children, we have to find out who did this." — Patsy Ramsey

One thing we find time and time again in our investigations is something as constant and inexorable as the law of gravity to a mountain:

Murderers are also liars

Although liars aren't always murderers, when investigating murders, liars make more likely murder suspects, and accessories to murder than folks who don't lie. So we must ask ourselves early on:

- Has John Ramsey lied?
- Has Patsy Ramsey lied?
- Has Burke Ramsey lied?
- Has anyone else lied?
- **Who has lied the most**, and who has reason to lie the most?

Most of us aren't murderers or liars, so we tend to take what murderers tell us at face value. This is why the average reader might have missed the amber flag in the quote we dropped above. Here it is again; see if you notice something in it on your second flyby.

> *"For the safety of all of the children, we have to*
> *find out who did this."*

If you had lost a child, if your child had been violently abused in your home, there would be a sense of anger and outrage. There would be an incontrovertible sense of *finding justice for JonBenét*. Oddly, those four words are almost completely missing. Have John or Patsy ever said them? Did they say those words to CNN [on January 1, 1997] at their first opportunity? Because instead of a desperate, even embittered, search for justice we're seeing something slightly different – justification. Justification of pageants, justification of what one did and how one acted. It becomes holding court with the media rather than getting a criminal tried in court.

A murderer doesn't want to be caught, so what they tend to reveal about a crime or crime scene has basically two goals:

- Exonerate the storyteller [through false admissions or misleading omissions or both]
- Mystify the investigator [through providing superfluous information in the form of noisily flapping false flags].

Because most of us aren't criminals, we make the mistake of imagining a crime both as a) an exception to a rule and that b) unexceptional behavior around an exceptional crime is somehow normal [and exonerable].

Criminals spend a lot of effort trying to communicate either what they felt or what they tried to do, often not to merely place these on the record, but to dispel suspicion that they were seen not to have felt [or behaved, or acted] as one would expect.

The reality of a crime tends to be the opposite of trying to do something, thinking carefully and waiting. Crimes tend to be very intentional, and the covering up is part of this crisp and panicked intentionality. Innocent people also are highly intentioned. People who discover someone injured or missing are far more practical about trying to help these people they care about.

Let's jump briefly into something specific so this doesn't feel so theoretical. We're going to dip into one of the very rare in-depth interrogations the Boulder cops got with Patsy Ramsey.

From forumsforjustice.org:

PATSY interrogated June 23 1998 [referring to the morning of December 26th, just after the 911 call]: *And I called them and told them that she's been kidnapped, she is missing. And then I walked out through here, and **opened the door**, and started waiting for – front door – started waiting for the police to show up. (INAUDIBLE). I was standing on the (INAUDIBLE) and pretty soon a squad car came – you know, officer came up. And I remember thinking because it said somewhere in the note, if you do that, if you call somebody, that's not good. Blah, blah, blah. And I just remembered thinking oh, my God, I hope they are not watching me. I mean, what if they are watching, if the policeman comes, I mean all this was just rushing through my head.*

There's plenty wrong with this excerpt. Do you see it? What's all wrong is the juxtaposing of the urgency [oh my God, thoughts rushing through Patsy's head] with the complacency [blah, blah, blah, pretty soon a car came, you know an officer came, uh, went to the front door]. As terrified as Patsy is about calling the police, she doesn't seem to actually tell them about the contents of the note. At the very least they could park down the road, or around the corner, right? But Patsy takes the note so seriously that she doesn't bother to even suggest this. That's how concerned she is about the safety and security of her daughter.

On the same line of reasoning, had Patsy truly realized she'd fucked up in calling people to their house, she could at least have sent the neighbors back home [no harm done], and the reverend [bless him, no harm done either], instead of having them camp in the crime scene all morning.

The other glaring giveaway revolves around the idea of intentionality. Patsy starts off her action plan – this is where she explains how she rushes to her daughter's aid by…waiting at the front door. She "waits" then adds that she "started waiting". Yes, much ado but really nothing. Of course a moment ago <u>Patsy had thrown down the phone on the 911 operator Kimberly Archuleta</u>. Now she's hurrying to the front door to wait for the cops. Patsy's waiting to speak to the cops…when she was just speaking to one! Instead of standing around picking her teeth Patsy could have spent that time studying the Ransom Note, calling friends and family to ask them to keep a look out, ask them for information and otherwise kicking off her own investigation. I'm not sure how wise it is opening the front door when it's still dark [this was just before 06:00, sunrise would be almost 90 minutes later during the winter] when someone has supposedly just broken into your home. But let's allow that one to pass. Assuming the whole family aren't feeling vulnerable or frightened, Patsy could step out that door and begin searching the grounds and the house from top to bottom for evidence of JonBenét. She could call JonBenét's name a few times. At least, that's what an innocent person would do.

Meanwhile, where are John and Burke while Patsy is standing around? Perhaps showering, and Burke is in bed. Ya think? Patsy's in her own private emergency crisis and for the rest of the family it's Christmas as usual?

A guilty Patsy would not only know where JonBenét was, but would know she's dead. If so, the next priority must be getting the misdirection to play out according to plan. That means manning the door, and chaperoning and manipulating each and every one who enters. It means controlling Burke and getting him the hell out of there before the cops can grill him. The priority for guilty schmucks is self-preservation and crime scene management, which involves waiting, talking, explaining and thinking. And that's why the only urgent rushing going on in Patsy's version is *going on in her head*.

I want to return to the reality of the Ramsey residence beyond what Patsy is saying. I think it's a misdirection, which means we're being asked to look away from…*what*? The reality at the Ramsey residence…. did it look and feel quite different to Patsy's twilight zone?

Assuming the Ramseys knew about JonBenét's murder, cover-up mode would have involved exactly that, covering things up. Getting rid of things. Perhaps a certain amount of cleaning. Some items may have been flushed down a toilet, others perhaps thrown into a hearth. Phone calls might need to be made, phone messages deleted, along with excess pieces of Ransom Note paper. What more than this? Well staging a crime scene might have involved wearing a certain kind of rubber glove [even kitchen gloves] and being careful to wipe away potential debris or DNA trails. The murder weapon would also need to be cleaned, disposed of or hidden in plain sight.

The biggest pickle would be getting three people's acts right, and this chatter possibly preoccupied John, Patsy and Burke just prior to French's arrival at 05:59. In our view the Ramseys would have called 911 only after they felt satisfied that they'd completed the execution of their charade. After the call there would be little for guilty assholes to do, for innocent people not knowing JonBenét's status, they'd be propelled hither and thither in fright fuelled sprints, possibly calling out JonBenét's name.

From <u>forumsforjustice.org</u>:

PATSY: *Anyway, he came in and – **and I was just rattled**. I think John came in, and I think he kind of walked us over to this sun room area, and tried to – tried to calm us down and, you know, tried to explain what happened. And then they kind of took over.*

Instead of trying to get help for JonBenét [yes, it's unnecessary because she's dead], Patsy talks about getting help for herself and John. The guy tries to calm them down – see, they're the victims.

Wouldn't genuinely upset parents demand from the cop what they were doing; who else was coming? Wouldn't they urgently feed him information, especially poring through the note?

What we invariably fail to see as investigators is the most obvious psychology of all: true remorse. Instead of "innocent" criminals blaming themselves for what they could have or should have done, instead of obvious displays of emotion, the criminal typically either excuses or explains their own behavior or blames another [often the police]. The big hole in most of these cases tends to be the victim. The victim soon becomes nameless and invisible, the facts are lost in miasmas of sleep and amnesia, and the narrative soon becomes entirely based on the narcissism of the "alleged" criminal. It's all about saving oneself, not saving a dead person.

If psychopathy isn't driving the criminal psychology at play, invariably there's an ugly unseen narcissism at work. If sex isn't the reason for murder, it's money, though sometimes it's both.

Is sex a factor in this case? We think it is, *and it isn't*. A cryptic and unsatisfying answer right? In the next chapter we begin the process of unravelling just this mystery.

Misdirection – the heart in the hand

"I think the purpose in life is to prepare us for eternity." — John Ramsey, <u>CNN</u>

"It's not only critical to be a part of the church, but it's important to find the gift God has given you to fulfill your purpose in life ... Anything we can do to help people reach those goals, that's what we want to do." — John Ramsey

"Make not your thoughts your prisons." — Shakespeare, Antony and Cleopatra

The point of misdirection is **to hide from view.** How it works in practise is that we need to see something without seeing it, or else to be distracted by something. Hiding from view – in this sense – doesn't necessarily mean removing from view. It doesn't mean concealing, or putting out of sight, but it does have something to do with our ability to see, and our ability to recognize what we are seeing.

One of my favorite of Einstein's sayings talks to this idea of subtlety buried in the noisy field of view.

"It's not that I'm so smart, it's just that I stay with problems longer." — *Albert Einstein*

True crime and especially this case requires some focused attentiveness. We want to see where the rabbit hole goes, but we must not be so caught up in our spelunking that we forget to return to the surface, and in effect, **the source of the rabbit hole**. Because we may find <u>one rabbit hole misdirects us away from another</u>. By its very nature, when inside one rabbit hole we are beneath the surface and unable to see into another. Each rabbit hole pretends to represent the truth but as it turns out, *there is more than one truth.* This is the essence of misdirection.

From <u>urbandictionary.com</u>:

[Misdirection is a] metaphor for the conceptual path which is thought to lead to the true nature of reality. Infinitesimally deep and complex, venturing too far down is probably not that great of an idea. Taking hallucinogenic drugs can be considered "tripping" down the rabbit hole, but it is also explored through philosophical and existential thinking.

The origin of the term is from the rabbit hole in Alice in Wonderland which leads into Wonderland.

Ever heard of <u>the satanic leaf-tailed gecko</u>? <u>Ever seen one</u>? How about an <u>arctic hare</u> or <u>arctic fox</u>? Ever seen <u>a bat-faced toad</u>? A <u>grey cicada</u>? A <u>snow leopard</u>? Look again – carefully this time…in the middle, to the left – <u>a snow leopard</u>. Are you sure you can see <u>a grizzly bear</u> when it's in an open field right in front of you? How about the <u>blue-scarfed Christmas-tree giraffe</u>? Or the <u>lesser snowy Christmas-tree giraffe</u>? The <u>pyjama boy Christmas-tree giraffe</u>?

Misdirection is sometimes as simple as camouflaging reality – in manipulating a set of circumstances so that the viewer cannot see what he is seeing. Because we tend to believe what we see, it's easiest to fix what we see rather than what we believe. Does that make sense?

This narrative addresses that far harder task of challenging beliefs, and as you've seen, there's a lot to challenge. A sown seed left to germinate for long enough grows a trunk and branches and is eventually difficult to chop down. A thorough true crime narrative needs to be like a wood-borer beetle. It needs to overcome the tree of Knowledge of Disinformation.

The purpose of misdirection is simple. The reason the satanic leaf-tailed gecko looks like it does isn't so it can appear on a documentary narrated by David Attenborough, but rather so that *it won't appear* in one.

Misdirection in nature is an approximation of misdirection in human nature and necessarily – true crime. The point is to gain life, gain treasure, sometimes it is to gain ego gratification or simply freedom – but the mechanism works by misleading others. The point most simply expressed is *to gain*. But that's not all it is. We can gain all these things anyway without misdirection – we can gain life, treasure and remain free simply by working hard and behaving ourselves.

But not everyone likes to play that game, and hard work is hard work. In the next instalment of Lessons in Child Psychology we'll illustrate the psychological dimension behind misdirection and the drive to gain. Suffice it to say there's a lot to be gained from misdirection – there's plenty of treasure to be made in misdirection, and the point of it is it's much *easier money* than the harder thing, which is the ordinary WYSIWYG work ethic.

You can make an honest and WYSIWYG conventional living digging holes, or as a street sweeper, or as a cub reporter like Clark Kent or Lois Lane, or you can be creative, and fudge your way to making millions, or in Ponzi King Bernie Madoff's case, $65 $18 billion.

Lawyers make a living out of it; criminals, businessmen and beauty queens if they can get away with it do too. Is there anyone else? You mean besides half the animal kingdom, besides entire species of fish, butterfly and crab depending on misdirection for their survival, besides sole Survivors across 32 seasons of the *Survivor* reality television series winning $1 million apiece and all employing misdirection, besides naughty little boys – no, the real question isn't who is, but who isn't?

Remember that line from a mastermind is misdirection, Roger "Verbal" Kint in *The Usual Suspects* [1995]?

> *"You never knew, that was his power. The greatest trick the Devil ever pulled was convincing the world he didn't exist."*

The greatest trick the Ramseys pulled, as far as we're concerned, is to write a Ransom Note and then have everyone forget about it. Besides that sleight of hand, there's another. People seem to have forgotten about the ground zero in this crime scene – JonBenét's corpse. The crazy thing about this case is that there's so much misdirection and the Ramsey residence was such a fucking mess from top to toe, it's hard to tell: what's misdirection and what's just a godawful mess.

The flashlight, pineapple bowl, tea glass and pillow on the kitchen counter are all examples of potentially meaningless misdirection. The broken open window, the suitcase, the duct tape, the cord around JonBenét's wrists, the garrotte – these seem more staged. But what about the heart drawn in red pen on the palm of the little girls' right hand. We have a lot to deal with in misdirection, so let's deal with the heart on JonBenét's hand right now.

From forumsforjustice.org:

HANEY June 23 1998 : *On the 25th, Christmas, when you put JonBenét to bed, did she have any marks on her?*

PATSY: *Not that I noticed.*

HANEY: *Any scratches, cuts, bruises?*

PATSY: *Not that I noticed.*

HANEY: *How about, did she have any marks from markers or anything like that?*

PATSY: *I didn't notice anything that night when she went to bed. And, you know, I know there was a red heart on her hand or her forehead. I don't know when that – I mean, you know, I didn't – I didn't inspect her when I put her to bed.*

Notice Patsy repeating three times that she didn't notice any injuries to JonBenét. If Patsy had been an accessory to covering up the crime, not only would she have been aware of the injuries, she may well have caused them herself, or perhaps witnessed someone – perhaps John – actually making them. We assume this was *post mortem* of course.

The other thing to note is that Patsy adamantly doesn't notice anything and then sort of interrupts herself to say she did notice something. She doesn't want to talk about injuries, but I guess a scribble on her hand is a mark, right? Patsy volunteers the info of the red heart on her hand. The *"I'm not sure if it was on her forehead fluff"* is window dressing to make it seem as though what she's saying is casual and not strategic. If it is strategic – is my point – then it is misdirection.

From acandyrose.com:

HANEY: *But when you put her to bed, let's talk about that. We will go into a little more detail later, because we have some photographs and we want to talk about that. You were – at least changed part of her clothing when she is asleep?*

PATSY: *Uh-hum, right.*

HANEY: *Doesn't – (INAUDIBLE). Did you notice anything?*

PATSY: *(No response.)*

HANEY: *Would she have washed her hands at a particular time?*

Is Haney angling in a step by step narrative to the heart on the hand?

From acandyrose.com:

PATSY: *Well, at dinner, she rarely washed her hands.*

HANEY: *Would she, or perhaps she had been eating crab and you have that slimy stuff all over?*

PATSY: *Yeah, I think she is going to wash her hands. But I didn't see her. I don't know.*

HANEY: *Getting her ready that early afternoon, four or five o'clock, did you give her a bath, did she take a bath?*

PATSY: *I don't think so.*

HANEY: *You don't think you gave her one?*

PATSY: *Uh-uh.*

HANEY: *Do you think [JonBenét] took one?*

PATSY: *No, she didn't take one (INAUDIBLE).*

HANEY: *Showers?*

PATSY: *Uh-uh.*

Interesting. The family are about to head out to a Christmas party and then a few Christmas visits after that and Patsy doesn't bath her daughter. We've already been told that JonBenét was riding her bicycle on the patio in front of the house. Riding a bicycle in thick winter garb over a soggy, snow-melted lawn is liable to leave kids a little – if not a lot – stinky and sweaty. In any event, Patsy wants to reinforce the notion that the red heart on JonBenét's hand wasn't an artefact from earlier in the day, it was recent.

Haney wants to know – if it was recent – who drew it? Was it likely that JonBenét did, or one of her friends, or Patsy herself. Now bearing in mind the theme of this chapter let's see how Haney's thorough questioning of Patsy unfolds.

From acandyrose.com:

HANEY: *Would [JonBenét] have washed her hands before getting ready to go?*

PATSY: *I'd like to think so, but I just don't know for sure.*

DeMUTH: *At the Whites, did somebody say, oh, here, get ready for dinner? Did somebody tell her to go wash her hands at the Whites, do you remember anything about that?*

PATSY: *I don't know.*

DeMUTH: *How was she about washing her hands?*

PATSY: *Just typical kid, you know, if she can get by with it, she wouldn't do it. You know, but I was pretty much always (INAUDIBLE). (Gesturing.)*

Well, whatever that means Patsy.

From acandyrose.com:

DeMUTH: *Had you referred to that at all Christmas Day?*

PATSY: *I don't know. I don't remember exactly, but I may have.*

This sounds like Trip DeMuth asking if Patsy had asked JonBenét at any point on Christmas Day to wash her hands. Patsy remains impressively unhelpful. She's neither here nor there – it's all maybes, not sures and I don't knows. So DeMuth decides to cut the shit.

From acandyrose.com:

DeMUTH: *How do you know there was a heart on her hand?*

PATSY: *Because it was on there in the morning, that's why.*

On there – do you see how disassociated that is? It's a very specific answer for once, there's even a testiness to it, yet the only part of her response that's vague is the part referring to JonBenét directly. **On there.**

From acandyrose.com:

DeMUTH: *And you remember it from the next morning?*

PATSY: *Uh-hum.*

PATSY: *Uh-hum.*

DeMUTH: *When you say the next morning, did you remember it from the previous evening?*

PATSY: *(Shaking head.) (No response.)*

Patsy can't actually say the words.

From acandyrose.com:

DeMUTH: *Did she – I mean did it get there, was that something she would do or –*

PATSY: *Well, she and Daphne, you know, a lot of times drew on themselves.*

DeMUTH: *Did you ever see a heart on her hand before?*

PATSY: *Not specifically a heart.*

DeMUTH: *What might you have seen before?*

PATSY: *Just markings, you know, just erratic marks maybe, she had been coloring, pen or ink marks, or like fingers from markers or something.*

DeMUTH: *Did you ever draw anything on the palm of her hands?*

PATSY: (Shaking head.)

Patsy can't even verbalize a denial. She can't say the words. And because of her disassociation with JonBenét's hand ["on there"] and her inability to verbalize not seeing the heart the previous evening, I'm sniffing *some* misdirection here.

Think about it – if JonBenét's time of death was close to midnight then the heart could well have been scribbled on during the commission of the crime relatively early on. If the Ramseys were involved, was the note written first, or was JonBenét's corpse "made-up" first?

It seems logical to assume the priority had to be JonBenét's body – what to do with it, where to put it, how to put it, all the ancillary mopping up, wiping down and dressing up of the environment around it, and then getting down to writing the perfectly appropriate <u>Iliad</u> of Ransom Notes.

In our view the misdirections here appears to show that Patsy drew the heart on JonBenét's daughter's hand.[24] And we agree with Patsy that it was drawn either late on Christmas night or early the next morning. I don't think it was drawn as a mark of love between mother and daughter; instead I think it was drawn to stir an inference of sexual abuse.

Does this inference conflict with the contents of the Ransom Note? Yes it does. Does that mean the Ransom Note was written before the drawing of the red heart on JonBenét's hand? We don't think so. The Ransom Note is in conflict with itself, but so is the crime scene, let alone the autopsy.

Lisa and I have very good reason for seeing a strong inference from Patsy that *an unknown someone* drew a red heart on the girl's hand – not blue or black. A titillating red. Who would do that? Well, exactly. The more pertinent question though is *why did attention need to be directed to a sexual assault?*

---

24 At the time of writing we believed Patsy drew the heart on JonBenét's hand. The current position is that a child, either JonBenét or someone else, drew the shape in red ink on JonBenét's hand.

In <u>Detective James Kolar's</u> book[25] Kolar suggests Burke sexually abused her. And further, there are studies and statistics of prepubescent children showing sexually driven aggression.

The sexual impulse here, interestingly, is not based on gratification but other factors. Although we think the sexual aspect of the crime itself is negligible, we agree with Kolar that there were broader sexual circumstances involved [which we will elaborate on in *The Craven Silence 3*] but that nevertheless have a bearing on the case.

Before returning to Haney and DeMuth's interrogation, we ought to address additional observations, from Kolar first – suggesting his line of reasoning isn't remotely spurious and secondly, from the fairly recently revealed Grand Jury indictments.

1. According to Kolar Patsy's mother Nedra gave Patsy several sinister sounding books. One, titled *Why Johnny can't tell right from wrong?*, specifically addresses sex education, suicide, and violence. Another tome provides support for parents with kids who grow up too fast.[26]

2. The <u>1999 Grand Jury's</u> True Bills, kept hidden until <u>October 2013</u> [14 years] referred explicitly to charges <u>against John Ramsey</u> for "[permitting] a child to be unreasonably placed in a situation which posed a threat of injury to the child's life or health" and <u>against John Ramsey</u> for "[rendering] assistance to a person, with intent to hinder, delay and prevent the discovery, detention, apprehension, prosecution, conviction

---

25 Kolar, who also appeared in the *CBS* documentary *The Case of: JonBenét Ramsey*, is the author of the bestselling Foreign Faction. While in-depth, Kolar refrains from presenting his entire theory of prosecution, possibly due to legal concerns.

26 In the Mindhunting chapter we address other potentially incriminating reading material in the Ramsey library.

and punishment of such person for the commission of a crime, knowing the person being assisted has committed and was suspected of the crime of murder in the first degree **and child abuse** resulting in death."

The media didn't quote from bills referring to Patsy, who had died seven years prior, but one can reasonably assume the content applying to John applied equally to Patsy as well.

At this point I don't expect the reader to swallow allegations of sexual mistreatment and cruelty. If the idea of a nine-year-old damaging his six-year-old sister's genitals irks, perhaps that's because the misdirection has mostly succeeded. The point is, we think the red heart is meant to misdirect attention *from Burke*. We think both parents may have been aware of a fairly chronic level of abuse by Burke, not just on Christmas Day, but beyond. The Ramseys may have correctly assuaged that a court could, or would find them criminally culpable of negligence not merely on Christmas Day, but beyond.

In *The Craven Silence 3* we will hone some of these ideas into a more elegant whole. But let's round off this assessment by reminding the reader of a previous blow to the head JonBenét sustained when Burke hit her in the face with a golf club. A harmless accident, and accidents happen to children all the time, don't they? Or, more ominously, yet another wild outburst from Burke which the Ramsey parents failed to address. This may have been one transgression from Burke in a series, and simultaneously, a failure to address it from the parents, making them co-transgressors in their own right. Make sense?

Mindhunting – the search for predatory psychology

SAWYER: Polygraphs – have they taken a lie detector?

BYNUM: Not to my knowledge. — <u>Diane Sawyer</u>
ABC PrimeTime September 10 1997

"They didn't run away. They were here to face whatever they had to face. I think that's important for people to know." — <u>Pam Archuleta</u>

The most important thing people want to know about this case is that JonBenét's family – individually and collectively – didn't kill their daughter and then cover it up. It's not one thing, it's two. If someone in the family killed JonBenét and others covered it up we're still talking about two or more accessories to several crimes – murder, obstruction of justice, abuse, reckless endangerment, felonious rendering of assistance etc. etc.

That reality, especially the murder and covering up part of that delicate little girl – if it is true – is almost too much to take, too shocking at times to even contemplate. But are Archuleta's claims valid? Did the

Ramseys "face whatever they had to face"? Did they take a lie detector test for example?

If we can't rely as much as we'd like to on the crack detective from Colorado Springs, who can we rely on? Can we rely on the guy on the other side of the helix – Detective Steve Thomas?

From nytimes.com:

A former Boulder, Colo., police detective who spent almost two years investigating the killing of JonBenét Ramsey says in a new book that he and other investigators concluded that the 6-year-old girl had been killed by her mother, Patsy Ramsey.

The detective, Steve Thomas, who resigned from the police department in mid-1998, writes that he concluded that Mrs. Ramsey strangled her daughter in a panic on Christmas night 1996 after accidentally causing a serious wound to the little girl's head. He also contends that the girl's father, John Ramsey, after realizing what had happened, "chose to protect his wife" rather than help the authorities determine what had happened.

Can I be honest? From where we're standing we have to throw one crack detective's work down the drain and toss a fair amount of the other's revenge-for-bedwetting theory out the window. It's regrettable isn't it?

The questions we're having about JonBenét's death [**Did Burke murder his sister or not?**] are echoed in the aftermath as well. It's simple – **did the Ramsey parents take a lie detector test or not? Did Burke?**

As we'll soon see, simple doesn't mean easy, and the answers to seemingly easy questions are difficult, and downright troubling. Why is that? Isn't that pointing to a mountain of misdirection?

Whatever one may say about the tests themselves, what's deeply troubling about this avenue of inquiry includes the people we ought to have complete faith in – the folks who do the tests, the folks who endorse the testers. Who are they precisely? The FBI. And a guy called Gelb. We'll get to Dr. Edward Gelb and the FBI eventually.

We'll get to the polygraphs and deal with the lawyers in more detail later. But first we want to take a cursory look, but as we do, take special care to note:

> The lawyers – after the Ramseys – are a vital layer
> in the veneer.

They are part of the veneer, just as the Ramseys have created a veneer. But they are behind the scenes making that veneer *work*.

Here's a snapshot from tripod.com:

BYNUM: *John and Patsy Ramsey are two very, very hurt people, obviously, based on what's happened to them. But in terms of the kind of people they are, they are caring, considerate, kind and very, very, very decent people.*

SAWYER: *(on camera) Do you think the Ramseys are capable of murder?*

BYNUM: *The Ramseys, in my opinion, based on everything I know, are absolutely incapable of murder and incapable of harming that child.*

There's "that child" reference again. Mike Bynum, can't you even say "JonBenét" either? The other thing with Mike, he's buddies with the family, and he's a lawyer, and he's defending them on television, and they're defending themselves on television. Not so much to the cops at the time – the time being between the murder around Christmas 1996 and 1 January 1997 [and we're about to get to that].

Of course Bynum is going to be calling the Ramseys very very very decent people. One thing we agree with though is we don't see them as murderers. Not necessary not capable of murder, I think everyone is capable of murder – anything is possible right – but in this instance, that line of questioning doesn't apply. Steve Thomas line of reasoning we think was closer to the mark but still a good ways off.

From tripod.com:

SAWYER: *You're saying there has never, for a moment, been a flicker of even doubt in your mind?*

BYNUM: *In my mind, that is absolutely correct.*

SAWYER: *Because I was wondering if you ever asked them directly, "Did you do it?"*

BYNUM: *I am not going to get into specific discussions, but let me tell you, no, I never asked that question. I would never ask that question.* ***My faith, my belief*** *and what I've told you is unchanged.*

SAWYER: *(voice-over) When Bynum, who had lost an infant grandchild of his own, learned that JonBenét had been murdered, he rushed to a friend's house, where the Ramseys and their nine-year-old son Burke had gone to stay.*

(on camera) Can you tell me about what you saw when you walked in that door?

BYNUM: *I think I can. John and Patsy were there with family and friends, their minister. And just after I got there, everyone was -- sorry --was kneeling in the living room and* ***praying together****. And when they got through, I went up and hugged John and -- and then I went over to Patsy. She was sitting on the couch. And I had to help her up and -- and give her a hug. So that was what I found when I got there. Everyone was devastated. It was difficult.*

We've already addressed the flip side to Bynum's narrative via Pam Griffin in the seamstress "as Patsy's saviour story". Bynum is referring to the same sharing of condolences [on December 27th].

From tripod.com:

SAWYER: *(voice-over) And there is someone else who was there that night who says Patsy Ramsey had collapsed.*

But it's not Pam Griffin, it's *a very neutral source.*

From tripod.com:

Dr. FRANCESCO (PH) BEUF, JonBenét's pediatrician: *She was just lying on the floor.*

SAWYER: (voice-over) *His name is Dr. Francesco Beuf. He was JonBenét's pediatrician. He talked to me by phone about whether Mrs. Ramsey's grief was real.*

Diane Sawyer is a great journalist right? Getting the inside story from the defense lawyer and family doctor. This is an incredibly affluent family so it makes sense to ask people who take money from the Ramseys – quite a lot – in exchange for their services. Is anyone getting an income going to bite the hand that feed it? Diane?

From tripod.com:

Dr. FRANCESCO BEUF: *Oh, for God's sake, she was **as devastated as anyone could be by a terrible loss like that**. They called me to provide some tranquilizers for her. She was absolutely shattered by this.*

Didn't Pam Griffin say Patsy was dehydrated but nevertheless rushing to meet every single well-wisher? My understanding of devastated people isn't that they go on CNN at the first opportunity, but that's me. My understanding of people who've suffered a traumatic loss is a period of denial and even anger. When my own mother died unexpectedly in 1989 I wasn't really that interested in talking to people other than my close personal family. It's a deep grief and one feels one needs to deal with it privately.

I remember when I returned to school the principal asked me if he should explain to the school what had happened, also suggested – since it was my final year – of taking my average grades so I wouldn't have to write matriculation [college graduation] exams. I demurred on both counts.

From tripod.com:

SAWYER: *And Mr. Ramsey?*

Dr. FRANCESCO BEUF: *He looked absolutely devastated. To me,* **they were the most appropriate reactions in the world.** *God knows, I wouldn't know how I'd react if one of my children had been murdered, particularly in such horrible circumstances. He paced and paced and paced. He and I went out for a walk for a while that night. It's the wreckage of two human beings.*

SAWYER: *(voice-over) Even so, we were told the Ramseys volunteered to give hair, fingerprint, blood samples. And John Ramsey offered to be formally interviewed by the police if he could do it in the house near his family. Bynum says it didn't happen only because police wanted both parents, and* **Dr. Beuf said Patsy Ramsey wasn't able to talk.**

Interesting. So it's not a case of Patsy refusing to talk, or Bynum's advice to not let Patsy talk, it's on *doctor's orders* that she not talk to the police. But hey, CNN's okay. The bottom-line is no matter how you spin it, the police wanted to talk to Patsy and Patsy wouldn't or couldn't.

The police also wanted to talk to John Ramsey, but he set conditions, and bottom-line, he didn't talk to the police in a way that satisfied all investigators tasked with the crime in the immediate aftermath [between Christmas 1996 and New Year's], or for another 120 odd days.

In terms of the "sick letter" lawyer trick, we've just seen exactly the same thing with Oscar Pistorius. I was actually in court during his sentencing. His shrink also described him in court as "a broken man" and someone who should be "hospitalised immediately". So Oscar didn't testify at his own sentencing hearing. Of course at the same time that the sentencing hearings were going on <u>Oscar was involved in filming a documentary about why he didn't purposefully murder</u> his girlfriend. The documentary was released, including footage of the sentencing trial 2-3 weeks before the judge announced the verdict. The footage of the sentencing trial was important because it could be used to timestamp when the recording was made. It didn't help that that eager interviewer tweeted details about his departure from London to South Africa and his arrival back in London.

Like the Ramseys, a large swath of the public didn't buy his bullshit, and many in the media didn't either. But the judge seemed to as <u>Oscar won a sentence for murder that surprised many for how light it was.</u>

But let's get back to Beuf and his unbiased assessments of the Ramseys. The most appropriate reactions **in the world**? <u>Are you out of your fucking mind?</u>

From <u>tripod.com</u>:

Dr. FRANCESCO BEUF: *I had advised that it was not good to have Patsy there because she was under heavy sedation and would not have been able to function. And then the story came out that the Ramseys had refused to be interviewed by the police. That is just flat wrong. I sat there.*

Flat wrong, eh doc?

From <u>tripod.com</u>:

SAWYER: (on camera) *Why did they get a lawyer?*

BYNUM: *I went, as their friend, to help. And I felt that they should have legal advice -- nothing more, nothing less.*

Nothing more, nothing less. Yes.

From <u>tripod.com</u>:

SAWYER: *So you're the reason they got a lawyer?*

BYNUM: *I'm the one.*

SAWYER: *It did not occur to them first?*

BYNUM: *They certainly never made any mention of it to me.*

SAWYER: *I'm trying to imagine, if I am in the middle of this agony and my friend says to me, "You better get a lawyer" I think I'd go, "What? What?"*

BYNUM: *Well...*

SAWYER: *This horrible thing has happened to my child. There's a note here. I should get a lawyer?*

BYNUM: *Well, first of all, that was not the words that I used. I told John there were some legal issues that I thought needed to be taken care of. And John just looked at me and said, "Do whatever you think needs to be done," and he and Burke -- he went into a room to talk with Burke and so I did.*

SAWYER: *What made you think there were legal issues?*

BYNUM: *I was a prosecutor. I know how this works. I know where the police attention's going to go, right from the get go.*

SAWYER: *(voice-over) And he says that's exactly what happened. By Saturday, two days after the murder that the police were openly hostile. An assistant DA gave him some news.*

The flip side of the "openly hostile" police were things like John Ramsey calling his pilot pal Mike Archuleto [yes, Patsy's pal Pam's husband] at 06:45.

From pbworks.com:

*~1:30 PM John Calls Pilot. "Twenty minutes... after Arndt moves [JonBenét's] body, John is overheard placing a phone call to his pilot **to ready the plane** to head for Atlanta. **Police instruct them not to leave town,** so they stay at a friend's home in Boulder."*

It's difficult to overstate just how fucked up this is. Your daughter has been murdered, and within about twenty minutes of "discovering" her body, you're ready to skip town? You don't ask permission, and what's more, there doesn't seem to be an ounce of fuck spared to actually try to find JonBenét's phantom murderer. Of course these are clearly the most appropriate reactions in the world. And then it gets even worse.

From tripod.com:

BYNUM: *[John Ramsey] said the police are refusing to release JonBenét's body for burial unless John and Patsy give them interviews. I have never heard of anything like that. I said to the DA, "I don't know whether or not this is illegal, but I'm sure it's immoral and unethical." I just was **not willing to participate and facilitate or do anything** other than to say "no." Not only no, but **hell, no, you're not getting an interview**. And I did say that.*

Incidentally, part of that October 1999 Grand Jury indictment includes this:

> *"…feloniously…**prevent the detention**, apprehension and prosecution, conviction and punishment of such person…"*

Bynum seems awfully confident on national television in September 1997 about his role in not willing to facilitate or do anything. If John and Patsy Ramsey were ultimately to face charges for – essentially – obstruction of justice, wasn't Bynum part and parcel of that? It's called aiding and abetting, isn't it? Aiding and abetting in one word is *accessory*.

If Bynum was an accessory to anything, I wonder who else was too. I mean, like the pilot, and the pilot's wife. You know, the Christian lady who prayed with Patsy, wrote a book for Patsy and said this for Patsy:

"They didn't run away. They were here to face whatever they had to face. I think that's important for people to know." — Pam Archuleta

We get it Pam; they didn't run away <u>they flew</u>. If you really want the original soundbites – not from the cops, not from the lawyers and not from the Ramseys – Newsweek has an excellent clip which unfortunately has no "sharing" functionality. At <u>this link</u>, about 25 seconds into the irritating self-loading and self-starting video, we see actual footage of the Ramsey jet arriving back in Boulder at dawn. Notice the reporter indicating that the Boulder authorities were unaware that the couple had left Atlanta. Nine days since JonBenét's death – in other words right off the fucking bat – the public were dumbfounded at what was going on. But on the ground rumors were flying, friends were cloying up, while other folks had started whispering and wondering why the Ramsey's hadn't been detained. Eventually someone had to address the clamour and the growing discontent that was already all over the front pages of the newspaper.

Leslie ~~Aahole~~ Aaholm, the City of Boulder Spokesperson at the time, told a press conference on January 3rd *"we had **no legal right** to detain the Ramseys from leaving the state to bury their daughter. There was **no legal grounds**. They were not under arrest, nobody has been ruled in or out as suspects."*

This was a major flaw in the investigation: THIS. You've actually got Boulder's top brass shrugging their shoulders and kicking the can down the road for the Ramseys. You can actually pick up a twinge of resentment from Aaholm when she spits out the word "daughter". It's like – what is wrong with you people, of course they're going to leave town to bury their daughter.

If you'll indulge me, let's get back to that Newsweek <u>link</u> again, concentrating on the 1:35 section. In the clip Tom Foreman, a television reporter, is clearly standing immediately in front of the Ramsey residence on January 3rd 1997. Investigators wearing <u>baby blue forensic suits</u> are moving through the front door of the Ramsey residence in the background – clear evidence that while the Ramseys have gone AWOL the cops are <u>doing their damnedest</u> combing through their home to find clues; to whatever they can.

The ABC news report confirms "no evidence of a break-in" and crime labs then already studying hair and DNA evidence "from the family". Just 9 days after the crime they're describing the Ransom Note as "a decoy" while simultaneously questioning the Ramseys appearance on CNN.

From <u>denverpost.com</u>:

In their first public comment on the case, John and Patsy Ramsey grant an extensive interview to CNN in which Patsy Ramsey proclaims "there is a killer on the loose." John Ramsey calls the idea that he or other members of his family could have committed the crime "nauseating beyond belief." That night [January 1st, 1997], five detectives from Boulder fly to Atlanta.

But it seems the Ramseys return to Boulder without consulting those five detectives. Meanwhile, all hell is breaking loose at the Mayor's office – on the same day.

From <u>Romper.com</u>:

On January 3, 1997, [Mayor Leslie] Durgin held a press conference broadcast live via CNN. The press conference was held not only to provide updates, but to respond to statements made by [JonBenét] Ramsey's mother, Patsy, in an interview earlier that same week — exclusively made to CNN as well. In the CNN interview, Patsy said "there is a killer is on the loose." At the news conference, Durgin rebutted Patsy's claim, saying: "Boulder is safe." But with the media frenzy surrounding JonBenét's murder ramping up, Durgin's words rang hollow.

This context from ABC's Tom <u>Foreman in Boulder [January 3rd</u> <u>1997]</u> is true crime gold:

"City officials insist JonBenét's parents are still co-operating fully, but to many it appears they are travelling wherever and whenever they want to without telling police, and answering questions only when it suits them. The parents have hired a private investigator [this is just 9 days after the crime!] a media consultant, separate attorneys, and they're offering a $50 000 reward but late this afternoon, city officials had to admit they're not even sure where JonBenét's parents are at this time."

That's a shitty reward for a millionaire, wouldn't you say? Not much of an incentive for anyone to solve this case, and seems it's just done [like hiring the private investigator] for appearances.

Meanwhile what are we to make of this?

"They didn't run away. They were here to face whatever they had to face. I think that's important for people to know."

Well obviously they didn't face up, and what's worse, didn't have to. What we're really wondering is how important it was to know something that doesn't seem in the least accurate.

"There was no <u>legal</u> grounds..."

There seemed plenty though, didn't there? No signs of a break-in, and by January 3rd, the Ransom Note is traced to Patsy's notepad – this is extremely incriminating.

From <u>denverpost.com</u>:

Friday, Jan. 3: Investigators announce that the Ransom Note appears to have been torn from a tablet of paper found in the house. If authorities are correct, this means that JonBenét's killer wrote the note after arriving at the house. John and Patsy Ramsey return to Colorado after JonBenét's funeral.

But how is this obfuscation even possible? How does it happen? Easy actually. Take the chummy legal culture of Boulder, throw one of its most affluent members in the deep end and watch the sharks congregate. The lawyers would play the little city "like a harp from hell" as one famous villain put it. It wasn't about friendship, or coming to the aid of someone in trouble. Rather, it was an incredibly lucrative opportunity for lawyers to do what they do best – lawyering.

And over the years John Ramsey's enormous wealth would become theirs.[27] It was really just a very simple transaction – all his wealth for decades of worry-prone freedom. All the lawyers had to do was keep the Ramseys out of jail and to do that, they had to keep him out of court. And best of all, they had the trump card in their pocket.

The man whose job it was to prosecute the case was waiting at the end of the road for the can to reach him. And after so much kicking the can down the road, what would Alex Hunter do when the can finally clonked against his shining shoes?

---

27 From thedailybeast.com: *Since the murder, Ramsey has sold three big homes, in Atlanta, Boulder, and Charlevoix. He has shed his plane, his boats and his cars, stopped golfing, stopped sailing. Now he is exhausting his IRAs...The next thing to go will be Patsy's oversized antiques—a Louis XV divan, Romantic paintings in thick rococo frames, sofas with throws draped over them, just the way his wife left them...Only in rare moments does a glimpse of vulnerability slip through his guard. I ask him how his losses have affected him. "We couldn't sell our house in Boulder and **our attorneys finally took it off our hands for half the price we paid for it.** I was in a daze."*
From Wikipedia: *[John Ramsey's] net worth was reported at $6.4 million as of May 1, 1996. In 2015 John told Barbara Walters in an interview that the death of JonBenét and the ensuing investigation and cost of the case had cost him the entire family fortune.*

Playing Chess with Polygraphs

S AWYER: *Polygraphs -- have they taken a lie detector?*

BYNUM: *Not to my knowledge.*

SAWYER: *Should they? Will they?*

BYNUM: *Not if I ever have anything to say about it.*

SAWYER: *Why?*

BYNUM: *Oh, that's – that's ouija board science, number one. And I will also tell you, to my knowledge, that request has not been made of John and Patsy.* — Diane Sawyer ABC PrimeTime September 10 1997

"I'm amazed that the whole world doesn't think we're guilty ... based on what they've been told." — John Ramsey to Barbara Walters, March 14, 2000

The craziest thing about the "Polygraph narrative" is its gargantuan scale; it's a complete narrative entirely on its own. One could devote a book exclusively to rollercoastering through that farce.

At this point we're going to take you through the highlights, but at the end of the day, the polygraphs are a lot like the police co-operation mirage. The Ramseys can retrospectively claim that they did [eventually] speak to police. Ditto they can retrospectively claim they did [eventually] take a polygraph or ten.

When we poke thoroughly through the Scalextric of this case, when we descend through the clunky depths of Lego strata, when we plumb the basement level of a SuperMario game, we eventually reach a dark obscurity with a clue twinkling in the midst of it.

On the 17th of March 2000, John and Patsy Ramsey were interviewed on ABC News 20/20 by Barbara Walters. It wasn't so much an interview at all as PR for the release of their book *Death of Innocence*.

Their book was released a little more than two weeks prior to the Walters interview on March 1, 2000. Curiously, Amazon currently shows the release of the mass-market paperback as January 1, 2001. You can say what you like about this "discrepancy", the dailycamera. com published excerpts out of their book on March 15, 2000. In other words, a local Boulder newspaper had seen their book two days prior to the Ramsey's interview with a sub-par Barbara Walters. Ten days after hitting *ABC* the Ramseys gave Larry King a double dose on *CNN*.

Let's go to Larry and then boomerang back to Barbara.

From cnn.com [March 27, 2000]:

KING: *Good evening. It's a great pleasure to welcome the Ramseys to this edition of LARRY KING LIVE. It is a live appearance. Their book is "The Death of Innocence," just published. They are the co-authors. They will also be with us tomorrow night. There's the cover of the book.*

This will be a two-night appearance, both evenings live... We're going to get the whole story, as much as we can cover in two nights of programming. We hope to cover as much of it as we can. First on, something directly current... You had said recently in an interview that you were willing to take a lie detector test, and apparently the Boulder police are now saying let's set it up.

Will you do it?

By "recent interview" Larry's talking about their interview with Barbara Walters two weeks prior. It's important to stress though that having written a book, by March 2000 more than three years after

JonBenét's death they haven't even taken a lie-detector test. If they're innocent, what's the problem?

Now notice how John answers?

Will you do it?

<u>John starts by dropping his head and looking into his interlocked hands</u> resting on Larry's counter.

From <u>cnn.com</u>:

JOHN: *We have – we were asked, "Had we been asked to take a lie detector test?" We said no. We were asked, "Would we?" We said certainly we would. We would expect it to be fair, and we would expect the results to be public.*

Hold up right here. Larry asks John if he'll do a lie detector test and John's answer is to reiterate that they were asked, and how they were asked. Larry knows how you were asked John.

Now notice the "certainly we would" isn't yes, it's a conditional yes, just as talking to and co-operating with the Boulder investigators in the days and weeks and months after JonBenét's murder was conditional as well.[28]

But let's be fair. Consider the position the Ramseys are in. They can't very well say no. But, and here's the rub, *they can't say yes either.* So their best bet is a conditional yes, and then an endless nit-picking over those conditions, trying to tie up the cops so that they eventually throw in the towel. This strategy allows them to postpone and delay, and if they do eventually do a test, they can prepare exhaustively with their defense team.

From <u>cnn.com</u>:

---

28 Conditional on police reports provided, <u>being interviewed together</u>.

KING: *And then you would take – well, by fair, what's the determination of that, Patsy?*

PATSY: *Well, I think it has to be someone of...*

KING: *National repute.*

PATSY: *National repute.*

KING: *FBI man.*

PATSY: *Independent, you know, a professional polygrapher.*

See one can't very well have biased Boulder cops interviewing them and twisting the results to make them look guilty. Far better to let the Ramseys pick their preferred biased cops, who'll twist the results in their favour...is that it? This may seem like a conspiracy theory, but take a note of this dodge because we'll be coming back to it.

From cnn.com:

JOHN: *Yes, we've been told that – that this is a dangerous thing to take a lie detector test, because they're a subjective science. They're not allowed in court as evidence.*

KING: *Unless both sides agree.*

Larry wasn't born yesterday. Good for you Larry! But John wants to nit-pick...they'll do the test but it's not worth doing anyway...especially not if you live in Colorado.

From cnn.com:

JOHN: *In Colorado, even if both sides agree, they're not allowed in court.*

KING: *In the right hands, though...*

JOHN: *But in the right – we have nothing to hide. And if they work and if it will advance the cause of finding the killer of our daughter, we'll do it. Simple.*

Simple? Is playing chess with polygraphs simple? Is anything about the JonBenét Ramsey case simple or straightforward?

From cnn.com:

KING: *Before we get into the story, to be a suspect and live with the death of a child as a suspect as well, you – how do you get through that?*

PATSY: *Well, first of all,* **we have never been deemed suspects.**

See what I mean. It's never simple, although in this case Patsy, it kind've is. Larry, do the honors.

From cnn.com:

KING: *Yes, but* **the public regards you as suspects.**

PATSY: **We've been said to be under the umbrella of suspicion,** *whatever that means.*

KING: *What's that like?*

PATSY: *Well, it's – it's kind of – no-man's-land, you know?*

KING: *Is it no-win?*

JOHN: *Well, we lost our daughter. That's the worst possible thing that could have happened to us. Anything that has happened in the aftermath pales by comparison.*

What does Patsy mean by "a no man's land"? Who lives in a "no man's land"? A child? But John has a nice panacea for Larry's tricky question. The worst thing that could ever happen to them is the death of their child. Nothing else is worse talking about. But they're suspects in her murder, and they're antsy about taking a lie-detector test, so… talking about the case is a no man's land too. Except that they've written a book and that's why they're on Larry King Live.

Let's boomerang back to Barbara two weeks earlier, hitting the Ramseys with the same question.

From acandyrose.com:

WALTERS: *Why didn't you take a lie detector test?*

PATSY: *No one ever asked us…*

WALTERS: *Really?*

PATSY: *… to take a lie detector test.*

WALTERS: *Police never asked you to take a lie detector test?*

JOHN: *No.*

PATSY: *No.*

Well they were asked immediately after they gave this interview. But John, suspecting their denial rings hollow, hedges their answer with a little semantic chess.

From acandyrose.com:

JOHN: *I was asked, during my interview with Steve Thomas,* **a hypothetical question —**

WALTERS: *One of the policemen.*

JOHN: *One of the policemen that investigated this murder. He said, if I were to ask you to take a lie-detector test, what would you say? And I said I would be offended. That's what I would say. I wasn't interested in proving my innocence at that point. That…that [OVERLAP] was… a non-issue.*

Do you see, it's a slightly different twist, but it sure doesn't sound like:

We'll do it. Simple.

Or:

We said certainly we would

It's just starting to feel a whole lot more complicated. No, that's the wrong word. There's simple and there's complicated, this is something else, something more cynical, more strategic. This is *convoluted*. And it's because of these convolutions – which go on seemingly forever – that the Polygraph Pickle has evolved into a sizable soapie in its own right.

Meanwhile, Patsy goes back to the scene of the crime and says they didn't co-operate with the cops on the polygraph thing because, in her own words [cue whisper]: "there's someone out there."

From acandyrose.com:

PATSY: *We were frightened... there was a murderer loose.*

But Patsy that was three years ago. Barbara, you're not gonna let this one go are you?

From acandyrose.com:

WALTERS: *Mr. Ramsey, would you now take a lie-detector test—*

JOHN: *I would, certainly.*

WALTERS: *Would you, Mrs. Ramsey?*

PATSY: *Yes, I would take a lie-detector test.*

Okay let's leap out of that freak show to The Today Show, evidently their interview with Katie Couric took place the same day as Larry King. The PR for their book was in full swing but so were a slew of uncomfortable questions, and this one snagged on all the talk show hosts.

From acandyrose.com:

COURIC: *Did you all take a lie detector test?*

JOHN: *We were never asked to take a lie detector test. That's another...*

It's important to be clear though that the answer to Couric's question – three years after JonBenét's murder – is no. Then and there they hadn't taken a polygraph.

From acandyrose.com:

COURIC: *Why not volunteer to take one?*

JOHN: *It didn't occur to me, first of all. That wasn't our motive. I understand that lie detector tests are not admissible in court anyway. It's kind of a voodoo science. I would, if I was asked, certainly I would. But* **the fact is, I was never asked**.

COURIC: *And you never volunteered?*

JOHN: *I never volunteered. It never crossed my mind.* **I was not interested in proving my innocence.** *I was interested in finding the killer of my daughter.*

That's odd because John and Patsy are on a book tour, they're talking to Katie Couric to promote their book, and the book is called *Death of Innocence*. One wonders does the title refer at all to JonBenét, or is it really about John and Patsy? Is their story about the death of their innocence? The entire narrative is about proving why the aspersions of guilt hurled their way are spurious. And yet:

"I was not interested in proving my innocence."

Of course that's why the Ramseys went on *CNN* on January 1, 1997, because they weren't interested in proving their innocence. It's also the reason why the headline in the *Denver Post* the day after that ignominious interview read: RAMSEYS WARN OF KILLER.

From cnn.com [January 1, 1997]:

CABELL: *Inevitably, speculation on talk shows will focus on you. It's got to be a sickening –*

JOHN: *It's nauseating beyond belief.*

John's nauseated by speculation surrounding his guilt, including speculation of an elaborate cover-up but:

"I was not interested in proving my innocence."

So let's see what the first conditions are surrounding a non "hypothetical" polygraph test? Recall that John didn't wish to be interrogated by Boulder Police unless they could come to him, unless interviews with Patsy could be done simultaneously rather than separately and later…they were only prepared to be interrogated if the police first handed over all their information first. In the end, that's exactly what they did.

From cnn.com [March 21, 2000]:

KING: *Would you do it?*

JOHN: *We would expect it to be fair, and we would expect the results to be public.*

KING: *And as you said earlier, you would make your lie detector public.*

JOHN: *We would insist that it be made public. If we're going to do it, let's make it public.*

PATSY: *Make everything public. You know, I said, you want to see an interview? Publish the interview that I had with Tom Haney. Let's talk about…*

It's quite subtle but what the Ramseys are actually doing is manipulating the process of taking the Polygraph. Do you see, they want to decide who conducts it and how, and then they want the results made public. They're exerting a lot of pressure on the authorities, and trying to get them to blink. They did exactly the same on ordinary issues of co-operation, allowing the evidence and the investigation to play out in the media, making grand public statements of willingness, but not quite ever getting around to talking to the cops about what they so publically claimed to be willing to talk about.

There's a lot more meat on the bone we've plucked out of ribcage of the Misdirection skeleton, but let's touch on something else to settle matters of scope, as opposed to just the scale[29] of this colossal case.

---

29 Scope deals with variety, scale deals with size or output. We will return to the slippery convolutions of the Polygraph narrative in *The Craven Silence 3*.

Soap and Jack Crawford

Jack Crawford: <u>Just do your job</u>, but never forget what he is.
Clarice Starling: And what is that? — The Silence of the Lambs, 1991

Jack Crawford: *Starling, when I told that sheriff we shouldn't talk in front of a woman, that really burned you, didn't it? It was just smoke, Starling. I had to get rid of him.*

Clarice Starling: *It matters, Mr Crawford. Cops look at you to see how to act. It matters.* Jack Crawford: *Point taken.* — The Silence of the Lambs, 1991

In this chapter we'll briefly consider two aspects that also play into Mindhunting. We want to know what Patsy's overall approach is to "cleaning" or "washing". We won't go into this in exhaustive detail, but we need to touch on it.

The other aspect we'll look into is the reading material of the Ramseys. What speaks better about someone's mental machinations than their bookshelf? The willingness to take a lie detector test, Patsy's attitudes about cleaning, and the Ramsey library are three attempts to poke holes into the cheese. So far we've poked our way into *something*.

Lisa and I don't see the Ramsey parents as perpetrators of the debilitating and likely deadly head blow to little JonBenét's skull, but if it was Burke, we still need to understand why they felt they needed to cover for him.

To find our way through the morass of misdirection into the sparkling crystals of the Ramsey's authentic mind space and the real motives driving these people, we're going to have to get creative. With Patsy we need to navigate through the domestic cleaning ritual, assuming there is one. With John we need to see what is filling his head when he's mooching about at home. <u>Worth playing for?</u>

1. Cleaning Lady

We're heading back to the goldmine we have on Patsy in her own words from the June 23rd, 1998 Boulder Police interrogation of JonBenét's mother

From acandyrose.com:

DeMUTH: *Was there ever an occasion when you would draw a smiley face on the palm of her hand or on her hand somewhere?*

PATSY: *As a matter of fact, I discouraged her doing that because we always did what we called the pageant scrub the night before we have a pageant. We would wash her hair real good, and scrub her fingernails, and, you know, and oftentimes she would have, you know, marker all over herself or something, on her leg or something. Say, honey, now don't do that, wipe it off. We had to use **nail polish remover**, sort of try to dilute it and get it off. So **I kind of discouraged that as much as possible.***

There's a fascinating psychology at play here on so many levels. First off we get a sense that being in these pageants couldn't have been much fun for JonBenét. How much fun does a "pageant scrub" sound? Secondly, it's not just the preparation just before the pageant that's arduous, but all the other behavior JonBenét was expected to avoid. From a long way off we can see how this fastidious approach to being clean clashes with our knowledge of a troubled little girl who was bedwetting virtually on a nightly basis. The third thing to note is Patsy's claim that she would never draw a smiley face on her daughter's palm in the name of cleanliness seems to miss the joy and fun of a normal mother daughter relationship. Patsy may think the appropriate response is a sort of mercenary approach but it rings cold to us. Why use it then? Probably because Patsy – two years down the track – needs to push the possibility of a perverted interloper as the author of the heart on the hand as hard as she can. She's doing this, we believe, to extricate herself from the umbrella of suspicion – whatever that is.

We could leap forward from here, since we've already touched lightly on Patsy's approach to "cleaning", but let's stay with this a little longer because I want to draw out something that will reinforce the sense of scope we're casting towards.

From acandyrose.com:

DeMUTH: *There was something regarding that you would draw a smiley face when she was feeling down to perk her up. What would your reaction be to that?*

PATSY: *That I would do it?*

DeMUTH: *Yes.*

PATSY: *I don't remember doing that.*

But you are an artist Patsy. You're the most likely person besides JonBenét to be drawing anything. Well, besides JonBenét and Burke. Artists are familiar with staining materials and also removing stains. They have the sort of cleaning products to remove tough stains, and they're in the habit of disposing of dirty/contaminated fabric. Do you see where I'm going with this? Let's go even further now.

We ought to see Burke and his sister as an artistic unit in their own right. With their mother interested in arts and crafts, both Burke and JonBenét were at that age when kids particularly love to draw. We know Burke did a few drawings for various shrinks and we can clearly see JonBenét did her own art, including on herself, as many children do. But what more than that?

Well, there is something…

From denverpost.com:

Patsy Ramsey's painting of two small children on a beach begs for poignant interpretation. A young boy is shown sitting with his arm around a smaller girl. The two face the calm turquoise water in what appears to be a moment of peaceful, innocent reflection.

The gentle scene had to be an image of Ramsey's son, Burke, and daughter, JonBenét, didn't it? Um, well, maybe not.

It's actually an important point. Has Patsy drawn this sketch from a family photo, or from memory, or conjured it up from a tender space in a mother's heart? None of the above – Patsy's basically stolen the idea from somewhere else and embellished it, making the netherworld of painted Burke and painted JonBenét at the nether seaside an impossibly bright and gaudy one. Patsy's version has a bright, plastic blue sea drowning the sky and the two figures under it. Another irony in the portrayal is the loving older brother's arm wrapped tautly around the smaller child's neck. Remember JonBenét was garrotted. There's something nauseatingly insensitive about this.

There is something more loosely natural in the original work – titled "Pals" – than in the imitation, where the arm is lower and seems to almost approximate the neck of the child. In Patsy's version suggestive of Burke and JonBenét still "pals" after her murder, the arm and the neck seem one and the same.

In the original artwork there's a much lighter sense – there are sailboats, a merry sun, reflections in the water and soft shadows behind both children. The children are drawn together but still comfortably apart. Patsy's version is a deluge of claustrophobic color, closeness and drowned perspectives.

From denverpost.com:

The painting was among several of Ramsey's artworks featured in a show in Charlevoix, Mich., just days after [Patsy] died. It was reproduced in The Denver Post on July 2, and sparked yet another controversy in the life of this bewildering figure who has appeared alternately tragic and cynical – depending on the moment – for nearly 10 years.

Once again, Patsy has left us with cause for suspicion and evidence to be analyzed endlessly, but curiously, no conceivable motive. When the image of Ramsey's artwork appeared in The Post, a reader recognized it as strikingly similar to one called "Pals" from the collection of artist Betty Morris Hamilton of Guntersville, Ala. Side by side, the resemblance is unmistakable. Ramsey's colors, though more intense, are much the same as those in Hamilton's original. The position of the arms, the streaks in the hair, the shades on the sand all look like Hamilton's work.

I called the artist in Alabama, expecting indignation. Instead I got tenderness. Hamilton looked at the image of Ramsey's painting. She paused. Then in her sweet Southern drawl she suggested that maybe Ramsey had used her artwork "as a guide."

Hamilton probably felt both complimented and – since Patsy was recently dead – drawn towards sentiment in defense of a fellow artist.[30]

---

30 Hamilton probably also felt a sense of Christian solidarity to Patsy, a fellow Christian. From denverpost.com: "I've always wanted my paintings to bless people," she said. "I consider my artistic ability a gift from God. It doesn't belong to me. If this painting blessed her in any way, it accomplished what I intended. How can I feel bad about that?"

I do a lot of profiles on artists as part of my regular photojournalism work and although I can be effusive, I eschew sentiment when it's unwarranted. There is something disgusting about a mother copying the sentiment of another artist when it comes to portraying and purporting the innocence of one child, alongside another whom the entire family – including the model in the portrait – are allegedly guilty of killing.

I see the same **bright pageantry** in this picture as we see everywhere else – **it's classic Patsy isn't it?**

Let's jump away for a second, just to reinforce this idea of "classic Patsy". We'll do so by referring to a statement by a former cleaning lady in the Ramsey residence, Linda Wilcox.

From acandyrose.com:

WILCOX: *Okay. It was the summer of '95. It was probably two or three weeks before they left for Michigan. JonBenét was 4, getting ready to turn 5 that August, and her and Burke both caught the chicken pox. I was there cleaning in the kitchen. Burke was upstairs itching like mad. He had them all over, he was in bed with the t.v. in his room, playing videos. JonBenet was in the t.v. room, sitting at a small table, in her nightgown, doing something quiet, **like coloring**. The child had a fever, she's sitting there coloring; Patsy is in the kitchen on the telephone with the doctor. I figured, oh, she's going to call the doctor to find out what to give the kids and the conversation went, "well JonBenét's got chicken pox and she's got these spots on her face and we need to have a photo shoot in about 3 days. Is there anything you can give her to **get rid of the spots**?" This is the child she loved with the whole of her heart?*

There's enormous metaphor in this paragraph. There's a sick child marching to Patsy's orders, and needing to appear healthy and pretty for some public demonstration. It's bright pageantry and thus classic Patsy all over again.

Now let's drill even deeper into Patsy's psychology.

From acandyrose.com:

DeMUTH: *Did anybody have a particular liking or **habit of drawing hearts?** Did JonBenét draw hearts routinely?*

PATSY: *I don't know. Typically children do a lot of different things.*

DeMUTH: *Some little kids have this – (MULTIPLE SPEAKERS.)*

HANEY: *Line dine job –*

PATSY: *She drew suns and things and birds and things like that.*

DeMUTH: *What was your reaction when you saw that heart on her hand?*

PATSY: *Well, I just thought Daphne must have done it or something, you know, they were playing the night before. You know – you know, **my mind ran things out.** But Santa Claus made a point the night that he was at our house at the party and was, you know, **reading this dialogue that I had written up,** and then he told this story about, you know, how Christmas should be Christmas all the time, all year long, and he said, "and where is Christmas when it's not really Christmas," something like that. He said particularly JonBenét, and he pointed to JonBenét. And she said in her heart. Pointing. So I mean, you know, I just turned around. I am trying to figure and figure and put things together, but, you know, that – I am sure you all have too, but –*

If Patsy's lawyers coached her prior to this grilling, and I'm guessing they did at length, then they would have warned Patsy not to gift the investigators with information. Don't volunteer anything. But at the same time, I can see the lawyers providing Patsy with packaged answers to misdirect the cops once they started honing in on anything. So while Patsy had Bill McReynolds buried in her handbag [so to speak], she wasn't going to bring him out unless the cops prodded her sufficiently.

That way the reveal could seem appropriate, and Patsy was pretty good at things looking and seeming appropriate. Well, to a point, and then she was terrible.

There's another red flag buried in that response – do you see it? It's in Patsy's point about "writing up a dialogue". Patsy's a former journalism major and she does quite a lot of writing – her newsletters, she even gives Santa a dialogue to base his performance on and – we're guessing – Ransom Notes.

What's clear from the last waffle quoted above is the ruse to implicate Bill McReynolds. During the same interrogation John Ramsey would – without hesitation – drop Bill's name as soon as Smit asked him to specifically name a suspect. With both Patsy and John separately and apparently spontaneously dropping his name, the Boulder cops and an unassuming detective [and Smit was that] might take the bait. Well Smit did, didn't he?

The smarter question to ask wasn't whether the Ramseys suspected McReynolds or why, but if they suspected him why wait two fucking years to tell anyone about it? Surely it would be eating at any other parents who had lost a child in similar circumstances – this guy, we think it's this guy, go get this guy. But by playing dumb they could delay the whole process and still come out of it with a rough sketch that made them look like they were helping.

From acandyrose.com:

DeMUTH: *You knew her best. That's why we need to ask about her habits.*

PATSY: *That was a pretty good little heart, you know, I mean – pretty well drawn.*

Patsy's implying here that an adult must have drawn it. Well, an adult besides her.

In our view an adult did draw it. An adult used a red pen and drew on the upraised palm in a way that would be clearly visible. The red was intentional too, sending a different message than say a green, yellow, black or brown heart. Patsy drew the heart on her daughter's hand as part of the cover-up intended to signboard the crime not merely as murder, but as a sexual crime as well. In *The Craven Silence 3* we'll cover the sexual misdirection in more detail. Now to John.

2. Jack Crawford

Who is Jack Crawford and what does he have to do with John Ramsey?

From Wikipedia:

Jack Crawford is a fictional character who appears in the Hannibal Lecter series of books by Thomas Harris, in which Crawford is the Agent-in-Charge of the Behavioral Science Unit of the FBI in Quantico, Virginia. He is modeled after John E. Douglas, who held the same position...

There's speculation that Jack Crawford was in the Ramsey residence that awful night, and assisted the Ramseys in psychological mindfuckery involved in both staging and covering up the crime. But how could a fictional Jack Crawford do this? He could if he was buried inside the Ramsey's reading material. Let's check, and then see where this line of questioning leads us.

From acandyrose.com:

BOYLES: *We'll talk about the police interview and we'll talk about the books by the bed. One of the stories we broke was about **John Douglas' book Mindhunter being seen in the crime scene photos**. You know a little bit about books by the Ramseys beds...*

WILCOX: *Well, they each had a pile of books in the corner by the bed. Even though they had nightstands. Originally the nightstands weren't there until they redid the upstairs. And even afterwards, **they tended to*** *just throw the books there. So, **I kind of knew who read what**. So, Patsy's side had things like, you know poems for women and not really what I would consider true trash-like Harlequin romances, but more like Mary Higgins Clark, woman novels. Some of them, I had even read. John's side of the bed was usually some kind of suspense-thriller. He tended to buy books by, what I call, by the numbers, I mean whatever's number 1 on the bestseller lists. Occasionally it would be something like the 7 habits of successful people, or financial things or even a (didn't hear) occasionally. But, generally it was some kind of suspense novel."*

As we continue our effort to interrogate John's actual headspace we want to assess not just if he would be involved in a cover up after the fact, but how he would do it. <u>What's the thinking</u>?

To this end we're interested in <u>one particular book</u> called *Mind Hunter* by <u>John E. Douglas</u>. Here's why.

From <u>acandyrose.com</u>:

On page 298, Douglas talks about the case of a kidnapping/murder of an 18-year-old girl that took place in Columbia, SC in 1985. The kidnapper made several phone calls to the victim's family. He said a couple of things (quoted from the tapes made of the calls) that sounded familiar:

(p. 303) "You will receive instructions where to find us" (ibid.) "Listen carefully." (p. 311) "Okay, listen carefully."

When the victim's body was found, Douglas says, "The sticky residue of duct tape was on Shari's face and hair, but the tape itself had been removed – further indication of planning and organization." (p. 303) Later, the suspect, again in a call to family, said, "She said she was ready to depart, God was ready to accept her as an angel.' He described having sex with her and said that he'd given her a choice of death – shooting, drug overdoses, or suffocation. He said she'd chosen the last one and **he'd suffocated her with the duct tape over her nose and mouth**." (p. 306)

We know, from the fact that the duct tape which had covered JB's mouth had a perfect lip-print on it, that it had been placed over her mouth when she was unconscious or after death. Why? There are also accounts of female victims having foreign objects inserted in their vaginas (p. 256, 366).

A few other things in the book echoed some similarities with JonBenet Ramsey case. When he's talking about tracking down a someone who in the early 80s was sending letters threatening politicians, including the President, he talks about the significance of the signature on these letters – **C.A.T.**

(p. 360) "There was a lot of speculation about what C.A.T. stood for or symbolized. I told the Secret Service not to spend too much time worrying about that, since it might not mean anything at all. There is often a tendency to read too much into every detail when, in fact, the UNSUB might just like the sound of it or the way it looked written out."

The Ransom Note was signed SBTC. This signature was possibly used because it seemed appropriate to how a Ransom Note should be signed.

Mind Hunter was first published in 1995 and went on to become a #1 *New York Times* Bestseller. Although the book is said to be part of the crime scene photos, I haven't thus far been able to source those images in my research. So what does John say about it?

From acandyrose.com:

KANE: *Okay. What about Mind Hunter, John Douglas' book was there in the house, had you purchased that?*

JOHN: *No. It was there in '96? Interesting.*

KANE: *Was it interesting?*

JOHN: *I never never heard of John Douglas or that book before.*

KANE: *So you never read that?*

JOHN: *No. I bought one of his books the next summer ['97], his newer book.*

John's answer sounds the same as his answer to whether he'd do a lie-detector test. Let's try Patsy on the same thing.

From acandyrose.com [June 1998 interrogation with Haney and DeMuth]:

HANEY: *How about the book Mind...?*

PATSY: *No.*

HANEY: *Do you recall that? Do you recall seeing it around the house?*

PATSY: *Huh-uh.*

HANEY: *You were not reading.*

PATSY: *No.*

HANEY: *It is a book by John Douglas.*

PATSY: *I don't know.*

HANEY: *Do you know who he is?*

PATSY: *John Douglas I know.*

Inexplicably the investigators then meander off in another direction.

From acandyrose.com/Enquirer August 4, 1998:

In a dramatic development in the JonBenét Ramsey murder case, police found a "how-to murder manual" in the bedroom of the little beauty queen's parents! The true-crime book describes a 1985 murder with amazing similarities to the brutal killing of JonBenét, who would have turned 8 on August 6.

And incredibly, it was written by John Douglas, former head of the FBI's behavioral science unit – and **one of the first experts hired by JonBenét's father John after he and wife Patsy set up their own investigation team.**

We'll be looking into Douglas in *The Craven Silence 3.* In theory Douglas ought to be an even slicker investigator than Lou Smit,[31] right?

From acandyrose.com :

"The book was among several found during a search of John and Patsy's bedroom after JonBenét's body was discovered in the basement," said a source close to the case. *"One of the investigators recently read through it in detail and was stunned at what he saw in one chapter.*

"For someone planning a murder or staging its aftermath, it could amount to a how-to manual." The book *Mind Hunter…describes the case of Larry Gene Bell, who abducted and murdered high school senior Shari Faye Smith and a 9-year-old girl near Columbia, S.C.*

On Christmas night 1996 the Ramseys were thrown into a difficult situation. Unfortunately their predilections – in terms of reading fiction, entertainment, social climbing and whatnot – meant rather than ameliorate their situation, they apparently chose another option when it came to dealing with their daughter's demise: psychological pageantry.

This – *Mind Hunter* – appears to be the inspiration, from acandyrose. com:

And Douglas, who helped solve the killings, lists circumstances in the case that were later eerily echoed in the JonBenét murder:

31 Lou Smit and Linda Arndt both saw the book Mind Hunter in the Ramsey master bedroom on the third floor; Lou Smit picked it up via crime scene photos and Arndt in situ. Sergeant Tom Wickman also reported seeing the book first-hand in the parents' bedroom.

~ 160 ~

*- After snatching Shari, the killer **called her mother**. His first words to her were, "Listen carefully."*

- Shari was suffocated with duct tape, which was later pulled from her mouth and nose.

- Before she was killed Shari wrote a "last will and testament" to her family on a legal pad. The fake JonBenét Ransom Note was written on a yellow legal pad.

- Shari's killer collected pornography featuring bondage. JonBenét's hands had been bound with cord before she was murdered.

- Shari's sister Dawn later won the Miss South Carolina beauty title and went on to finish as a runner-up in the Miss America pageant.

Seems a lot to be mere coincidence, right?

From acandyrose.com:

Both John and Patsy were questioned about the book in June, and they dismissed the similarities between the book and JonBenét's murder as sheer coincidence…But Gregg McCrary – Douglas' fellow FBI profiler who was also approached to work for the Ramseys and turned them down – declared: "The longer you are in my business, the less you believe in coincidences. I believe the JonBenét crime scene was staged. Many times when people stage a crime scene it's based on their perception of what a real criminal would do - and they get that information from books or movies. The grand jury will have to [weigh] whether these are a series of coincidences - or something else.

To get to the emotional reality behind the thinking we need a bullshit free assessment of John. Let's go back to Wilcox and get the scoop from her.

From acandyrose.com:

BOYLES: *You contacted me after the Boulder Police contacted you. You've spoken with them, now it's been 20 months. Why did you call me and why did you want to have this meeting?*

WILCOX: *One, I keep hearing a lot of little things, **misconceptions**, that I wanted to clear up. The other, I personally have a very hard time with the Ramseys going on national television, blatantly lying and not having anyone speak up to contradict what they are saying.*

BOYLES: *An example?*

WILCOX: *An example, when John Ramsey says to the camera, I didn't know she wet the bed, or not very much. I happen to know myself, he walked upstairs, she had wet her bed, I came in on a Monday morning and he said, "Could you change her bed? She's wet it again." The thing that strikes me as odd, I knew her between 2 1/2 and 4. During that time, she did wet the bed but it wasn't chronic. It was every now and then. Early on, I mean 2 1/2 year olds always do, I mean it seems like they always have accidents. But, **it got progressively worse**. I would think that a 6-year-old would wet the bed less than a 4-year-old or a 2-year-old. **It actually got worse**, it was moderate, she didn't have rubber sheets at that point, a pull-up would hold it. But her and Burke both wet the bed. Burke was 7-years-old and he also wet the bed. I didn't think it was odd at the time, because it sometimes runs in families and it's more common in boys. **And, their parents were lazy**.*

When Lisa and I spoke to world renowned psychologist Dr. Lillian Glass about the bedwetting issue afflicting both of the Ramsey children, Glass provided an excellent term that really sums up the whole process that was underway. Glass called it *regressing*.

It's a word that means:

- Deteriorating
- Reverting

- Going backwards

Growing children are like growing plants. Put them in the wrong environment and they struggle. Even a good environment can turn on a child, leading to the same thing – regression. For a child to grow parents must be like attentive gardeners. A flourishing plant is easy to overlook when it first begins to wilt; by the time it is seriously deteriorated it is often too late.

The laziness description rings true because the Ramseys also never ate dinner at home – always at restaurants. The messy home, the mere facts that shit was being smeared over walls in the first place suggests negligence – or something worse – from the parents. But what could be worse than negligence?

From acandyrose.com:

PETER BOYLES: *You told me a story about John Ramsey coming over and turning off the vacuum while you were cleaning the house. Tell the audience that story.*

WILCOX: *Okay, first and foremost, the major...**Patsy's major job was to make sure nobody annoyed John**. One of the things that really annoyed him was lots of noises, you know, [inaudible] noises, things like that. One day, I was there, it was during the summer, so Patsy and the kids were in Michigan, it was the summer of '95, probably June or July, I was in the master bedroom, upstairs, on the 3rd floor, vacuuming the floor, which was my job. I was finishing up. John Ramsey had come in during that time, probably through the garage, went up the stairs, turned off the vacuum, turned around and walked away.*

BOYLES: *He didn't say anything to you?*

WILCOX: *Not a word.*

BOYLES: *Just turned it off and walked away?*

WILCOX: *The look on his face said it all.*

BOYLES: *What were you doing, other than your job?*

WILCOX: *Nothing, I was vacuuming the floor.*

BOYLES: *And he came over, turned off the vac, didn't say anything to you and walked away.*

WILCOX: *Right. He didn't like the sound of the vacuum.*

Does this sound like a particularly attentive parent? Even so, inattentiveness isn't a crime. So what does it point to? My impression is two very spoilt, very entitled, very self-centred and very proud parents. Both seem to be caught up in the pageantry of social climbing. As parents, in my view, they suck.

The one doesn't like marks on skin, the other doesn't like noises. Patsy scrubs, John silences. How could this – which seems neither-here-nor-there – have played out at the actual crime scene? Is a little bit of neglect really harmful? Larry, over to you.

From cnn.com [May 28th, 2001]:

KING: *Did you try anything to revive her?*

JOHN: *I took the tape off her mouth, I tried to untie her arms. They were very tightly bound. I couldn't get the knot undone. And then I just – I – I picked her up and I just screamed, the kind of scream you scream in a dream when you – you're trying to speak but you can't. It's just a scream.*

It's very dramatic of course, but what's missing from John's story is the obvious – does he check whether she's breathing? Does he check a pulse? Does he try to talk to her or rouse her? Does he check for injuries? Are her eyes open? Is she warm to the touch?

Instead of all these things John's more interested in contaminating duct tape and rope tied around JonBenét's wrist. This is his first priority, John, not JonBenét.

It's important to <u>note the rope is wrapped around her left pajama sleeve</u>, not pulled tightly around the skin of her wrist. John incorrectly implies both arms were tied when only one was. It's also a misnomer that her arms are tightly bound. Besides being easy to slip out of the knot, the cord itself is fairly flimsy.

John also picks JonBenét up and screams – **he says**. It's not clear if Fleet White screams or John screams, or both men. According to Linda Arndt it's <u>Fleet White who screams for an ambulance</u>, yet <u>John needs to be told by Arndt that JonBenét</u> – who is stiff and cold, and smelling – is dead.

From <u>acandyrose.com</u>/websleuths:

7NEWS has confirmed it involves a book by a well-known FBI profiler John Douglas. The book is called Mindhunter. 7NEWS has confirmed that investigators discovered the book in the Ramsey's bedroom. Sources tell us one of the parents was reading it, but we don't know which one. The Ramseys have been questioned about it. The book describes many of the cases Douglas worked on while he was at the FBI. Investigators are particularly interested in a chapter that explains how the FBI helped catch Larry Gene Bell, who was convicted and sentenced to death for kidnapping and killing two girls in South Carolina in 1985. Experts say there are several similarities between the case described in that chapter and the Ramsey case. While the book doesn't mean anything by itself, when you put it together with all the other details of the murder, it's an important piece of information. We tried to contact the Ramsey's lawyers about this, but they did not return our call.

So who read Mind Hunter – John or Patsy?

From <u>acandyrose.com</u>/websleuths:

The book was read by Patsy. It was found on the floor on HER side of the bed... What's so interesting about this revelation is that Patsy took the book with her when she and John permanently left the house the day of the murder. Now I ask you, if your child had been brutally murdered hours earlier in your own house and you had to move out of the house because it was a secured crime scene, and you had only a few minutes to grab some essentials to take with you, would you even consider grabbing a book????? And of all the books in the house, she only grabbed that one book!! Smoking gun? A jury sure might see it that way.

The speculation is interesting but I tend to go with a more direct source – Wilcox. From Wilcox's description of Patsy's reading tastes [poems and the like] this doesn't sound like a fit for her. It's a perfect match for Wilcox's description of John's reading preferences:

suspense-thriller… whatever's number 1 on the bestseller lists.

This was both. If true, what could it mean? Well it supports our theory that both John and Patsy were the authors of the Ransom Note, and both were actors or agents in the cover-up. We believe John used the ideas in Mind Hunter to script the Ransom Note accordingly. The mistake he made, if he was involved, was scripting too much, and then the biggest rookie mistake of all, using a pen and pad from the home itself. But Jack Crawford couldn't think of everything now, could he?

DNA, Dream Teams, Defamation Lawsuits & Unclassified Documents

"This was not a case of 'Twelve Angry Men.' There wasn't much argument at the end." —anonymous grand juror who voted to indict the Ramseys, thedailybeast.com

"…they never had a chance to present their version of the truth… [But]…there are probably a number of people who, if the killer were to be identified through the DNA evidence…they will probably still believe that somehow John or Patsy Ramsey were involved." — Lin Wood, nbcnews.com

"This case will be a war of experts." — Dr. Henry Lee

A classic example of defense lawyer deceit is the argument that the Ramseys weren't afforded a chance to address the Grand Jury. The argument is that even the justice system was biased against them, but the argument only "works" for lay folk unfamiliar with the basics of the justice system. The Ramseys weren't supposed to address the Grand Jury, just as O.J. Simpson wasn't asked to address the Grand Jury either – and didn't testify on his own behalf at trial anyway.

From ohiobar.org:

[The Grand Jury process is] usually one-sided, and…very different from a trial. Unlike a public trial, the accused person is not present… nor is his/her counsel present (even if he is called as a witness). Also, witnesses are not cross-examined. Not even a judge is present in the grand jury room…

Another misconception, not just in this case but in many, is that DNA in and of itself conclusively exonerates or implicates possible suspects. Let's examine what was found at the scene and see if it leads to anything definitive.

DNA

Blood was found in the following areas on/around JonBenét's body. DNA tests concluded that all blood evidence found belonged to JonBenét.

1. JonBenét's thigh area, which was wiped down.
2. The right shoulder area of JonBenét's white shirt, likely from her nose/mouth.
3. The inner crotch of JonBenét's panties.
4. The white blanket.
5. The pink nightgown.

DNA testing was conducted during the following timeframes:

- **1997** – Initial collection and testing from family and other possible suspects.
- **2001** – New testing conducted on JonBenét's underpants resulted in 1-2 markers, out of 13, being defined.

- **2003** – An additional spot of blood on JonBenét's underpants was tested and resulted in 9-10 markers being defined.
- **2008** – New "Touch DNA" (skin cell) technology was introduced and applied to the waistband of the pants on JonBenét.

FINGERNAILS

No blood or tissue was found underneath any of JonBenét's nails after they were clipped during autopsy.[32] This supports the lack of a significant struggle with her attacker.

Three potential sources of DNA were found. The female source was believed to be JonBenét. The two other sources were male and unidentifiable. One found under a right hand fingernail, the other under a left hand fingernail. Adding to the uncertainty of sources, the medical examiner, Meyer, may have cross-contaminated evidence when he used the same pair of clippers to clip all ten nails. The standard procedure is to use a sterile set of clippers for each individual nail.

Since Patsy couldn't confirm in her interviews when JonBenét had last been bathed, there was a possibility that DNA from multiple sources could have been under her nails for a period of time. Steve Thomas notes that DNA can be deposited by something as simple as brushing your nails across your face. Since the DNA found was not blood or tissue, it could have come from any surface that JonBenét had been in contact with that day or in the days prior.

JONBENET'S UNDERPANTS

Unidentified male DNA was found in JonBenét's underpants. It was found in an area of the fabric that also contained two spots of

---

32 Source: Steve Thomas' book *JonBenét: Inside the Ramsey Murder Investigation*.

JonBenét's blood. Lin Wood argued that since it was "commingled" with JonBenét's blood that it was a strong indicator it came from the killer. But what if the DNA was on the fabric prior to the addition of the blood?

From thedenverpost:

DNA tests done in 1997 and 1999 only narrowed the genetic material believed to be in saliva in the blood spots to a male outside the Ramsey family. Investigators sought a match of the DNA profile with a U.S. database in 2003 but found none.

From jonbenetramsey.pbworks.com:

"Investigators in the JonBenét Ramsey case believe that male DNA recovered from the slain child's underwear may not be critical evidence at all, and instead could have been left at the time of the clothing's manufacture. In exploring that theory, investigators obtained unopened "control" samples of identical underwear manufactured at the same plant in Southeast Asia, tested them – and found human DNA in some of those new, unused panties."

The panties that JonBenét was wearing were indeed brand new, they were the size 12-14 "Bloomies" that Patsy had bought for her niece, Jenny Davis. JonBenét typically wore size 4-6 panties.

Another plausible theory floated by internet poster Why_Nut was that foreign DNA on the panties could have come from the seat of JonBenét's brand new bike.

In the same report where Lin Wood suggests the commingled DNA points to the killer, he also says that there are common markers in the DNA from the fingernail evidence and the underpants evidence. But common markers aren't a match. The sources of the DNA may be linked, but they also may not be.

JONBENET'S LONGJOHN PANTS

Twelve years after JonBenét's murder, Touch DNA was used to test the waistband of JonBenét's pants. Unidentified male DNA that matched DNA previously found in JonBenét's underpants, was found on the waistband. This led to Mary Lacy, the District Attorney who took Alex Hunter's place, issuing a letter to publicly exonerate the Ramseys.

While this linked DNA evidence at the outset appears to be damning, it's also important to understand Touch DNA, and the transference of DNA in general.

Finding DNA evidence on a human doesn't necessarily mean the source of that DNA was in direct contact with the person. If person A sneezes on a table, then I sit down and put my sleeve in the same spot, my sleeve will likely now show signs of DNA from person A.

If JonBenét's killer wasn't wearing gloves, doesn't it make sense that their Touch DNA – skin cells - would be all over her body, her clothing, the paint caddy, the blanket, etc.? Likewise, if the killer was wearing gloves, you'd expect there to be no Touch DNA at all.

JonBenét was found in the basement of her home, where all sorts of items were stored over time. In the pictures you can see window screens, lumber, paint, boxes and other supplies stored. Items that had been handled and used by workers. If JonBenét's pants and undergarments had been removed in the basement either during an attack or staging, old DNA from some other source could have been transferred to her clothing.

James Kolar drives this point home when he reveals in his book *Foreign Faction* that there were [at least] six unique and unidentified genetic profiles – five male and one female – found at the scene. It's highly unlikely that JonBenét was attacked by six strangers who came and went undetected. So, if there are that many sources of unidentified

DNA at the scene, one can conclude none are reliably linked to the killer at least not without any additional corroborating evidence, of which there's none. Here are some of the sources:

Male #1 – fingernail scrapings

Male #2 – fingernail scrapings

Male #3 – Touch DNA on the waistband of pants

Male #4 – Touch DNA on the wrist bindings

Male # 5 – Touch DNA on the garrote

Of all the touch DNA found at the scene, the most interesting in my view, is the DNA found on the pink Barbie nightgown in the wine cellar. It belonged to Patsy and Burke.

HAIR

The following hairs were found and tested at the immediate scene:[33]

1. A Caucasian [possible] pubic hair on the blanket – unidentified

2. A dark hair or hairs were found on the sleeve/shoulder area of JonBenét's white shirt – unidentified

3. Animal hairs were found on JonBenét's hands – unidentified

4. Animal hair, alleged to be from a beaver, was found on the duct tape – unidentified

SEMEN

1. Found on the blanket inside the suitcase that was underneath the window in the basement – tested conclusive for John Andrew [JA was out of the state with his sister, Melinda, on Dec 26. The blanket was one he used while at college.]

---

33 Source: jonbenetramsey.pbworks.com.

While investigators and technicians were busy trying to make sense of the contaminated scene, the Ramseys were busy with their legal team suing everybody and their brother. What's interesting is the majority of the lawsuits filed by Lin Wood were either on behalf of Burke, or in the defense of Burke.

Defamation Lawsuits

Filed November 1999. $25 Million Libel Suit. Burke Ramsey vs **Star** and **American Media**. On May 25, 1999, Star published a front page photo of Burke and JonBenét with the headline "JonBenét was Killed by Brother Burke." Settled in March of 2000 for an undisclosed amount.

Filed May 2000. $35 Million Libel Suit. Burke Ramsey vs **Globe**. In a 1998 article, Globe published *"Burke, 11 is the Killer – say Crime Investigators – and Burke will NEVER stand trial!"* Settled for an undisclosed amount in March 2001.

Filed May, 2000. $4 Million Libel Suit. John and Patsy Ramsey vs **Time Warner Companies, Inc**. In May 1999, Time published *"Extra: Tabloid Solves JonBenét Case! Star Magazine reports that police now think the brother did it. Don't laugh."* A confidential settlement was approved in July 2001.

Filed May, 2000. $4 Million Defamation Suit. Burke Ramsey vs **New York Post**. On May 13, 1999, the front page of the magazine read *"Parents' Deal Could be Bombshell. Brother, 9, Murdered JonBenét: Mag."* This case was settled out of court.

Filed May, 2000. $11.75 Million Libel Suit. Burke Ramsey vs. **Windsor House Publishing Group, Eleanor Von Duyke and Dwight Wallington**. Windsor's book, published February 1998, Burke is portrayed as sexually molesting JonBenét, being mentally ill and guilty of murder. This case was settled out of court.

Filed March 2001. $80 Million Libel and Slander Suit: John and Patsy Ramsey vs. **Steve Thomas**, author of *JonBenét: Inside the Ramsey Murder Investigation*, co-author **Don Davis** and publisher **St. Martin's Press**. Settled in March 2002 for an undisclosed amount.

Filed June 2001. $70 Million Libel Suit: Burke Ramsey vs. **Court TV network**. In 1999, a Court TV show and internet promotions identified Burke as a suspect in JonBenét's killing. This case was settled out of court.

Filed February 2004. John and Patsy Ramsey vs. **Fox News Channel**. In 2002 Fox aired a JonBenét special on the 6th anniversary of her death which indicated the parents may be involved. The case was dismissed by a federal judge.

In *The Craven Silence 3*, we'll be dealing with the lawsuits that were filed against the Ramseys in 1998, 2000 and 2001.

The following are the key players of the dream teams on both sides. With their friendships, and mutual business and political connections, the Ramseys certainly seemed poised to avoid prosecution at all costs.

Boulder DA Dream Team

Henry Lee, World renowned Forensic Scientist and Crime Scene Analyst. Lee was hired by Alex Hunter in February 1997, along with Barry Scheck to assist the team. Lee has worked on numerous high profile cases, mostly for the prosecution, but worked for the defense in the O.J. Simpson case. He's the Director at the Henry C. Lee Institute of Forensic Science at the University of New Haven. He's served as an advisor for more than 80 law enforcement agencies worldwide. Lee was also invited to be an investigator on the recent CBS docu-series *The Case of: JonBenét Ramsey*.

Barry Scheck, American lawyer specializing in DNA. Scheck was hired by Alex Hunter in February 1997, along with Henry Lee to assist the team. Scheck is also best known for his defense work in the O.J. Simpson case. He's also the co-founder of the Innocence Project which uses DNA evidence to exculpate individuals of crimes for which they've been wrongfully convicted.

Pete Hofstrom, Assistant District Attorney, Chief of the Felony Division. Hofstrom started as a paralegal for Alex Hunter in 1974, worked his way up, and eventually became the # 3 prosecutor in the DA's office. In a Vanity Fair article, Bardach wrote that Hofstrom regularly had breakfast with one Ramsey defense lawyer. Steve Thomas made the comment "defense lawyers love Pete Hofstrom." Just like Hunter, Hofstrom was not a proponent of trials. When the police were withholding the release of JonBenét's body over the Ramseys not being cooperative, it was Hofstrom who ended the showdown. He went directly to Ramsey attorney, Mike Bynum, and said "We've got a problem." Alex Hunter eventually removed Hofstrom from the case.

Alex Hunter, District Attorney from 1972-2000. At the time that JonBenét was killed, Hunter had not taken a case to trial in over ten years. He was notorious for settling cases outside of court. Hunter did not want to empanel a grand jury, but did so only after feeling political pressure as fallout from the resignation of Detective Steve Thomas. When the grand jury, after a year of work, voted to indict the Ramseys in 1999, Hunter refused to press charges. Upon his retirement, he told the Denver Post, "it's been a good life."

Mary Lacy, District Attorney from 2001-2009. Prior to becoming DA, she spent 10 years as Chief of the Sexual Assault Unit. She issued a formal apology letter to the Ramseys in 2008 after a Touch DNA test resulted in additional unidentified male DNA at the scene.

Lou Smit, Retired Detective. Smit had previously worked on over 200 homicide cases. He was asked by Alex Hunter to join the investigation team in March 1997, but resigned from the case after only 18 months due to differences with the Boulder PD. He believed the Ramseys were innocent and the evidence pointed to an intruder. Smit introduced the theory that a stun gun was used on JonBenét. He continued working on the case as a consultant. He passed away in August 2010.

Bobby Brown, former Colorado Springs Detective and protégé of Lou Smit's famed Apple Dumpling Gang—a group of retired law enforcement officials famous for solving some of the nation's toughest cold cases. Brown ran Bobby Brown Investigations and has expertise in polygraph tests and hostage negotiations.

James Kolar, Lead Investigator from 2005-2006. In 2012, Kolar published his book *Foreign Faction: Who Really Kidnapped JonBenét?* In an effort to disprove the intruder did it theory. He resigned in 2006 because he felt certain important leads were not being pursued in the case. Kolar was one of the investigators selected to be a part of the CBS docu-series *The Case of*: JonBenét Ramsey.

Mike Kane, Deputy District Attorney, Special Prosecutor. Kane was hired by Alex Hunter in May 1998, recruited from the Pennsylvania Department of Revenue, to be in charge of the grand jury proceedings. Kane had previously worked as a prosecutor in Denver and had extensive grand jury experience. In February 1999, he wrote to Lou Smit telling him his request to give evidence to the grand jury was denied. He also demanded that he surrender all of his evidence and sought court permission to permanently erase it.

Tom Bennett, Retired Detective, Chief Investigator. Bennett had over 30 years of experience as a police detective. He was hired by DA Mary Keenan in June 2003 to work 20-30 hours per week on the case. He resigned in 2005, and James Kolar took his place.

Bill Wise, First Assistant District Attorney. Wise, Alex Hunter's law and business partner, and best friend, was one of the first people Hunter hired after taking office in 1972. They owned real estate together with one of the Ramsey attorneys. He was widely believed to be one of the sources of the leaks to the media. Bill Wise retired at the same time that Hunter did in 2000.

Gordon Coombes, Investigator for the Boulder DA from 2008 to 2011. He was a part of the team while they were analysing the new technology of Touch DNA.

Ramsey Dream Team

Mike Bynum, Ramsey family friend, business partner and lawyer. He had previously worked in the DA's office with Alex Hunter. Bynum went to the Ramseys house to console them on December 26, and immediately offered them legal help. He chose the politically-connected firm Haddon, Morgan and Foreman for the Ramsey's representation.

Harold Haddon, John's lead defense lawyer and partner in Haddon, Morgan and Foreman. Haddon was the manager of US Senator Gary's Hart's campaign. His wife, Beverly, was a lobbyist and also active in politics. Haddon is also the attorney for investigative journalist, Paula Woodward.

Bryan Morgan, Defense lawyer and Partner in Haddon, Morgan and Foreman. Morgan was also good friends with Assistant DA Pete Hofstrom. He attended the same Episcopal Church as the Ramseys.

Patrick Burke, Denver attorney. Burke was hired to represent both Patsy and Burke. Patrick Burke was a former assistant Colorado attorney general and ex-federal public defender.

Patrick Furman, Professor of Law, University of Colorado. Furman was hired in early 1997 to be one of Patsy's defense attorneys.

Jim Jenkins, Atlanta-based lawyer. Hired by John Ramsey to represent Melinda, John Andrew, and his ex-wife Lucinda.

William Gray, Civil attorney hired by John and Patsy. Gray and Alex Hunter were limited partners in a commercial complex in Boulder. Bill Wise was a general partner as well.

Ollie Gray, Private Investigator hired by John and Patsy. He implicated Michael Helgoth in the death of JonBenét. Gray suffers from Parkinson's Disease and still works on the case today for no pay.

John San Agustin, Private Investigator hired by John and Patsy. Gray and San Agustin, who also worked for no pay, spent time investigating the neighbors and registered sex offenders in the area.

John Douglas, former FBI profiler, author of the book Mind Hunter: According to Douglas, attorneys for the Ramseys hired him in early 1997 to assess whether or not John Ramsey was capable of killing his daughter.

From Amazon: *During his twenty-five year career with the Investigative Support Unit, Special Agent John Douglas became a legendary figure in law enforcement, pursuing some of the most notorious and sadistic serial killers of our time: the man who hunted prostitutes for sport in the woods of Alaska, the Atlanta child murderer, and Seattle's Green River killer, the case that nearly cost Douglas his life.*

As the model for Jack Crawford in The Silence of the Lambs, Douglas has confronted, interviewed, and studied scores of serial killers and assassins, including Charles Manson, Ted Bundy, and Ed Gein.

Pat Korten, Public Relations specialist hired by the Ramseys. Korten was a former U.S. Justice Department spokesman and radio talk show host, and had ties to the Reagan Administration.

Lin Wood, Lead Attorney for John, Patsy and Burke Ramsey since 1999. Wood specializes in civil litigation and represents other high-profile clients such a Dr. Phil McGraw, Beth Holloway and Gary Condit.

Unclassified Documents

In 1999, although the Boulder Grand Jury voted to indict both Ramsey parents, District Attorney, Alex Hunter, did not sign the documents and chose not to file charges. The documents remained sealed, and unknown to the public, until 2013. Only four pages of the indictment have been shared with the public.

The following true bills were returned by the Grand Jury:

COUNT IV (a) Child Abuse Resulting in Death

On or between December 25, and December 26, 1996, in Boulder County, Colorado, **John Bennett Ramsey** did unlawfully, knowingly, recklessly and feloniously permit a child to be unreasonably placed in a situation which posed a threat of injury to the child's life or health, which resulted in the death of JonBenét Ramsey, a child under the age of sixteen.

COUNT VII Accessory to a Crime

On or about December 25, and December 26, 1996 in Boulder County, Colorado, **John Bennett Ramsey** did unlawfully, knowingly and feloniously render assistance to a person, with intent to hinder, delay and prevent the discovery, detention, apprehension, prosecution, conviction and punishment of such person for the commission of a crime, knowing the person being assisted has committed and was suspected of the crime of Murder in the First Degree and Child Abuse Resulting in Death.

COUNT IV (a) Child Abuse Resulting in Death

On or between December 25, and December 26, 1996, in Boulder County, Colorado, **Patricia Paugh Ramsey** did unlawfully, knowingly, recklessly and feloniously permit a child to be unreasonably placed in a situation which posed a threat of injury to the child's life or health, which resulted in the death of JonBenét Ramsey, a child under the age of sixteen.

COUNT VII Accessory to a Crime

On or about December 25, and December 26, 1996 in Boulder County, Colorado, **Patricia Paugh Ramsey** did unlawfully, knowingly and feloniously render assistance to a person, with intent to hinder, delay and prevent the discovery, detention, apprehension, prosecution, conviction and punishment of such person for the commission of a crime, knowing the person being assisted has committed and was suspected of the crime of Murder in the First Degree and Child Abuse Resulting in Death.

The following is John Ramsey's response to the release of the Grand Jury indictments:

From thedailybeast.com:

After the documents were released on Friday, one of Ramsey's attorneys, L. Lin Wood, said they "validate John Ramsey's position that the Boulder District Attorney should release the entire grand jury record and not just 4 pages from an 18-month investigation that produced volumes of testimony and exhibits. The grand jury's true bills on Counts 4(a) and 7 are nonsensical. They reveal nothing about the evidence reviewed by the grand jury and are clearly the result of a confused and compromised process. The Ramsey Family and the public are entitled to the benefit of the full and complete record, not just a historical footnote. Fairness dictates that result."

*He added that the grand jury didn't have "the benefit of the **conclusive 2008 DNA testing that led to the unequivocal, public exoneration** of the Ramsey family."*

Arndt [Again]

"If I get kicked off this thing, I'm going to take out myself and everyone else." — Detective Arndt to Steve Thomas[34]

"JonBenét Ramsey. What comes to mind immediately is injustice." — <u>Nancy Grace</u>

If it's starting to crystalize now why this case has gone unsolved across two decades, if Lou Smit and Steve Thomas both went wildly off track on this case, it's hard to find anyone who trumps Linda Arndt on the same count. If you need someone to totally fuck up a case, short of hiring a pack of Police Academy misfits, it works to get a loose cannon involved. How loose was Linda Arndt?

From <u>forumsforjustice.org/Rocky Mountain News</u> :

"Last year [2005], I was told just about this time of year [mid-year] that [Patsy] was on her deathbed and gravely ill," said Arndt, the former Boulder Police officer who was the lone detective in the Ramsey home when JonBenét's body was found in the basement on Dec. 26, 1996.

"That spurred me to reach out to her and find her again, which I did. She responded." ...Their renewed contact in May 2005, Arndt said, "was

---

34 *JonBenét: Inside the Ramsey Murder Investigation.*

a heart-to-heart connection, common decency, showing courtesy and empathy to someone who really had a lot of tragedy."

It's the Lou Smit thing all over again. Smit got so close to the family he got sucked in, and so did his detective work.

Here's Steve Thomas' take on Arndt's role – consciously or not, intentionally or unintentionally – in derailing the investigation.

*Their [the Ramsey's] main successes in January, however, were stalling the requested interviews and blocking the testing of evidence. That underscored my belief that they had moved away from any pretence of finding a killer and were deep into trial defense preparation. I feared they would hinder the investigation whenever possible. I hand-delivered a letter to Commander Eller from attorney Patrick Burke that laid out their conditions for us to interview the Ramseys. The points, which were plainly unacceptable, included having the session take place the very next day in the office of another Ramsey lawyer. Patsy would have both a doctor and a lawyer at her side, probably be available for only one hour, and be **questioned only by Detective Arndt**.*

<u>It's tough to get any more obvious than that.</u> If the Ramseys wanted to railroad the investigation into their daughter's murder, they saw Arndt as a key player in it. Like Lou Smit, I'm sure Arndt was flattered by their "confidence" in her. Basically it was a scenario of an affluent upper class family rolling out the red carpet for the downtrodden, overlooked, poor Ms Blue Collar detective. The Ramseys valued Arndt's input, the Boulder Police not so much? So who did Arndt gravitate further and further towards? Cookies and scones, hugs and bouquets, or rough criticism and scepticism? By the way, we're not joking about the bouquets.

Here's Steve Thomas again:

Back in Boulder, Linda Arndt was a happy detective. She had won a victim's assistance award in April and came into the SitRoom to show off a vase of beautiful flowers, which she said were from "John and Patsy." ...and <u>Detective Jane Harmer</u> *looked at me in disbelief. "What the fuck was that all about?" she asked. Detectives normally do not receive flowers from suspects.*

What the fuck indeed. Harmer herself would later provide this nugget to Dateline in September 2016:

"I think that the Grand Jurors heard the evidence and came up with that conclusion [to indict] and I would agree with their conclusion."

All fair and well, one step forward...except Harmer then fucks up that feel-good epithet by adding that she was part of the team that unanimously voted not to indict the Ramseys. Two steps back.

From <u>Dateline [1:22:04]</u>:

HARMER: *"It literally took everything that I had to keep that [indictment] a secret."*

MANKIEWICZ: *Do you think the prosecutors could have gotten a conviction if they tried that case?*

HARMER: *I do not.*

MANKIEWICZ: *So the DA was right not to go for it?*

HARMER: *This was, uh, very much a team decision. The investigators and the attorneys were all in agreement.*

MANKIEWICZ: *That's gotta be frustrating.*

HARMER: *Very, very frustrating. But, you only get one shot.*

MANKIEWICZ: *Meaning that if you wanna try someone and don't convict them, you can't try them again.*

HARMER: *Correct*

From Steve Thomas:

The detectives were concerned about one of their own. Linda Arndt, who had been a good cop, [but] now seemed unhappy, withdrawn, or outright hostile. It looked as if the problems she had encountered as the first detective at the Ramsey home were eating her up inside.

Think about it – Arndt screwed up straight off the bat by allowing John [a suspect] to search his own house, and then to contaminate JonBenét's body even further by covering her corpse under a blanket. As pressure was brought to bear on the investigation – largely thanks to the media and Ramsey lawyers orchestrating the whole circus – Arndt was caught in the crossfire. She soon found herself in an untenable situation, and felt she had to choose sides.

From Steve Thomas:

*In early March Arndt had a private meeting with Patsy. [Arndt] drove to the home of a Ramsey friend, where **Patsy greeted her with a hug**. Arndt reported that she [lifted her clothing] to prove to lawyer Patrick Burke that she wore no recording device...when I asked what they talked about during the hour-long chat, [Arndt] looked me in the eye [and said, repeated]: "I can't tell you."*

In a weird sense, Arndt became Patsy's patsy. If Patsy had sworn Arndt to secrecy, one wonders whether Arndt provided the Ramseys with inside information about the investigation side of things. It's logical to assume she did, especially when the Ramseys [actually their lawyers] were demanding access to police evidence on them in exchange for a very limited interview. Due to the inexperience of the Boulder cops, they co-operated. The Ramsey lawyers knew they would eventually have to submit their clients for a fairly unlimited interrogation, but if they could bullshit and buy time they could sew up holes and prep their clients adequately.

From Steve Thomas:

Team Ramsey would also get to examine the actual Ransom Note, receive exact one-to-one copies of both the Ransom Note and the practice note, and get photographic negatives of important evidence pictures. When we protested to Deputy DA DeMuth about the treasure trove being given away, he responded, "They'll get it anyway if they are ever charged."

It should be pointed out that DeMuth – who was picked by Alex Hunter as the prosecutor for this case – appeared to join the Dark Side himself. It's not clear whether DeMuth was already with Team Ramsey before or after interrogating Patsy in mid-1998. Irrespective, DeMuth – after a 17-year stint with the Boulder District Attorney's office, was later employed by John Ramsey's lawyer Mike Bynum.[35] DeMuth gave up criminal law for a lucrative career prosecuting corporate and civil cases. The point is, if DeMuth, who was relatively high in the pecking order, could be swayed,[36] is there any doubt Arndt wasn't?

From Steve Thomas:

*I considered it an act of treason and refused to participate in handing it over. I just couldn't do it... While Detective Trujillo was in the lobby giving the material to defense lawyer Patrick Burke, **Detective Arndt came up and gave Burke a hug.***

From forumsforjustice.org/Rocky Mountain News :

[Arndt] talked about what the contact between the two [Arndt and Patsy] meant to her.

---

35 DeMuth went to work for Ramsey's lawyer Mike Bynum in September 2000. From dailycamera.com: David Sanderson said Trip DeMuth's move shows the Boulder County District Attorney's Office is a "deeply rooted, incestuous establishment."

36 Although DeMuth has not admitted being a proponent of the "intruder" narrative, his investigative line of inquiry appeared to have supported this, which would indirectly have been support for Team Ramsey.

"Knowing that she was dying, that was the impetus I needed to finish, to fulfill the promise that she asked of me," said Arndt, 45.

The day was Jan. 8, 1997. Arndt was at the Child Advocacy Center in Niwot where JonBenét's older brother Burke – now 19 – was being interviewed by a child psychologist.

"Patsy and I were alone for over an hour, and she shared a lot of things in that conversation. She did, and I did," Arndt recalled. "And one of the things she demanded of me, she looked me in the eye and grabbed my hand and said, 'Promise me, promise me you will stay on this case and you will find out who did this to JonBenét.'

"I don't remember my words, but I gave her my word that I would. And I cannot hold her story any longer."

I'm not sure exactly what Arndt means by "I cannot hold her story". I don't think it means "I can't keep bullshitting for Patsy". Instead I think it means: "I'm writing a book about Patsy." Whether Arndt ultimately kept her word is also open to discussion. In September 1999 Arndt <u>felt, or rather implied there was "no doubt"</u> that John Ramsey was involved in JonBenét's murder – at least that's how I read her cryptic but not so cryptic fingering of JonBenét's father to *ABC* news. Since promising to find justice for JonBenét, it's not clear what Arndt did besides quit her job and lose a defamation suit to boot.

It's also not clear whether Christianity played a role in addling Arndt's mind as far as this case is concerned. When Arndt describes Patsy as "a lady of grace and courage and spirit" I tend to think Christianity did its duty instead of people with jobs doing theirs. Whatever was putting pep in her step in the first quarter of 1997, Arndt's colleagues were none too happy about it.

From <u>forumsforjustice.org/Rocky Mountain News</u> :

Arndt wasn't allowed by department brass to stay on the case. *She was pulled off in April 1997, quit the force two years later and unsuccessfully **sued the department** for defamation. Arndt, who still lives in the West but is no longer a police officer, is now occupied, she said, "putting my life back together, trying to find my way back in the world."*

What a mess. When you have a department bickering with itself, and lawyers laughing all the way to the bank, how can a little girl hope to have the true story told? Will Arndt's memoir be published? Will Arndt finally keep her promise to Patsy?

From forumsforjustice.org/Rocky Mountain News :

In her first in-depth print interview, Arndt remembered Ramsey as "[someone]…imprisoned by secrets. This whole case has been imprisoned by secrets."

There's an aspect to that statement that seems to be insightful. The theory that Burke did it infers not merely a double bind but *a triple bind*. But is that what Arndt's suggesting?

From forumsforjustice.org/Rocky Mountain News :

Arndt was reluctant to reveal many details of her contact with JonBenét's mother in the final year of her life. "I gained nothing and risked everything to contact her. And it was just the right thing to do," Arndt said.

*"There's no way to undo the wrong that was done (to the Ramsey family). But (it was) just to acknowledge what you could or couldn't do, and **apologize** for any error on my part and to **offer myself** in any way that was helpful to her."*

One gets the same sense of "compassionate leave" from Lou Smit. The Ramsey family are the actual victims here; they're honest, decent people…

From <u>forumsforjustice.org/Rocky Mountain News</u> :

Arndt would not discuss her theories of the case, saying only that she doesn't hold the "prevailing view" within the Boulder Police Department, which increasingly keyed on Patsy Ramsey. [But when] asked if what she is writing will eliminate anyone's suspicions about Ramsey, Arndt stopped short of saying so.

"I don't know that (the book) will exonerate. It will give people a context that they have not had before, and it will give them an understanding for everyone involved – but, particularly, for Patsy."

This loosey-goosey statement possibly sent chills down John and Burke Ramsey's spines, if they ever had a chance to see it. In any event, hers was yet another bit-part player scuppering a ship called The JonBenét Ramsey Investigation. All the spotlights trained on the Ramsey residence, on the Boulder cops and officials, seemed to yield to rust, mildew and mishaps. Eventually the last one went on the fritz, flickered and died.

<u>When all other lights go out</u>, we're left in the dark basement. In time, if we stay where we are, despite the dark, if we listen carefully, despite the cold, our eyes and ears begin to adjust. As a ghostly apparition seems to appear out of the murk at our feet we're aware of the simple circumstances surrounding this case. There's less a mystery of who killed JonBenét, we think, than there is a lot of furtive intrigue in Boulder's corridors of legal power. The mystery isn't who killed the innocent child but rather who was responsible for the behind the scenes shenanigans that frustrated the investigation?

But is that much of a mystery either?

FLASHLIGHT

Her tragic story is a dark reflection of our culture and its obsession with both fame and death in equal measure. — Newsweek

Lessons in Child Psychology #4

In lesson #3 we turned a spotlight onto Becker's stinky comparison – money with feces – but <u>we're not done yet</u>. Now we want to burrow down into this psychology on our hands and knees, feeling with our fingers, holding a slim torch between our teeth, and following the whiff of death wherever it wafts.

It's down-and-dirty work but since it's never been done sufficiently, let's get it done and dusted. While we're crawling in the dark, sniffing at skirtings, poking cracks and corners, it's important to have a basic idea of motive floating in the back of our minds.

The prosecutor in the Jodi Arias case, <u>Juan Martinez</u>, notes the following in his book *Conviction*:

"It seems the majority of the homicides that pass across my desk have some sexual element to them. If it isn't about sex, it is usually about money."

Murderers are often motivated by money or sex, sometimes both. Could that be true in a Christmas scenario involving a kid brother and his baby sister? Could the same be said for JonBenét's parents?

In this narrative, and more particularly these "psychology lessons" we'll focus more on the money side of that equation. In *The Craven Silence 3* we'll plumb the sexual dimension in more detail.

To understand money we have to drop through the basements of time to get an archetypal grip on what this thing called money actually is, and what it means to human beings in psychological terms. To guide us down that dark elevator shaft is the man behind Terror Management Theory.

Money gives power now – and through accumulated property...power in the future. Man has become dependent on social symbols of prestige that single him out as especially worthy... The symbols of immortal power that money buys exist on the level of the visible, and so crowd out their invisible competitor... — Ernest Becker[37]

While Becker expresses himself at times with an austere voice perhaps more suited to the natives of Laconia and ancient Sparta,[38] we shouldn't overlook their contemporary import to the common Christmas context. To demystify Becker's psychology we need to personalise his message to the fuzziness surrounding Feliz Navidad.[39]

What are your fond and not so fond memories of Christmases past as a child? In the chapter, A Page out of a South African Diary, I'll provide some additional background into the similarities between my family and sibling situation and the Ramsey's.

My father – a successful businessman – was also often absent, but Christmas was a special time for me. Typically we went away to the coast during the holidays. The whole family travelled in a white 1973 Mercedes Benz. I remember my father occasionally banging the dashboard because the analogue indicators, like so many watch dials, would get stuck.

---

37 *Escape From Evil.*

38 The "laconic phrase" typifies terseness. Spartan laws and Spartan society were admired in ancient times by the likes of Socrates for their brevity.

39 Spanish for "Merry Christmas". The etymology of "Christmas" can be traced back to 1038' and the Italian/Catholic term *Cristes-messe* to 1131, while the idea of a banquet, feasting and a triumphant star is also attributed to Mithraism in the 1st – 4th century AD.

Part of the magic of those trips were the carefully disguised Christmas treasures packed in with the luggage. Often they were buried in a way that defeated the cursory curiosities of innocent children. Other times the secreted treasures peeked fortuitously through a plastic bag or bulging suitcase.

If we had a chance to sneak a peek at the attached card the excitement was even greater – we children would surreptitiously spread the news to one another. "I saw your present!" "What was it?" "How should I know?" "Well what did it look like?" "How should I know?" "Well how big was it?"

We may not see it immediately, but Christmas for kids is like the lottery for adults. There's a "how much did I win?" element to it as much as there is the "I wonder if I got lucky?" element. When adults scratch their "lucky" numbers the thought flickers that perhaps this time the gods will unload their bounty on them – not just them, *only* them.

Man succumbs easily to the temptation of created life, which is to exercise power mainly in the dimension in which he moves and acts as an organism. — Ernest Becker

What is the JonBenét Ramsey dimension to this? Well we've heard John Ramsey speaking on television early on, saying that the statistics show crimes committed against children in the home point overwhelmingly to family members as accessories, especially parents. What do the stats say *exactly*?

From childwelfare.gov:[40]

---

40 Endorsed by the U.S. Department of Health and Human Services, and the following US-based subsidiaries: Administration for Children and Families, Administration on Children, Youth and Families, Children's Bureau.

In 2014, parents, acting alone or with another parent, were responsible for 79.3 percent of child abuse or neglect fatalities. More than one-quarter (28.0 percent) were perpetrated by the mother acting alone, 15.0 percent were perpetrated by the father acting alone, and 21.8 percent were perpetrated by the mother and father acting together. Nonparents (including kin and child care providers, among others) were responsible for 15.7 percent of child fatalities, and child fatalities with unknown perpetrator relationship data accounted for 5.0 percent of the total.

In plain English that translates to the odds in this scenario favouring:

1. Patsy 28%

2. Patsy and John 21.8%

3. Burke 15.7%

4. John 15%

5. Intruder 5%

Although there was an ominous spine-tingling sense that it was wrong, I remember a giddy feeling building up as the countdown to Christmas was underway, that gifts I guessed I was about to receive would reinforce my status as a valued son in the family. My mother and I had an especially close relationship, so how would this translate… well…*materially?*

The gifts a child might anticipate receiving [encouraged via a thorough shakedown of the home's contents while mom and dad were out, or distracted] could elicit barely contained, often sickening feelings of expectation. Having discovered a hidden horde and later fully examined it, my brother and me, and later my sister, would breathlessly bubble over to each other on what we thought we were getting based on the number, size, shape and heft going on beneath the carnival of wrapping-paper.

The meretricious value of these gifts communicated more than merely their monetary-value, they also communicated how well our parents knew us, and further, how and where exactly they saw us evolving not only on our own terms, but *in terms of one another*. A certain toy indicated a certain level of responsibility and development, a certain value imparted from the family endowment was an endorsement of our value as individuals. But there was something else. At Christmas siblings were able to see in a transparent and gratifying, but at times terrifying manner, how parents had appraised the value of one's siblings compared to oneself. Was it fair? Had one unexpectedly superseded another? Did one come out of this contest ahead or behind?

Many parents who have experienced Christmas as a holocaust have had to do Day After Christmas Damage Control. Gifts needing to be exchanged for the extra-large or chrome polished version.

Some little voice on a child's shoulder should tell them "no" to mercenary inquiries about gifts being analogous to human value, but another voice whispers menacingly into the ear of the little boy, "yes, do you see, they love her more!"

If this seems juvenile, consider the pomp and ceremony surrounding engagement rings. Grown [heterosexual] women around the world anticipate that one day a [heterosexual] man will romantically serve up a massive piece of his treasure – hewn from months or years of sweat and toil [in other words living death] in the form of a glittering rock. This symbol of his love, protection and insulation against life's knocks [including death] is intended to impress not merely the bride, but the rest of the world too. Which is why as soon as an engagement is announced all eyes turn to the engagement ring: "How big is it?" "How much did she win compared to me?" The union is touted as a journey to "happily ever after" just as the Christmas fairy tale is attended with a jovial "Ho ho ho" and an appeal to be "Merry".

But <u>there's a very dark psychological underbelly to all this,</u> especially when expectations aren't met. I participated in a cycling event sponsored by a huge hotel chain, and a very wealthy friend of a friend's wife lost her expensive wedding ring. I tell you, the whole day became a holocaust, with armies of people including the hotel staff searching on bended knee for that ring. In the end I think she found it herself in the drain of the basin.

And so, what about on that Christmas morning in Boulder, 1996? Were expectations sky high? We believe they were. But *were they met*?

~ Philistines Philippines and Engineers

"Did I help pound nails? No." — John Ramsey
deposition, December 12, 2001

On our journey through the basements of human psychology, the flashlight catches on something bright. Is it a coin? Is it a ribbon? Is it a medal or a badge?

Sometimes a glimpse of something turns out to be, at closer inspection under a flickering flashlight, something *entirely different*. To know what we're looking for, let's swim through the mantle of human history, and paddle towards the notion of a defunct identity.

Whoever or whatever a Philistine once was, they are no more. What's worse, Philistines never wrote their own texts, so who they are tended to be taken from second-hand sources – and usually their rivals and conquerors.

From Wikipedia:

...the Deuteronomistic history books... [portray] them at one period of time as among the Kingdom of Israel's most dangerous enemies. In contrast, the canon of Eastern Christianity...uses the term "allophuloi"... which means simply "other nations".

As we float throat the basements of human history and ticking clocks, the flashlight casts strange shadows on dark walls. It's difficult to see what something is when the shadow behind it either drowns the thing itself, or distracts us from it.

Are the enemies in the JonBenét case the cops? Are the cops "Philistines" in the Biblical sense? How about the conventional sense?

The dictionary.com gives us the conventional definition as:

A person who is lacking in or hostile or smugly indifferent to cultural values, intellectual pursuits, aesthetic refinement, etc., or is contentedly commonplace in ideas and tastes.

To call someone a Philistine is to call them lacking in conventional values, smug about cultural values, intellectually smug and contentedly ensconced in their smugness. Were the Boulder police smug and disconnected from their community, or were the Ramseys?

Are we accusing John Ramsey and Patsy of being Philistines? Of course not. The Ramseys were very, very, very decent people according to their first lawyer, Mike Bynum. They were also deeply Christian folk. Let's float a little closer to that aspect of human history.

From livescience.com:

Stories in the Hebrew Bible say that the Philistines clashed with the ancient Israelites many times. One of the battles supposedly took place between a Philistine force led by the giant man named Goliath and an Israelite force that included a man named David who would go on to become king of Israel. In the story David kills Goliath with a slingshot and the Israelites go on to rout the Philistine force. Whether David or Goliath ever existed — or if a series of wars between the Philistines and Israelites occurred — are matters debated by scholars.

If history is analogous to this case, then either JonBenét is a modern martyr for David, her death precipitating slings and arrows that led to exposure and undoing of corrupt law enforcement. Or something different. Perhaps the Ramseys and their lawyers, and Boulder's chummy legal culture have emerged as the Goliath in this story. And perhaps the story is not yet over, the little corpse – or some other small person, a reporter, an eBook writer, a mere documentary – could bring the colossus of corruption crashing down.

Our flashlight catches on the top of a pyramid. When we swoop closer we see a small black king standing in the dust with a smug look on his face.

From livescience.com:

...many archaeologists think that the Philistines came to the Levant during the 12th century B.C., possibly as refugees searching for a new home. The 12th century B.C. is also the time when Ramses III engaged the Philistines in battle, supposedly defeating them....

But as it turns out, the great and famous Pharaoh lied about defeating the Philistines. Is the flowery story of a heroic little David slaying a Giant Philistine and then defeating their mighty armies mythical too?

Today scholars aren't sure what a Philistine even is, that slice of history has emerged over time as an unsolved mystery no one particularly cares about. But the conventional wisdom [written by their enemies of course] is that Philistines were lumbering assholes.

Let's get out of the mantle of human history and find our way back to the cold concrete of one particular Basement in Boulder. As we rise through the strata of the Ramsey house, #755 15th Street[41] we find a pair of boots. We see a piece of string tied in a knot. We see a framed photograph of a man and a woman on a powerboat called *Miss America*.

---

41 Now 749 15th Street.

From John Ramsey's deposition with Darnay Hoffman, December 12, 2001, via the dailycamera.com:

HOFFMAN: *You say that — and I understand that you were in the Navy; is that correct?*

JOHN: *Yes.*

HOFFMAN: *All right. When you were in the Navy, would you describe, if you remember, pretty much what area you were responsible for as a serviceman?*

JOHN: *Well, I was a Civil Engineer Corps officer.* **I was stationed in the Philippines for two years.** *I was the civil engineer for the Naval supply depot in the Philippines. I was transferred to Atlanta where I was the base engineer for the Naval Air Station in Atlanta.*

It's time to sow a seed which we'll harvest in *The Craven Silence 3*. It's a pity Hoffman didn't interrogate John in-depth about his two year stint as a naval officer in the Philippines. What was that like? I have served in the Air Force. I've been to U.S. army bases abroad such as Itaewon in Seoul, South Korea. I've travelled throughout the Philippines too, including Manila and Palawan where the U.S. military has bases. I've also travelled through Thailand, which was where a major suspect in the JonBenét case was extradited from. What do these two apparently obscure south-east Asian nations – one a massive archipelago – have to do with JonBenét a million miles away? Well, not *nothing*.

We'll deal with military personnel on tropical islands in the next narrative. Now, let's return to the engineering side of things.

Gambetta and Hertog find strongly suggestive evidence that engineers are more likely to become terrorists because of the way that they think about the world. Survey data indicates that engineering faculty at universities are far more likely to be conservative than people with other degrees, and far more likely to be religious. They are seven times as likely to be both religious and conservative as social scientists.— Washingtonpost.com

I'm not suggesting for a moment that John Ramsey was a terrorist. What we're shining a flashlight on is the psychology common to engineers. What can we add to the psychological profile of engineers besides that they're typically religious and conservative?

*Gambetta and Hertog speculate that engineers [have]... a marked preference towards finding **clear-cut answers**. This preference has affinities with the clear answer that radical Islamist groups propose for dealing with the complexities of modernity: **Get rid of it**. They quote the famous right-wing economist Friedrich von Hayek, who argues that people with engineering training "**react violently against the deficiencies of their education** and develop **a passion for imposing on society the [missing] order**...by the means with which they are familiar."* —Washingtonpost. com

Is John Ramsey religious, conservative and someone who prefers clear-cut answers? There's some evidence to indicate checks on the first two, but what about the latter? Let's shine that light a little closer...

From John Ramsey deposition/dailycamera.com:

HOFFMAN: *Would you describe what you were doing as an engineer?*

JOHN: *Contract management. We ran all the base utilities, **maintenance and repair**, road construction, **long-term planning, site planning**.*

HOFFMAN: *Were you actually involved in any hands-on engineering projects?*

JOHN: *I had a staff that did that. I was in charge of the staff.*

So we see John was good at organizing people, delegating a staff, getting a team of people to execute according to a shared plan, a shared goal; a shared outcome. Site planning involves the spatial awareness of a piece of land and building, its orientation and architecture. Among other things, site planning tends to assess and organize are access, circulation, privacy, security, and other factors.

What's curious, in fact unique, about the Ramsey crime scene is the access and circulation through the scene of foot traffic. The Ramsey residence was a private residence, and apparently secure prior to 06:00 on December 26th 1996. And yet soon after the 911 call the crime scene was stirred up by the stomping of a dozen family friends, invited by the Ramseys. Whose idea was it to circulate strangers through the crime scene? Who would think to give access through the residence at 06:00 on the day after Christmas?

From John Ramsey deposition/dailycamera.com:

HOFFMAN: *So were you ever involved in any of the actual construction?*

JOHN: *Did I help pound nails? No.*

HOFFMAN: *Or do anything like that, any sort of manual labor work.*

JOHN: *In the military?*

HOFFMAN: *Yes, in the military.*

JOHN: *I did not.*

HOFFMAN: *When you were not in the military, did you do that?*

This is an important question. It's also interesting that John says he did no manual labor in the military. Even as an officer there's a period where almost all new recruits do physical labor, often as part of basic training, and often beyond that as well.

But does John's answer, that he did no physical or manual work in the military, square with reality? Well, we're not sure that it does.

From study.com:

*Military engineers, especially those in officer roles, supervise soldiers and civilians in planning projects and missions. Many military engineering projects are a complex interplay of public and private sectors, so military engineers in leadership roles must make sure that civilian contractors and active duty members understand their roles in enhancing mobility, security and survivability. These duties can range from enforcing sanitation measures on a base to formulating new training procedures. Whether they're providing humanitarian aid to war-torn countries or combat support to soldiers, many **military engineers can expect their daily tasks to be physically demanding.***

We also know from Patsy's 1995 newsletter that John seemed to enjoy physical stuff like golf and boat races. Piloting an aircraft is also a physical experience in the sense that flying requires something of an intuitive touch, much as swimming and sailing does.

From John Ramsey deposition/dailycamera.com:

JOHN: *I enjoy remodeling and doing work with my hands, yes.*

Just not in the military, eh?

From John Ramsey deposition/dailycamera.com:

HOFFMAN: *Did you do any remodeling in your home in Boulder?*

JOHN: *We did quite a bit of remodeling. I did not do any of the work there, as I recall.*

HOFFMAN: *Did you have occasion to do remodeling in any of your other homes?*

JOHN: **We have remodeled every home we have owned.**

HOFFMAN: *Have you personally done any remodeling in any of these homes?*

JOHN: *Yes.*

You remodel here, there, everywhere, you just <u>didn't do it personally in the Boulder residence</u>? And yet <u>the remodelling in the basement of the Boulder home was incomplete</u>. And he's the guy who said he broke <u>the basement</u> window when he locked himself out?

From John Ramsey deposition/<u>dailycamera.com</u>:

HOFFMAN: *When you were in the Navy, you went through basic training, naturally?*

JOHN: *I went through officer candidate school in Newport, Rhode Island.*

HOFFMAN: *And would you just describe briefly what your basic training was like?*

Hoffman's no slouch. He's twisting John's arm now, forcing him to concede.

From John Ramsey deposition/<u>dailycamera.com</u>:

JOHN: *It was physical training; it was navigation, celestial navigation, seamanship, rules of the road relative to ship movement, and, generally, familiarization with military procedures and the military system.*

HOFFMAN: *All right. You say that one of the areas that you were instructed in was seamanship?*

JOHN: *Navigation and piloting. You were being prepared to captain a ship.*

HOFFMAN: *Did any of your basic training involve — and I don't know if they still do this — learning various nautical knots?*

JOHN: *No.*

Another clever little ruse from Hoffman. He adds: "I don't know if they still do this" to offer John <u>plausible deniability</u>. And John takes Hoffman's bait.

HOFFMAN: *Do you sail at all?*

JOHN: *I used to.*

HOFFMAN: *Did you pilot your own sailboat or did you —*

JOHN: *Yes.*

HOFFMAN: *— have someone —*

JOHN: *Yes.*

HOFFMAN: *— do it for you?*

JOHN: *No.*

At last Hoffman has gotten John to admit to something he does himself. He sails his own sailboat.

From John Ramsey deposition/<u>dailycamera.com</u>:

HOFFMAN: *Did you receive any training in sailing?*

JOHN: *No.*

HOFFMAN: *Are you familiar with the various knots involved in sailing?*

JOHN: *I am really not. **I should be**, but I am not.*

Well, yes, if you sail, you should be familiar with knots, shouldn't you. Mr. Hoffman, you may now slam-dunk the witness.

From John Ramsey deposition/<u>dailycamera.com</u>:

HOFFMAN: *All right. So how would you generally moor your craft?*

JOHN: *I would tie it up on a cleat.*

HOFFMAN: *Was there any sort of knot that you used that you could identify that has a technical term?*

JOHN: *I don't know the technical term for it.*

HOFFMAN: *Have you had occasion to be able to look at the knot that was tied around the so-called paintbrush garrotte?*

JOHN: *I have not.*

That's amazing. John's never examined the knot on the garrotte even though he supposedly found JonBenét and "rescued" her from the basement, even though he's apparently prepared to move heaven and earth to find the monster who murdered his daughter. He's even prepared to post ads in newspapers and offer a $100 000 reward. But he won't look at the garrotte knot.

From John Ramsey deposition/dailycamera.com:

HOFFMAN: *Is there any reason why you haven't?*

JOHN: *It is very painful for me, Mr. Hoffman.*

Why would looking at a knot be painful?

From John Ramsey deposition/dailycamera.com:

HOFFMAN: *I understand that. But with your nautical training, do you think that you could in any way be able to identify the sort of knot?*

JOHN: *No.*

HOFFMAN: *Okay. Do you know whether or not any — if your private investigators hired anyone to look at the way in which that knot was made and to give a report on it?*

JOHN: *Not to my knowledge.*

HOFFMAN: *Do you know if any of your investigators have been involved in trying to look at forensic evidence?*

JOHN: *What is "forensic evidence"?*

HOFFMAN: *Any of the physical evidence that might have been at the scene that you might have had occasion to have.*

JOHN: *Well, I think any evidence that was at the scene was in the possession of the police. I don't know that we had any physical evidence that —*

John, John, John. Wasn't the April 1998 interview conditioned upon your request for access to all the police investigative materials? All the fucking forensics.

From John Ramsey deposition/<u>dailycamera.com</u>:

JOHN: *I don't know that we had any physical evidence that —*

HOFFMAN [interrupting]: *Would the Ransom Note be considered physical evidence, in your mind?*

JOHN: *Absolutely.*

HOFFMAN: *Do you know whether or not your investigators had occasion to have anyone who was professional in this area examine the Ransom Note?*

JOHN: *I believe they did.*

HOFFMAN: *Do you know — well, first of all, were you ever given a copy of the Ransom Note?*

JOHN: *Patsy handed it to me that morning, yes.*

HOFFMAN: *Do you know what happened to the Ransom Note after Patsy handed it to you?*

JOHN: <u>*I gave it to Officer French*</u> *when he arrived.*

HOFFMAN: *Did you give the Ransom Note to any of the friends that you had invited to come over?*

JOHN: *I did not.*

HOFFMAN: *Do you know if the Ransom Note was passed around to other police officers? Did you have occasion to observe that?*

JOHN: *I don't — I don't know.*

HOFFMAN: *Do you know what happened to the Ransom Note after you gave it to Officer French?*

JOHN: *Not for certain. I think they took it and made copies of it.*

HOFFMAN: *Do you remember the next time you saw a Ransom Note?*

JOHN: *I think Linda Arndt[42] or someone gave me a Xerox copy of it that morning as we were waiting.*

HOFFMAN: *Do you know why she gave you a Xerox copy of it?*

JOHN: *No.*

HOFFMAN: *Did you ask for a Xerox copy of it?*

JOHN: *No.*

HOFFMAN: *You say you had an opportunity to read the Ransom Note when it was initially discovered by Patsy —*

JOHN: *Yes.*

HOFFMAN: *— is that correct? Would you tell me how much time you spent reading it?*

JOHN: *Not specifically. It was — I spread it out on the floor and **tried to read it as quickly as possible.***

HOFFMAN: *Do you remember when that — was it in the morning that Linda Arndt gave you a copy of the Ransom Note?*

JOHN: ***It was prior to finding JonBenét.***[43] *I don't remember specifically what time.*

---

42 From <u>dailycamera.com</u>: *Arndt briefly worked for the University of Colorado. After losing that job, she worked as a tree-trimmer making $8 an hour.*

43 Arndt differs from John Ramsey's version that he received the copy the same morning, prior to the discovery of JonBenét's body. From <u>acandyrose. com</u>:
Vargus: Did you give the Ramseys a Xerox copy of the Ransom Note?

HOFFMAN: *Do you know how she was able to make a copy for you?*

JOHN: *I do not.*

HOFFMAN: *Once she gave you a copy of the Ransom Note, did you at any point in the morning read it again?*

JOHN: *Yes.*

HOFFMAN: *Did you read it more than once?*

JOHN: *Yes.*

HOFFMAN: *Do you remember how many times you may have read it?*

JOHN: *No.*

HOFFMAN: *Would you say a dozen times?*

JOHN: *I don't remember. I mean, I was trying to figure out, to the best of my ability, who in the world had my daughter.*

HOFFMAN: *And were you looking at the Ransom Note for that purpose?*

JOHN: *Yes.*

HOFFMAN: *When you were looking at the Ransom Note, was there anything in the language of the Ransom Note that struck you as peculiar?*

JOHN: *The whole thing was peculiar.* **We were addressed as "Mr. and Mrs. Ramsey,"** *and then they switched to "John" personally.*

Actually that's wrong John. <u>The practise note</u> was addressed to Mr. and Mrs Ramsey. Or more accurately, to Mr. and Mrs. I. An "I" is the first down stroke of the capital letter R…

Arndt: On January 5th I gave a Xerox copy to Patsy Ramsey's attorney.
Vargus: Why?
Arndt: The attorneys for the Ramseys, respective attorneys, had asked for copies of the Ransom Note. And that request I had bumped up to the supervisor making the decisions.

From pbworks.com:

Additional sheets were missing from the pad and were never located at defendants' home....[and] there was another page in the pad that had written on it "Mr. and Mrs. I," which many believe to have been an early "false start" of the Ransom Note. (PSDMF P 51.) (Carnes 2003:24-25).

I don't know whether the astute Hoffman was asleep when John made this major slip, or whether he was shining his torchlight elsewhere, and was somehow caught up in his own misdirection. Perhaps Hoffman hadn't studied the Ransom Note in careful detail himself. I mean, not everyone can be sure that the Ransom Note is actually addressed to – who? Isn't it addressed to "Mr. Ramsey" and only him? John seems to have forgotten that, but unfortunately so has Darnay Hoffman. It's a pity because if this isn't a smoking gun, it's a very smoky and smelly one.

From John Ramsey deposition/dailycamera.com:

JOHN: *They asked for twenty dollar bills and hundred dollar bills, as I recall. The amount was a very odd amount. The way the note was signed was very odd. The cruelty that they threatened was bizarre. It was a very sick mind that wrote that note.*

Patsy's "Personality Changes"

"I bet your parents taught you that you mean something, that you're here for a reason. My parents taught me a different lesson, dying in the gutter for no reason at all... — Batman in Batman v Superman: Dawn of Justice

"The Miss America Pageant reinforces a belief that women are merely how they look and how they please." — Gloria Steinem

*Patsy Ramsey was **born to an engineer father and an ambitious mother** in Parkersburg, West Virginia, the eldest of three sisters. She **excelled at debating** at the local high school and was an active volunteer. In her first year at state university <u>she entered the beauty pageant</u> and won, **having studied it - and taken notes** - the previous year. Her failure to win Miss America upset her mother, who later cherished <u>the title for her granddaughter JonBenét</u>.* — Patsy Ramsey's obituary published in <u>the UK's Guardian newspaper</u>, June 27, 2006

The circle of the flashlight swings over pageant trophies. The once shining metal is concealed under a veil of grey dust. A name and a date inscribed on a trophy is lost in a tangle of old spider webs.

Having come this far, do we feel we have a handle on Patsy? Let's dust away some of those trophies, lift them up and see if we can find something new, something to help us on our way towards justice for JonBenét.

As we brush away the grime covering the name plaque, as we see her name appear blinking on a piece of brass – Patricia Ann Ramsey (née Paugh) – we can't help wondering:

Does a trophy wife live a trophy life?

Does a trophy wife end up like this trophy here, blackened, derelict, discarded?

Let's shine our flashlight over Detective Steve Thomas' deductions before we share more of our own thoughts on Patsy.

From nytimes.com:

By Mr. Thomas's analysis, Mrs. Ramsey had grown frazzled by Christmas night 1996 because of "an approaching 40th birthday, the busy holiday season, an exhausting Christmas Day and an argument with JonBenét" over a bed-wetting incident that led to "some sort of explosive encounter in the child's bathroom" that resulted in a mortal head wound.

*Mr. Thomas says he concluded that while **JonBenét's head was probably injured by accident**, Mrs. Ramsey, rather than summon help, panicked after her daughter fell unconscious. That, he says, led her to write a note suggesting that JonBenét had been kidnapped, after which she "faced the major problem of what to do with the body."*

One would imagine Steve Thomas, like Lou Smit, who was trained to solve criminal cases like this and was working first-hand on the case and on the crime scene, could have come up with a more likely scenario. Thomas' job was to solve this murder. We're <u>not sure if Thomas succeeded</u>, but he came far closer than Lou Smit did.

It's not that Thomas was mistaken about Patsy's strange behavior surrounding her daughter's death – because it *was* strange. But would Patsy really become so outraged, lose the plot so completely that she'd reach for a clubbing weapon and bash her daughter mightily over her little head? The daughter she'd invested her own Miss America dreams in, would she banish those to oblivion too?

What we think Thomas failed to reconcile is why John would stick by Patsy if Patsy had clobbered their daughter to death. John had already lost one daughter. He would brook no truck with Patsy if she's unilaterally killed JonBenét.

The psychology goes further though. If Patsy was the sort of person with violent mood swings, someone erratic who was always lashing out, and who could step so far over the line of human decency to murder her own daughter, it's unlikely John would have much invested in her, let alone the marriage. By the time of JonBenét's death, John and Patsy had been married almost sixteen years.

Were all sixteen of those years sweet marital bliss? It's doubtful, but if they had been horrible John would not have remained married to her for a further ten years *after their daughter's death*.

What Thomas' tale seems to miss is that murders don't just materialize randomly out of thin air. The behavior and psychology that undergirds it is there like an alien stowed away the whole way, not just at the end. So the question we need to ask is this:

Was there an alien on board?

If so, what was it? <u>What was it?</u>

From <u>nytimes.com</u>:

It was at that point [the bedwetting incident] Mr. Thomas concludes, that the accident turned to murder. He says that on the way to placing her in a remote room of the basement, Mrs. Ramsey realized JonBenét was still alive. "Only feet away was her paint tote," he writes. "She grabbed a paintbrush and broke it to fashion the garrotte with some cord. Then she looped the cord around the girl's neck." To make it look like a kidnapping, he says, Mrs. Ramsey tied the girl's wrists and taped over her mouth...

In this version John was fast asleep throughout, and so was Burke – were Burke's precious Christmas gifts and JonBenét's abandoned on the living room floor while Patsy traipsed hither and thither?

The evidence may partially fit Thomas' theory – and certainly we feel it's important to note Patsy's perfume [metaphorically] was wafting over crucial pieces of forensic evidence: the paintbrush and the Ransom Note and the thoughtful covering of the little girl with her favorite blanket. But having the evidence fit the crime tends to leave out the most vital piece of the puzzle – the psychology. The motive.

Thomas thinks he's explained it – the bedwetting angered Patsy. But did it really? Was Patsy a hands-on high-strung mum? Had she hit either of her kids before? <u>Was she someone with particularly high standards</u> when it came to home maintenance, cleanliness at the expense of the happiness of her children? Was she a disciplinarian? Or was Patsy simply evil?

Linda Arndt noted that John and Patsy didn't speak much to each other while the cops stampeded through the crime scene the morning after Christmas. This may seem like one parent resenting the murderous conduct of the other, but not having the guff to say anything out loud [then, or ever] seems a stretch. You see, there's *another explanation* for two parents occupying separate parts of the house/crime scene.

In the previous chapter we touched on John's experience and knowledge in site planning. We think John and Patsy stationing themselves at different locations in the house was a kind of *site maintenance*. What they didn't want, we think, was certain incriminating items discovered or disturbed. What they did want was to dramatically be seen to make particular discoveries at a particular time, and then have a plausible reason to touch their daughter and contaminate the scene, thereby being able to explain their DNA on JonBenét [assuming it was still there].

While Arndt singled out John's behavior as suspicious – especially where she caught him casually going through his mail in the kitchen at one point – from the Ramsey's perspective [as suspects] the looking-through-mail thing was simply part of John passing the time.

Each minute the body wasn't discovered the case against them grew weaker, each moment the body cooled would make it harder for the coroner to figure when she died. Every tick of the grandfather clock allowed them to slip through another noose hole, and then noose holes gave way to loopholes. On and on, tick tock tick tock, the evidence against them loosened its grip.

Invisible DNA could be dislodged or covered in the fibres and fragments of countless others. Each half hour that passed, the crime scene became muddier and more difficult to clean and unscramble. And if they had a dodo cop on the beat they could call the shots, they could draw out the discovery with appropriate prayers and pageantry.

Isn't that what they did – John *and* Patsy?

Or was Patsy simply evil?

From forumsforjustice.org:

Patsy enrolled at the University of West Virginia in 1975. Soon afterwards her parents moved to Charleston, West Virginia, where she lived until she finished college. Patsy and her younger sister, Pam, were involved in the pageant circuit, winning at county fairs and other local beauty contests. **Nedra had become a driving force behind the sisters' pageant participation,** *and* **both daughters always acquiesced to their domineering mother's wishes.**

A domineering mother [or father] can sometimes lead to grownups choosing partners who are the opposite. The opposite of dominant, bossy, and dictatorial is someone reserved. John was that. Or someone flashy and fun, like Jim Wharton.

From <u>Wikipedia</u>:

[Patsy] was high school sweethearts with celebrity WTAP sports anchor, <u>James "Jim" Wharton.</u>

The pageant thing set Patsy up for a trophy hunter – a young buck with big bucks, or a not so young buck with bucks. John was the latter.

From <u>forumsforjustice.org</u>:

In 1977, while still a college student, Patsy entered the Miss America pageant in Atlantic City as Miss West Virginia. This was **her third,** *and finally successful, attempt at the title of Miss West Virginia. Her sister, <u>Pamela Ellen Paugh</u> <u>won the same title three years later</u> [at 21 years of age].*

John seemed the kind of [older] guy who'd let Patsy live and let live, but was the casual undercurrent too casual, and if it was, what sort of alien malevolence could weasel its way in through the cracks?

From <u>forumsforjustice.org</u>:

Although Patsy was not selected as a finalist in the Miss America competition, she did receive **a talent – award for her dramatic reading** *of an essay she composed, "Kiss of Death,"* and was awarded a $2,000 scholarship.

Years after her competition in the Miss America pageant, Patsy stayed active in the organization and often served as a judge and worked on their fundraising campaigns. Her Miss West Virginia dress and sash were proudly put on display in her bedroom whenever the family home was opened for public tours. She once said that although people would forget her name or the state she represented, they would always remember her affiliation with the program and "hold it in the highest regard."

Patsy graduated magna cum laude with a degree in journalism from the University of West Virginia. In the summer of 1979 she moved to Atlanta, Georgia to take a job with **McCann Erickson Advertising Agency***.*

If John was an engineer, Patsy was a marketer.

The literal meaning of the word *engineer* of course is to: contrive, wangle, concoct, plot.

The literal meaning of the word *marketer* of course is to: sell, push, promote, puff…

Marketing fits in with Patsy's social expressionism, and the idea of selling and dressing up products and services in flowery advertising matched the pageantry of her earlier life.

From forumsforjustice.org:

Still following Patsy's moves, the rest of Patsy's family left Charleston, West Virginia after [Patsy's father] Don Paugh's retirement from Union Carbide and also moved to Atlanta.

This is important to note. Patsy was from middle class America. When she went to Atlanta, her middle class family went with, including her jobless dad and domineering mum. It's not clear when Patsy's parents moved after their daughter, before or after they met John, but what is clear is once Patsy hooked up with John, so – eventually – did her family.

From forumsforjustice.org:

*It was in Atlanta that John and Patsy met in 1979, only a year after his divorce from Lucinda, while both were living at the same apartment complex. They were married the following year on November 15, 1980 at Atlanta's Peachtree Presbyterian Church – a church that would be revisited for two family tragedies in the ensuing years. Many long-time friends of both John and Patsy thought the union between these two individuals was **strange because of the opposite nature of their personalities**. Patsy was extremely social and gregarious, while John was reserved and very quiet. **He was never open with his affection** even in the early courtship stage of their relationship. When out with friends for an evening, John sat at the dinner table while Patsy danced with other males in the group.*

As reserved and quiet as John apparently was, he wasn't quite a wallflower. He'd had a two year affair with a secretary before meeting Patsy, and John must have been attracted to something in Patsy's youth and flamboyance. She was a *bon vivant*, perhaps he wanted to be part of that too. And perhaps the pageantry in Patsy was the pilot in John.

Both are similar in a sense – pageantry is female spectacle while piloting is a kind of male pageantry – there's a uniform, a big machine, the mastery of the craft and of course, all aboard are enthralled by the man controlling the whole ride. But beyond steering a joystick, or adjusting a sash, what did Patsy have in common with John? How did their marriage work?

From forumsforjustice.org:

*After the marriage, Patsy worked with John at Microsouth a company owned by John and ran out of their home. John's business specialized in selling and setting up computers manufactured by other companies. **Patsy*** *gave up her career after the birth of her first child* and concentrated on social and charitable work. She volunteered for fundraising for the local children's hospital, and was a member of Atlanta's Garden Club and the local Junior league [the members are] the wives of the affluent community leaders and businessmen.

Something else gluing this pair of odd ducks together was Christianity.

From forumsforjustice.org:

*John did not actively participate in the Atlanta social life, but he did become a deacon at the church the family attended. After Patsy gave up her working career, **her and John's roles in the marriage became very defined** Patsy took control of the household matters, including the raising of the children and John was **free to pursue** his rising career in the computer industry and frequent travel schedule. Although Patsy was in charge of the household, John still kept **tight rein** on the family's financial affairs. Patsy was given a checking account to pay household bills and personal expenses, but generally **was not privy to information** on John's income and investment matters.*

Here's early evidence of life in the trenches for a trophy wife. Patsy's role became confined essentially to domestic duties. John could flutter away whenever it suited him, and he held all the cards, he called all the shots. Was this a satisfying life for Patsy? While dad was away, and he frequently was, it was just Patsy and Burke, until JonBenét came along. We'll deal with Burke later, but the fact that Patsy ultimately became ill, recovered, became ill again, recovered and then eventually died, belies a real subterrean struggle going on, on a physical level as well as spiritual and emotional. What was going on?

We think Patsy became lost in Boulder, and she found herself in dreaming a dream for JonBenét.

"Our family is almost too close..."

"We Didn't Mean For This To Happen."
— Patsy Ramsey

Early <u>in Lawrence Schiller's book *Perfect Murder Perfect Town*</u> someone hears Patsy say "we" [plural] "didn't mean for this to happen." If an intruder broke into the Ramsey residence and murdered JonBenét, there would be no reason to ever say something like that.

Imagine your best friend dies in a car accident. Why would you say to anyone, regarding his or her death:

"We Didn't Mean For This To Happen."

Of course if you'd worked on his car and fucked something up, if you were somehow responsible, though unintentionally drawn in, then it's exactly what you'd say, right? Of course as effusive as Patsy was, she was part of a broader culture not only in Boulder, but through the South. It wasn't so much a case of what happens in Vegas stays in Vegas but something…slightly different. Let's call it pageantry. Pageantry is all about appearances, and the Southern tradition Patsy belonged to was exactly that.

From <u>forumsforjustice.org</u>:

If there were any problems in the marriage, it was handled in the typical Southern tradition of 'sweeping it under the rug'... [so that] **by all outward appearances everything looked perfect on the surface.** *Some friends say the Ramsey family was too perfect almost "make believe".*

This is the part Lou Smit and Steve Thomas, we think, overlooked. This was a subtle but also fundamental sentiment keeping this case [and the Ramseys] together. That Smit couldn't see this, or wouldn't, and that Thomas saw past it is in a sense, in our opinion, a dereliction of duty.

It's one thing to see the crime scene as one littered with decoys and fake props, it's one thing to see the execution of the crime as a kind of diabolical make-believe, but it's something else entirely to fail to see this psychology through to its logical end. Patsy is one end, but John is also a loose end. And yes, there's another.

Let's turn the flashlight back to that June 1998 deposition, and get Patsy's own words on the aftermath to JonBenét's murder.

From acandyrose.com:

HANEY: *Prior to the diagnosis of your ovarian cancer, what was your relationship like with John?*

PATSY: *Great.*

HANEY: *Okay.*

PATSY: *Good, happy, healthy marital relationship.*

HANEY: *Sexual situation?*

PATSY: *Good. Two kids, lots of practice.*

HANEY: *How about following your treatment, was there a change?*

PATSY: *Well, for obvious reasons, there was – this was –* **big change** *in our, you know, sexual life, because I was undergoing chemotherapy* *for nine months, and had a complete hysterectomy, which **took several months to recover from**. Just **physiologically**.*

Not only is there a big change, but Patsy gives a big answer to Haney's question. It's odd in a way because it's a very personal question, and yet Patsy answers it in great detail.

A red flag that pops up here is Patsy's indication of a specific timeframe – "several months". A hysterectomy typically takes six weeks to recover from, physically at least. A hysterectomy is a surgical procedure to remove all or part of the womb. Some of the complications that can arise include urinary incontinence and chronic pain. In the next chapter we'll touch on the psychological aspects.

Think about Thomas' theory in this context though. Just how perturbed could a mother be by her daughter's bedwetting if she was doing the same herself? The ovarian cancer would have also made Patsy not only familiar with her own body fluids, but perhaps more comfortable with the idea of them.

From acandyrose.com:

PATSY: *And but I felt like it was even though we may not have had, you know, sexual intercourse per se, there were very loving, touching – you know, he was – he looked forward through that whole thing. **He was my saviour**, we will get through this, you know, five steps, chin up, you know – because I unfortunately saw a lot of cases of women in treatment where husbands or live-ins or that "see ya".*

HANEY: *But your relationship remained good?*

PATSY: *(Nodding).*

HANEY: *Would you say he is a pretty caring touchy, feely, huggy?*

PATSY: *Uh-hum.*

HANEY: *How about since JonBenét's death?*

PATSY: *Well, there for a number of months, I mean it was, you know, we didn't have sexual relations because I mean, you know, you have to be in a pretty good mood and pretty kind of happy frame of mind to go into all that, and I was pretty much in a fetal position crying every day all day.* **And I remember the first time that we did actually make love,** *we were at the lake house and we both started weeping, you know, just all kinds of feelings, you know, very emotional time. So...*

I'm not sure sure I'm following. It's June 1998, 18 months after JonBenét's death. Patsy's just said one has to be in a happy frame of mind to have sex, and now she's saying there was a wonderful weepy moment by the side of a lake when she can clearly remember making love for the first time. The way she puts it sounds like she lost her virginity with John:

"I remember the first time that we did actually make love..."

Were they having intimate relations often, post Patsy's hysterectomy?

From acandyrose.com:

HANEY: *Since the death I am sure you have been grieving a lot and how have you found, you know, support and comfort? Is it mainly through religion or family or –*

PATSY: *All of that. We have wonderful friends. Our family is very close.* **Almost too close,** *probably. You know, I mean they are all – you know, my parents, my sisters,* **it's just like an open wound.** *You know, to them. John's brother and (INAUDIBLE).* **We were a very close family** *and she was the apple of our eye, you know. And it's just the family is just – they pull together and they are there, because there is a lot of tension over it too, and it's just – you know, goes on and on and nothing is resolving and people still look at us, and you know, it's* **just lot of dynamics** *there. Very hard. But we are all Christians and know that JonBenét is in a better place, and we are going to be there some day. (INAUDIBLE).*

That doesn't sound like a simple or straight answer to: have you found support. This idea of an open wound and lots of dynamics and "were" [past tense] a close family rings a little hollow alongside the idea of a supportive family. Notice how Patsy refers to "wonderful" friends first and her family merely as "close" even "too close". Is the psychology starting to crystallize?

From acandyrose.com:

HANEY: *You mentioned that maybe you're too close. Do you mean the fact that now that you're in Atlanta, the physical proximity to all of the relatives, maybe that's too much or--*

PATSY: *No, I don't mean – I mean **it's just we are so close, we feel each other's pain like it's our own, you know.***

This is a major psychological giveaway, but Haney misses it. In a situation where the parents and son are accessories to murder, each one is going to be feeling a similar sense of culpability, and each should. Patsy doesn't realize it but by referring to this situation not in a good way, as in family warmth and intimacy, but merely being "too close", in an almost locked-in claustrophobic sense, she's really revealing her psychological cards in a big way. Make sense?

Turning Point

"Life is always at some turning point."
— Irwin Edman

*"…JonBenét is safe and with God and [the…]
grieving that we all have to do is for ourselves….
for our grief to resolve itself we now have to find out
why this happened."* — John Ramsey

*"She'll never have to know the loss of a child . She
will never have to know cancer or death of a child."*
— Patsy Ramsey

*"That's the one thing we want people dealing with us
to know, to believe that, we know that in our heart."*
— John Ramsey

*Friends say it was Patsy's deep Christian faith that
helped her cope with JonBenét's murder and her
illness. "This is just our earthly home," Patsy said
in 2004. "We're going to heaven, where JonBenét is.
That's when we'll really be home." — <u>People.com</u>*

"Devils don't come from hell beneath us. No, they come from the sky." — Lex Luthor in Batman V Superman

In Patsy Ramsey's version of events she wakes up early in the darkness before dawn on the day after Christmas and descends the spiral staircase to find a note on the final step. In her own story Patsy begins her version of events "coming down from the sky".

Patsy descends from the heavens to find a 3 page note. It's politely addressed to "Mr. Ramsey", not her. Patsy glances at it anyway. She doesn't read it, simply catches on the words "we have your daughter" the <u>sixth line from the top</u>. According to Patsy she reads no further – not even the very next line saying "she is safe and unharmed…and if you want [to see her], follow our instructions."

Instead Patsy goes "bounding" up the stairs. What's interesting is the note itself claims to be left by a foreign group who have gained access to their house, and stolen their child. Patsy doesn't seem the least bit worried they may still be there, even though its dark and she's alone. She doesn't check doors or windows where she is, she doesn't run to John either – instead she runs through the dark into what ought to be an inky room 90 minutes before dawn on the day after Christmas.

According to Patsy she also opens JonBenét's door. But wasn't it always open? Didn't JonBenét sleep with the door completely open? Let's go back to the deposition and see how Patsy handles this area of interrogation.

From <u>acandyrose.com</u>:

PATSY *[answering/indicating on a schematic to Haney what she did after finding the note on the stairs]: Okay, I came up, bounding up here. Over to here, pushed the door open. She wasn't there. I ran under --*

HANEY: *Let me just stop you there. When you pushed the door open, was there a light on in the room?*

PATSY: *There was -- her lamp light was not on. You know, there was enough light that I could tell she wasn't in her bed. Now, whether that was coming from the laundry area, whether daylight was breaking or whether there was -- you know, sometime we left a little night light here on in her bathroom, so you know, I -- all I know is I was able to see that there is no one lying in that bed and the covers are ruffled.*

It's a very simple question. Was there a light on, yes or no. Patsy's answer is a mouthful. First off, she seems to stumble [as if to say "There was a lamp…" or "There was a light on…" But then Patsy would have to explain why she walked in complete darkness past her daughter's room at the crack of dawn, and didn't bother to check on JonBenét. Second, no fucking way daylight was breaking 90 minutes early on December 26th. Third and perhaps most significant, Patsy misdirects about the bed and covers being ruffled. Haney didn't ask about the bed or the covers. But Patsy wants to stress that JonBenét was in bed and then she wasn't. We don't think she ever was. It's vital though that Patsy put JonBenét in bed – this must be non-negotiable otherwise her and John, and Burke for that matter, are fucked.

From acandyrose.com:

HANEY: *Did you go past that door?* *[In other words, did Patsy enter JonBenét's room?]*

PATSY: *No.*

HANEY: *You didn't enter that room at all?*

PATSY: *No.*

HANEY: *Did you -- did you think that possibly she had gotten out of the bed, was somewhere else in the room you didn't—*

Like the bathroom, where Patsy's "little night light" might have been glowing from? You didn't go in there, did you?

PATSY: *It just happened so fast, and I, you know, read that letter and said "we have your daughter", your mind goes berserk.*

Actually nothing happened so quickly. Oscar Pistorius wielding a gun at a locked door said the same thing. What's *happening so quickly* when Patsy is the only one up, the house is in complete darkness and silence [supposedly] and…nothing is happening? We can understand Patsy's heart is beating a mile a minute, and her mind is a cacophony of concern and panic [about herself and perhaps her son, oh and John too], but how are things happening so fast before the sun is up in the middle of the night, standing alone in a doorway?

From acandyrose.com:

PATSY: *I mean I was -- and then I went up there and my child is not in the bed. You know, I didn't, nothing against your questioning, but no, I didn't stand around and say I wonder if she is in here, I wonder if she is in there. I screamed for John.*

There's a glimmer of accuracy here. In the authentic version of events, yes, Patsy likely did not "look for JonBenét". Was there a lot of standing around in the wee hours, scratching heads, scratching letters on a notepad – we think so.

From acandyrose.com:

HANEY: *Okay, and that's why you were standing here?*

PATSY: *I am going this way and I lean on and said John -- you know, the landing is like here, is like this, then it turns and like that. And I leaned over, I mean my knees were like, you know, buckling. And oh, God, and he came down and I said, "she's gone, she's gone, there is a note, she's been kidnapped."*

There's something else, obvious, missing from Patsy's earnest portrayal of herself innocently and tearfully searching [except not searching] for her daughter. Can you see it? She fails to do the obvious which is **call out to JonBenét**.

Even Burke in his [we think] fictitious version, <u>describes his mother frantically coming into his room</u>, crying *"Oh my gosh, oh my gosh, of my gosh [not "oh my God…"?], running around my room, looking for JonBenét."*

But when she's at JonBenét's door she says nothing, and doesn't set a foot in the room. Strange huh?

From <u>acandyrose.com</u>:

HANEY: *So you're here at the base of the stairs?*

PATSY: *Uh-hum.*

HANEY: *You scream for John?*

PATSY: *(Nodding with no audible response).*

HANEY: *Do you remember exactly what words you used, was it more than just John or--*

PATSY: *I remember my voice was just cracking. I mean it was like "John", like that. I mean like, I can't even, you know, I hear my scream and I hear his scream when he* **came up** *from the basement, I mean it was just a horrible thing. You know, it was just --*

HANEY: *Where does John, and we will use a red marker now for John…*

John Haney, <u>are you out of your fucking mind</u>? Patsy's just told you **John came up from the fucking basement!** And you want to fiddle around with stationery?

From acandyrose.com:

HANEY: *Where does he first appear in there, at least in this diagram, if you can start there?*

PATSY: *He **comes down** those stairs there. (Indicating) and…*

And Haney let's that major slip through the cracks, and Patsy waffles on and on.

Later on the morning of that infamous day after Christmas in Boulder, they tell Burke JonBenét "is in heaven". Burke later says the same thing; that his parents told him JonBenét was in heaven.

In fact when Burke first heard the news JonBenét was in heaven, she was lying in the lounge under the Christmas tree waiting for the coroner to arrive. He eventually did at around 20:00 and didn't stay long. The point is when John, Patsy and Burke tell us that they told each other JonBenét was in heaven, she was actually in their living room – dead. It may seem a silly technical point, but earlier that day when Burke went to see Fleet White did Burke ask what had happened to his sister? Why ask when you already know? Why ask when you know and no one else does?

A few days later the family held a Memorial Service in Boulder to offer JonBenét's spirit to God [even though she was already in heaven], and then a few days after that a funeral for JonBenét in Atlanta [ditto] where they'd do the same again, this time with her body present. Isn't that a bit much? A Memorial service and a funeral?

From bardachreports.com:

It was not the first time that a carefully packaged appearance had backfired. On Sunday, January 5, media consultant Pat Korten [hired by the Ramseys] had arranged to have television crews outside St. John's Episcopal Church in Boulder.

*During the service, "there was a special handout personalized for the Ramsey family, offering prayers for them," says a parishioner who was present. "**We were appalled**, because a lot of people had qualms about believing them by then." Outside the church was a throng of photographers waiting to capture a sobbing Patsy, exiting on the arm of Barbara Fernie. "They totally used the church as a photo opportunity," says the parishioner.*

What's interesting is that rather than capture the Ramseys in tears, the photographers capture something else…as all three of them appear beside those golden sandstone walls beaming…they…they seem to be smiling, and Burke runs along ahead seeming to be having the time of his life. In video and documentary footage is clearer just how footloose and fancy free Burke appears to be coming out of the memorial service for his sister.

On December 31st, the last day of the year, the Ramseys held a funeral for their daughter. We won't go into that yet, but for now have a look at this clip of Patsy with Bill McReynolds. He would later be identified by the Ramseys as a prime suspect. Does he seem to rebuff Patsy's attempt to receive a hug from him?

And then, what happened next?

From forumsforjustice.org:

After the Georgia funeral, John, Patsy and Burke returned to Boulder, but were true to their word that they would never step foot in the house on 15th Street again. This time they stayed at the home of Jay Elowsky, a close friend and owner of the Boulder Pasta Jay's restaurant, at which the family had dined on Christmas Eve.

As we've mentioned before, the Ramseys typically ate their meals at restaurants rather than at home. If one seriously considers the import of this, we can see how Elowsky would consider the Ramseys not merely as friends but as among his best patrons, if not *the* best.

From forumsforjustice.org:

Elowsky had been an unwavering supporter of the Ramseys during the media blitz that engulfed Boulder after the discovery of JonBenét's murder. While the Ramseys were trying to avoid the press by secreting themselves at Elowsky's residence, Elowsky had a confrontation with overzealous photographers and [started] swinging at them with a baseball bat. When he was arrested and charged with assault, a 9 mm handgun was also recovered from where it had been hidden in a paper sack in his vehicle. With this sanctuary now violated, **the Ramseys moved to the Stine residence.**

Because of Elowsky's antics with the press and the resulting publicity, the Ramseys now refused to speak to him. Roxie Stine had become the most protective and secretive of all the Ramsey friends. She even invented code names for everyone staying in her home and those who were still considered friends, so that they could talk freely without giving away identities. John and Patsy were dubbed Ozzie and Harriet but Patsy was also often referred to as Queenie. Roxie and her husband called themselves June and Ward Cleaver, and Nedra was identified Dr. Ruth. The Ramseys remained at the Stine residence until Burke finished the school year in June, and they moved to the family home in Charlevoix for the summer months. By fall, arrangements were made for the family's permanent [transplantation] back to Atlanta.

Imagine that – murder suspects, moving in at a moment's notice and staying with the Stines for six months. Now is where we address the thing we've been trying to shine our damn torchlight on without success. Basements are funny places. The light plays tricks. What better light of illumination is there than first-hand accounts from former best friends?

From <u>forumsforjustice.org</u>:

*Friends of Patsy had noticed that **she had undergone several personality changes** which they found unusual even for someone who had lost a child through a violent act. Always [exceedingly] sharp witted **with an extraordinary memory**, Patsy now could not even remember day to-day events, much less any details about the funeral or days ensuing. She **became extremely paranoid and afraid to be alone**, and seemed to expect everyone around her to take care of her. There was no hint of the former gregarious, social whirlwind her family and friends had known in the past.*

Do you notice how this psychological assessment doesn't match the woman Haney has been talking to? That woman finds a Ransom Note and is so blasé about it she doesn't bother to read it. Her home has been broken into, her daughter abducted and yet there's no fear, paranoia or concerns about safety then, is there?

From <u>forumsforjustice.org</u>:

John arranged several trips to try to bring Patsy out of her state of depression. During a weekend at the Broadmoor, a resort hotel in Colorado Springs, Patsy refused to come out of the room. While still staying with Jay Elowsky, the trio went to Steamboat Springs in the Colorado mountains, but Patsy's behavior was so erratic, screaming and crying all weekend, that they came back early.

*She did seem to respond well to the family excursion to the Kloysters, a resort in North Carolina which was an annual trek with a group of friends from Atlanta, and to a Christian retreat in Estes Park, another Colorado mountain town, with a female friend. The family also spent several days in Spain with the Fernies, which **prompted rumors in the media that the Ramseys were moving abroad to escape prosecution**. Patsy, of course, made several trips to Atlanta to visit with her mother* *prior to the permanent move. All trips were planned with fake airline reservations to avoid being followed by the media and police officials.*

Forget about the fake airplane tickets. Let's walk down from JonBenét's open bedroom door, down that spiral staircase. Let's turn the clock past the 911 call at 05:52, French's arrival at 05:59, Arndt's two hours and ten minutes later. Keep going. Keep going. Keep going. Stop. It's 13:00 and bright outside. A lot of the snow has melted, and the air is crisp, though chilly.

Let's do this in slow-mo. Arndt makes the egregious error of "lifting the tension" by sending John to investigate his own [we believe] crime scene. Forget about John, we're not going to follow him and Fleet down. Let's turn towards a detective in the kitchen area concentrating intently. He stiffens. His eyes narrow. He looks up.

From websleuths.com/Steve Thomas:[44]

About the same time Ramsey found the body of [JonBenét], *a detective discovered what would mark a turning point in the investigation, the existence of a possible practice Ransom Note **in a tablet** belonging to Patsy Ramsey.*

---

44 *JonBenét: Inside the Ramsey Murder Investigation.*

A Page Out of a South African Diary

Bruce Wayne: You don't know me, but I've known a few women like you.

Diana Prince: Oh, I don't think you've ever known a woman like me. — Batman V Superman: Dawn of Justice

This narrative is about to go up a few gears. Those readers who know my work may feel they're in relatively safe hands. Even so this message is for them as well. You think you know a person, but you only know what they let you know.

So I'm going to let you in on a few things about my family life not to shock you, not to be self-indulgent. Instead I want to assure you the insights you're about to read have been *lived*.

They're insights not drawn from the theoretical or hypothetical, they're real. This is how my family matches up against the Ramseys. This is important if we're to trust the psychological insights drawn as truly authentic.

Here we go:

1. Upper-class/wealthy [CHECK]
2. Father involved in engineering/construction [CHECK]

3. Owned a boat [CHECK]

4. Mother, housewife [CHECK]

5. Former pageant queen [CHECK]

6. Hysterectomy with complications [CHECK]

7. One or both parents strong Christian/s [CHECK]

8. Keeping up of appearances [CHECK]

9. Mother deceased in her forties [CHECK]

10. Older brother, interested in math [CHECK]

11. Older brother, apple of parents' eye, then disassociated [CHECK]

12. Younger sister, sociable, apple of parents' eye [CHECK]

13. Sibling rivalry [CHECK]

As a middle child, I'm in the unique position to have an experience of both an older brother and younger sister. The bottom line is the sibling rivalry is there irrespective of the gender. In some cases because my sister was a girl, she won a lot of benefits and escaped punishment far more often than my brother or I did.

Did my older brother and I ever torture our sister – seven years younger than me? On one occasion, having made her burst out crying, one of us [I forget who] was desperate to silence the torrent of tears. Getting in trouble for hurting her, or fake-hurting her, could be pretty painful in itself. Usually offering a chocolate or similar bribe would stem the tide, and sometimes the speed at which my sister would stop crying was evidence that she hadn't been crying to begin with.

Eventually we discovered offering a real chocolate as reward was just as good as offering a fake one. The offer could halt the tearful pantomime entirely. Starting it up from scratch was fraught with problems; nor was it difficult to re-engineer the sobbing charade, but it stretched the credibility of her "injury" beyond belief. But the more the fake chocolate bribe was used the less it worked until eventually it didn't.

While there was a real pageantry at times to her tears no doubt at times we pushed her too far. Whatever one might say as older brothers about the fake drama that could "magically" elicit rewards for her such as comfort and attention, if we weren't careful those manipulations – when they succeeded – were very much at our expense. Reward for her typically meant punishment for us. In any event, if there was a power struggle, turning on the waterworks invariably turned things in her favor. And we didn't like that. She was, after all, much smaller and weaker – and theoretically her young age meant she was not as smart for the time being – as either of us.

There was an important incentive in controlling my sister's outbursts, the genuine distress as well as the fakery.

This brings us to the less bright side of our "upper class" lives. In our family we received corporal punishment, and sometimes it was severe. A hard hosepipe lash to the back of one's legs was a typical punishment, occasionally – especially when we were older, and if there was nothing else to hand – we got clunked on the head, or the elbow by the heel of mum's <u>wood-platform shoe</u>.

It wasn't uncommon to have bruises on our bodies, especially our butt. Sometimes our friends would see these when we got changed in the school locker rooms ahead of a scheduled Sports Class like swimming. We'd wryly observe that the corporal punishment we got from our parents made the stuff we got at school [where corporal punishment has since been done away with] seem like a joke in comparison. Of course it was never fun to get corporal punishment on a butt freshly bruised at home.

Back home, when either of us had fucked up and the tears were real, that was a disaster. We were a close-knit family, and a loving family and for a certain period, a very happy one. But in all happy families there are sometimes moments of twisted anguish.

This was one.

Now for the leaf out of a South African diary:

She was crying, and the chocolate bribe wasn't working. I can't remember how it happened or who started it, but my brother or me put a hand over my sister's mouth to muffle the sound of her crying. She then "screamed" through her nose, prompting the closing off of that too. The motive was damage control – to not allow her cries to reach my parent's [probably mum's] ears. Tears turned to laughter, laughter turned to release and then suddenly another artificial outburst of squealing and sobbing. It's fuzzy but I seem to remember my brother and I taking turns to block off the sound. In effect we were strangling her long enough to shut her up. As soon as she was quiet we'd release her, but then she'd scream again and we'd be forced to close all orifices making noises. And then there was a power shift. She stopped screaming but we continued strangling her, not to harm her, I suppose, but just because we'd suddenly discovered, as brothers do, that we literally had someone's life – and power of it – in our hands. It made us smile and her eyes widen with real anxiety. My sister remembers that unpleasant experience to this day, and we still find it funny, at her expense. That's harmless sibling rivalry for you.

STARRY STARRY NIGHT

Shadows on the hills

Sketch the trees and the daffodils

Catch the breeze and the winter chills

In colors on the snowy linen land

Now I understand

What you tried to say to me

And how you suffered for your sanity

And how you tried to set them free

They would not listen, they did not know how
Perhaps they'll listen now —Vincent/Starry Starry
Night by Don McLean

Lessons in Child Psychology #5

Is Christmas a competition for siblings? If it is, what does Becker have to say about the psychology involved when children [and adults] compete? Why do we do it to each other Mr Becker; why do we do it to ourselves?

Economic equality is beyond the endurance of modern democratic man....it is not merely that your house diminishes in real estate value, but that you diminish... – and so you die. Things have given immortality probably since the earliest states, but in modern times this one-dimensionality on the level of the visible has run wild...the ideology of modern commercialism has unleashed a life of invidious comparison unprecedented in history....modern man cannot endure economic equality because he has no faith...visible physical worth is the only thing he has to give him eternal life. — Ernest Becker[45]

If we're reading Becker right his point is that no one wants to be a wallflower, least of all at home. Patsy didn't, JonBenét didn't, Burke didn't; nobody does.

What is it we're talking about when we use the word "wallflower?" Well, it addresses the unholy core of this entire narrative, doesn't it? The core of the wallflower is the very same core of *The Craven Silence*. Literally then, what are we talking about?

---

45 *Escape From Evil.*

From <u>dictionary.com</u>:

...a person who, because of shyness, unpopularity, or lack of a partner, remains at the side at a party or dance...any person... that remains on or has been forced to the side-lines....

We want to live, we want to be alive, we want to grow, be significant and be seen as significant. We don't want to die, we don't want to regress, we don't want to diminish and fade into insignificance. We don't want to be pushed aside. We want to be the star at the top of the Christmas tree. We want our lives to be about us, and by implication, that means we must matter most.

And when we don't? At Christmas, what happens when we don't matter most?

He dies when his little symbols of specialness die...Immortality power...[resides]...in accumulated wealth...Primitive man lived in a world devoid of clocks...but guilt and time are inseparable...the Greeks and Romans were reluctant to admit that the old regenerative rituals no longer worked. [But] Christianity offered the impending end of the world...time was firmly set in a linear way while waiting for that end. We are still today ticking off the years, but we no longer know what for...
— Ernest Becker[46]

In December 1996 Burke and JonBenét, like millions of children before them, were also counting the days to Christmas. What is the point of keeping track of time? Well, Becker posits, perhaps it is a sense buried deep in our psychology, that everything is being wiped away. Everything, and if we're not careful, we might be too.

---

46 *Escape From Evil.*

So you have these very young children counting down the days and then the hours. The Christmas bounty is by its very nature a mystery. It's not necessarily what you want or what you don't want. And yet despite this chasm of knowledge, they count down with certainty and excitement to something… they just don't know what exactly.

Super Predators

"...the oldest lie [is that] power can be innocent."
— Lex Luthor in Batman V Superman: Dawn of Justice

"John Ramsey came through very, very sincere. When I left that interview, there was no doubt in my mind that he had nothing to do with the death of his daughter." — Lou Smit

"I wonder what it'd be like to crack a human skull."
— Words attributed to Michael Helgoth by John Kenady

Under the half-silver light of a starry starry Christmas night we stomp through crusty snow around the Ramsey residence. We're looking for a shadow entering or exiting. We're looking for footprints. We're looking for signs of an intruder.

But there's not much going on. Inside the house a flashlight swims past a window downstairs, upstairs. Swings hither and thither. We don't want to look at that though. Let's look at the outside of the house, the walls, the grounds, the garden, the patio.

There's a steel swing covered in hoar frost. And barely visible nearer the property boundary *there's something glinting faintly in the snow...*

We boldly approach a rusted steel sign lying in long grass and half covered by drifts of snow. The faded word MISDIRECTIONS is painted on it. Wind and weather have had their elemental effect on the word. It's rusted and cracked, but still legible.

MISDIRECTIONS

Directly underneath the battered sign is a hole. It's time we went in. This means brushing aside the starlit cobwebs covering the big rabbit hole entrance and then burrowing through the warren beneath. This is the "intruder" territory, a labyrinth of confusing twists and turns and dead ends.

On the first subterranean level we find ourselves floating through time. A television in the soil bursts to life. It's the 19th of September 2016 and a man who used to live here, in fact used to own this house, and has long been suspected of having *something* to do with his daughter's murder, appears on Dr Phil. His lips are moving but the television embedded in the chocolate cake earth makes no sound.

Look closer.

From people.com [19 September 2016]:

John, meanwhile, said his Dr. Phil interview will be his last with the media, assuring, "I have no intention to speak out ... in the future." He said, "The real story here is not that a child was murdered. The real story is what was done to us by [the system]."

We'll be dealing with "the real story" John is talking about in a series of narratives around the title *THE DAY AFTER CHRISTMAS*. Those narratives will probe in detail the legal chess playing and PR moves that ultimately succeeded in – we think – defeating the ends of justice.

We'll also be researching, with the help of expert and very experienced former prosecutors, various stratagems to bring this case back to trial.

Let's watch carefully as the man sitting in a seat mouths a few words to a large bald man sitting opposite him.

"*This is my final interview. I have no reason for speaking to the media again.*" — John Ramsey

We take a step and fall through the rabbit hole emerging in Melbourne Australia on the 6th of October 2016. An interview with John Ramsey is broadcast on KIIS 101.1 Melbourne, an Australian radio station. Meshel Laurie conducts a skilful interview, asking John some tough questions, and making the wry comment at the conclusion:

Meshel: *"I know you said you'd never talk to the media again; I don't know what made you decide to talk to me but I'm ever so grateful you did."*

John [stumbles over his words]: *"Ahm…it's my, it's been a pleasure. I really appreciate your questions and…uh…appreciate the opportunity to talk to your audience."*

As we move deeper through the rabbit hole we can hear Meshel's words looping through the dark:

"…you know a lot of things didn't pass the common sense test…"

And John muttering: *"…that is beneath even the lowest criminal mind…even…even hard-core criminals would not harm a child…and so it's a horrible crime and people want answers…and so the easiest answer is…well, it must have been the parents, case solved…they can't, or they don't want to admit or accept that someone could come into your home, take your child from their bed, and…murder 'em….I never dreamed that someone would come in and take my child…"*

I'm not sure what John's really saying when he says even the lowest criminal mind, even the most hard-core criminals wouldn't harm a child. What's your point John? That hard-core criminals are less likely to commit these crimes that happen in the home than the parents or siblings?

> *I never dreamed that someone would come in*
> *and take my child....*

Well, but you did. That's your theory, isn't it? Let's hold off that they never took your child to begin with, but this idea that you never dreamed it seems a little nonsensical when that's the theory you're pushing to folks over the radio, on Dr Phil, in your book.

But let's quit fucking around and seriously deal with that theory. The meat and potatoes of this narrative is misdirection, so let's be misdirected and see where it takes us.

From people.com:

JonBenét performed in child beauty pageants in the time before her death, and Burke speculated in his interview that the culprit "saw her at one of the pageants."

"I always thought it was a pedophile who saw her in one of the pageants and snuck in [to our house]."

Smit seemed to believe something similar – a sadistic paedophile. So let's look at the prime suspects listing all the worst of the worst Super Predators stalking Boulder [and the rest of the world] circa 1996. There's a warren leading to a blizzard of faded nameplates. There's Bob Enyart, someone called Gigax, Meyer – the neighboring Barnhill's basement dweller, Fleet White, Fleet White junior, Fleet White's wife, John Andrew [JonBenét's stepbrother], John Mark Karr...Somewhere down there even Santa is a suspect.

But for now we'll focus on just one, and arguably the best "intruder" suspect.[47]

Helgoth [and accomplice]

In February 1997 the <u>Boulder District Attorney Alex Hunter made an announcement</u> to the media. Eyeballing the camera, and it must be noted <u>somewhat cryptically</u>, Hunter stated:

> *"I want to say something to the person or persons that committed this crime - the person or persons that took this baby from us. The list of suspects narrows. Soon there will be no one on the list but you."*

Standing beside Hunter at that same press conference is a dark haired woman in a bright blue dress… is it Leslie Aaholm? Remember her? Isn't she the same dark haired City of Boulder Spokesperson, wearing a blue dress on January 3rd 1997, who'd said:

> *"We had no legal right to detain the Ramseys…nobody has been ruled in or out as suspects."*

It seems a lot can change in a month, or did it?

From <u>cnn.com</u>:

…<u>*Michael Helgoth, was also a prime suspect*</u>. *He was a Colorado native who died shortly after the murder.*

In fact Helgoth, an auto salvage yard worker, <u>died two days after Hunter's press conference</u>. Besides the timing of his death, the circumstances of his death seemed strange as well. <u>Ollie Gray, a detective</u>

---

47 We deal conclusively and completely with the other prime "intruder" suspects in *The Craven Silence 3*.

<u>hired by the Ramsey family in 1999/2000</u> honed in on <u>Helgoth as a top suspect</u>.

From <u>news.com.au</u>:

"There are probably three or four people who should have been investigated earlier and still need to be investigated," Mr Gray told NBC. "The latest development in this particular case as far as I'm concerned is Michael Helgoth. He was basically a hell raiser," Mr Gray said.

Helgoth's name reportedly came up early on in the investigation, but Boulder, Colorado investigators never got any answers because he committed suicide just months after the murder, reports the Daily Mail.

One theory held that upon hearing the Boulder authorities were closing in on him, Helgoth lost his nerve and killed himself. But Gray had a more imaginative theory. Because there were two sets of footprints left in the grit of the Ramseys basement, one from a Hi-Tec boot and the other unidentified. He saw the prints as belonging to a suspect. Both suspects, the argument went, could have easily gained access to the joint during the Ramsey's open house Christmas party, where as many as 1500 Boulder residents supposedly had free reign to move through the mansion. Was Helgoth one of them, and had he "cased the joint" with an accomplice? And as the cops zeroed in on the owner of the Hi-Tec boot, had Helgoth's accomplice lost his nerve and assassinated his partner? Was it a hit to silence Helgoth forever, especially given the media hurricane that had since blown up around JonBenét's murder?

From <u>news.com.au</u>:

Gray [said Helgoth] may have been killed by a co-conspirator in the murder.

"I don't think Mike did all of this by himself," Mr Gray added, *inferring that Helgoth may have been murdered by a conspirator to keep his mouth shut.*

*"Based on what we know now, I believe Helgoth and his accomplices committed the crime. **There's no doubt about it**,"* said Mr Gray.

Except there were doubts. And tantalising new leads. Had Helgoth been murdered or was it suicide? If it was suicide why had he shot himself through his own pillow? As for new leads, a bunch of low hanging fruit suddenly materialized. Lou Smit was one Ramsey detective who reached for these, but another Ramsey investigator, Ollie Gray was more vocal in fingering Helgoth and waving a victory flag.

From cnn.com:

It appeared to be a suicide. And what about the stun gun discovered next to his body? Investigators believe a stun gun had been used on JonBenét.

Prosecutor DeMuth told me this about Helgoth: "I remember that he had footwear that was consistent with the footprint evidence, he had a stun gun, he had reportedly made statements to a friend, very similar to the types of statements that we're hearing about today in the press with the arrest of John Karr."

Even more strange, a baseball cap with the letters s-b-t-c was found near Helgoth's body. Those are the same letters found in the Ransom Note at the Ramsey home. DeMuth says he believes Helgoth's DNA was tested and didn't match up.

One can be somewhat dismissive about the stun gun, and the hearsay, but the baseball cap seems somewhat compelling, doesn't it?

But there was more than just hearsay, there was a tape recording.

From dailymail.co.uk:

[Gray's] opinion was backed up by John Kenady, a man who used to work for Helgoth, who told the magazine InTouch; "There was a tape recording made by Helgoth. And in it, he said he killed JonBenét."

Mr Kenady also claims that someone close to Helgoth still has the tape, which was overlooked by police during the investigation. Mr Kenady claims that he first grew suspicious of Helgoth a month before the murder.

"In late November, Helgoth had told me that he and a partner were going to make a great deal and they each will bring in around $US50,000 or $US60,000," said Mr Kenady. "I will never forget we were walking toward his house and he said, "I wonder what it would be like to crack a human skull. I was amazed. I thought it was a very odd thing to say."

Junkyard worker John Kenady turns out to be a very useful source on Helgoth. He's able to give us virtually everything we need – the killer saying he murdered JonBenét, the killer saying he wanted particularly to know what cracking someone's skull felt like, the killer talking about $60 000 [half as much money demanded in the Ransom Note, i.e. Helgoth's 50/50 split]. There's also the stun gun. Is this guy too good – or too bad – to be true or what?

Let's step further into the rabbit hole with Helgoth's name on it…

From acandyrose.com:

*Narrator: These detectives do not see Helgoth as the actual killer, in fact, DNA samples taken at a post mortem show that he was not. But they think he may have been involved. One reason is that they've always believed it likely that more than one person was in the Ramsey home that night. The footprints suggest this as do the number of objects taken in and out of the house. These include a rope, stun gun, cord and duct tape. **It would have been difficult for just one person to have done everything that was done that night.***

As the Helgoth narrative gets fuzzier, it starts to point back to the Ramseys, do you notice? Yes, it would have been difficult for just one person to have done everything that was done to JonBenét that night. So if we're talking about an intruder, we actually need to think plural. That means the chance of DNA and other evidence is doubled.

From acandyrose.com:

And the Ransom Note also suggests that more than one person was involved. It says, "We are a group of individuals that represent a small foreign faction". It warns about the "two gentlemen watching over your daughter". Throughout, it refers to the kidnappers in the plural.

But would junkyard types use words like "attaché" for suitcase, and would abrasive, hard, sun beaten welders and mechanics advise the Ramseys to "get some rest" and refer to "good Southern common sense"? Why would Boulder's junkyard types refer to themselves as a "foreign faction"? How many junkyard types would even know what the word "faction" means? And why would American junkyard types not respect America, and yet not respect John's computer business?

From acandyrose.com:

The new team of detectives think Helgoth may well have been involved as an accomplice of an even more deadly killer. One who later murdered him to stop him from talking after Alex Hunter's unnerving press conference.

The problem is, by invoking Helgoth as a prime suspect, and then dragging in an invisible Mr. X, the investigation essentially throws out a whole new unsolvable dimension. Who is Mr. X?

From acandyrose.com:

In trying to identify a potential killer, they came up with an important clue. In the months before the murder, up to a dozen houses near the Ramsey's were broken into at night. There was a curious pattern to these burglaries. Little or nothing was taken. Detectives believe they were carried out simply for the thrill of stalking others at night. The break-ins stopped abruptly after the murder.

Well there are simpler reasons to these questions, just as there may be a simple or obvious reason why Helgoth committed suicide. Why would burglaries around the Ramsey residence stop after their house at 755 15th Street became a crime scene Media Central? A criminal would be crazy to continue habitual crimes with the Boulder Police Department and the media camped out for days and weeks afterward, and the entire neighborhood on edge for Patsy's [whispered] "killer on the loose".

From acandyrose.com:

The Boulder Police did not link [the burglaries] to the murder, but the new investigators believe they might be the key to everything because Helgoth too used to stalk people at night. It happened to John Kenady.

The new investigators of course are the Ramsey P.I.'s – Smit, Gray and San Agustin.

From acandyrose.com:

KENADY: *I was working on a car late one evening in my garage. I kind of get the feeling there's something out there and went right up to the window to look. I looked, and it was real quiet and I don't see anything. I look again and all I could see were a pair of eyes coming out of the black. I don't know why I figure well this could be Michael, so I said "Is that you Mike?" And he goes "Yeah" and I said "Well how long you been out there?" and he goes "Long enough" and ... he's gone. I thought it was kinda strange.*

Well, not really. His colleague is standing around, so what. Or not?

From acandyrose.com:

NARRATOR: *Helgoth used to stalk people at night dressed in black ninja clothing. When looking for his possible killer, detectives looked for a violent associate who shared his interest in martial arts and young girls. They immediately came up with one. A close associate who has since disappeared.* **A man who frightens those around him.**

Sounds scary, right?

From acandyrose.com:

FIRST MAN: *I tried to steer clear of that individual because he could have been, you know, a menace ... to me or my family.*

INTERVIEWER [UNSEEN]: *Were you personally scared of him?*

SECOND MAN: *Phew. On a level, I'd have to say "yes". Absolutely. I think he was capable of being violent towards anybody.*

KENADY: *[Helgoth's associate] threatened to cut one of his girlfriend's ears off. His ex-wife – he tried to kill her. They were only married probably five or six days.*

NARRATOR: *Helgoth's associate lived in this trailer park near the car salvage yard. The makers of this programme* **know his name, but have decided to withhold it,** *because* **he has not been charged with any offence.** *But the more that has been discovered about him, the more he fits the profile of a stalker and a killer.*

Amazingly, despite the compelling "evidence" against the evil Mr. X even the documentary filmmakers won't even reveal his name. Why? There's zero evidence linking him to the crime.

From acandyrose.com:

SECOND MAN: *He was very methodical. He wanted everything down to the last detail. He ... didn't want anybody else to have any control. If he didn't feel like he was controlling a situation, he would lash out.*

KENADY: *Martial arts, he liked those throwing knives, he was into ninja, he was into the dark clothing, he always wore a black t-shirt, black pants, black boots...*

NARRATOR: *Helgoth's associate was convicted following **a stabbing** here on the trailer park. Witnesses were too frightened to give evidence but court documents summarised his criminal record as **"violence – history of sexual assault"**. They also reveal that he was a convicted paedophile. He was imprisoned in the 1980s for a sexual assault on a child. It is believed that **he may have worked in the Ramsey home**, shortly before the family moved in. Unidentified animal hairs were found in the cellar where JonBenét's body was left. The hairs were of two colors. Helgoth's associate raised wolf dogs whose hairs exactly match those colors. Helgoth had bought two of these dogs.*

It's all extremely compelling. Is this Patsy's ominous killer on the loose? Is this the sadistic, brutal monster haunting the shadows?

When we step a little closer to the sign buried into the side of the rabbit hole we see that under Helgoth's name is another name. A few wipes reveals the name beneath the name: KENADY. The entire version of Helgoth we're getting is from Kenady, and although there's talk of confessions on tape, where are they?

As damning as all of this seems to be, it's still clearly misdirection. Why? Because what sort of skull cracking piece of shit would sexually assault a little girl, garrotte her and then sensitively cover her in her favorite blanket [the blanket itself, according to Linda Hoffman Pugh, had been retrieved from the upstairs dryer just outside JonBenet's bedroom door?]

Of course there's a far more obvious reason Helgoth and Mr. X aren't involved.

From cbsnews.com:

Colorado private detective Ollie Gray and his partner John Sangustin were hired by the Ramseys two years ago. Even when the Ramseys ran out of money, Ollie and John stayed on the job.

*They became **convinced of the Ramseys' innocence after seeing a lab report**. Days after JonBenét was murdered, her **parents were asked to give DNA samples to the Boulder police**. Their DNA was compared to foreign DNA found under their daughter's fingernails and in her panties, which may have been left by the killer.*

"This analysis eliminates the Ramseys," says Gray. "(The DNA) does not match John or Patsy Ramsey. According to the laboratories."

Well the DNA didn't match Helgoth either. If the DNA under JonBenét's fingernails is decisive evidence – it may be, but it may not be – it may decisively exclude the Ramsey parents as JonBenét's murderers. But does it exclude Burke? Was *Burke's DNA* ever added to the DNA archive?

BLACK STAR

"When the day comes for them to strike, they want you ignorant of everything, especially their intent to destroy you." — Edward W. Robertson, The Black Star

Lessons in Child Psychology #6

Was the star above the Ramsey Christmas tree that fateful Christmas of 1996 truly a genuine, shining star of peace in the family home and goodwill toward little sisters?

Man has changed from a giving animal, the one who passes things on, to the wholly taking and keeping one. By continually taking a piling and computing interest…man contrives the illusion that he is in complete control of his destiny. — Ernest Becker[48]

What happens when the hands groping to take and keep find a vacuum instead? What happens when it is Christmas and these material symbols of control aren't there? What happens when a man – or boy – discovers he is no longer in complete control of his destiny?

*What is the Matrix? Control. The Matrix is **a computer generated dream world**, built to keep us under control in order <u>to change a human being into this</u>. – <u>Morpheus in The Matrix</u>*

While Morpheus' analogy can be read as a call to revolutionary activism against involuntary lack of control and slavery, it can also be read in more contemporary terms. The world is based on Capitalism, built to keep consumers in servitude to the 1% running the whole thing. It's a system <u>designed to turn a person into this.</u>

The Matrix analogy has symbolic value, based on the symbolism of an underlying or overlying machine world. The vital difference between

---

48 *Escape From Evil.*

the symbolism of *The Matrix* and our present reality is that the human world is run by human beings. We may employ machines as slaves and assistance, but humans are running the show. The currency in which power – both personal and social – is reflected is money.

Earlier we referred to money as being analogous to excrement, and excrement to death. This is where we cover full circle. When a human being gives up his life energy – through work, or service, through physical labor, through some sacrifice of his or time and effort – the transaction that is really underway is <u>a conversion of human life/ energy into money</u>.

Another mainstream version of this is <u>*Survivor.*</u> Adults battle it out for 36 days on an island, putting their bodies, minds and morals on the line. At stake – money. And the winner tends to be seen as making the most deserving sacrifices of his own life, not only on his own terms, but everyone else's. The transaction is democratised but it's nevertheless a competition with one winner and 17 losers. By now the psychology of *Survivor* has become a canon in its own right, along with all the psychological strata – alliances, blindsiding, throwing people under the bus, voting blocs, immunity, backstabbing, betrayal, treachery…all under the guise of co-operative teams.

In our everyday lives we may not see the blood and sweat that we see on *Survivor* or in a war where bodies are strewn on steaming battlefields and literally lost in the trenches. But in the corporate sense, in the Capitalism sense, in the consumer sense – those cubicle slaves, those folks traps behind tills while everyone else piles on their Christmas shopping, those street sweepers and burger flippers are all furiously engaged in giving up their life time for money.

In a very real sense <u>the contents of Santa's Christmas sack is</u> a real symbol of <u>Life Magic</u>, just as a winning lottery ticket is a symbol but also the means to resurrect oneself out of the work slavery inherent to Capitalism.

In countless movies, from *Fargo* [released in 1996] to *Ransom* [ditto] to the thousands of other kidnap stories involving briefcases filled with money in exchange for a living person we see the same "real world" symbolism made manifest. A person's life becomes monetised. It becomes expressed as a monetary value and then a transaction is agreed – money for someone's life. Death for life. Life for death.

In the Ramsey scenario we believe there was an attempt to invert this familiar real life fairy tale. The Ramseys at the end of 1996 were the King and Queen of Boulder. And Kings and Queens exert tremendous power over their vassals – not just financial power but personal power too. The Ramseys were also charismatic, and their Christianity provided a sort of guarantee to back up their story, even in the face of ardent inquiry from the likes of "sincere" investigators like Lou Smit.

If one takes the hypothesis that Burke did kill his sister, and we add to that this idea of both parents then inventing a Ransom Note, what we end up in psychological terms is a perfect fit. Think about the transaction which is being brokered with the public and the police. It is this idea of exchanging a life for money. Further, it is the idea that the Ramseys will pay for the life they took [although in the fictional – as we see it – ransom letter they are paying a kidnapper]. Through this ruse the Ramseys maintain their financial and social power, essentially their claims to be King and Queen. In their minds, if the world knew what really happened, their crowns would be diminished or confiscated entirely.

And so the ruse is the payment [which never took place] of $118 000. Interestingly, if the Ramseys are the authors of their own Ransom Note, the money symbolising their daughter's life seems too little. This issue has been raised, but we raise it again here: that in the psychology of the Ransom Note, the amount the authors themselves see the value of their daughter's life, what JonBenét's life was worth to them is *incriminatingly low.*

When John Ramsey posted his reward for information leading to the arrest of someone involved he initially offered $50 000. Later this amount was raised to $100 000.

Over a period of time the Ramseys saw their wealth liquidated and converted into lawyer's fees, and though they lost homes, planes and boats, they've maintained a sort of "moral claim to the throne". This has entitled Ramsey counsel to sue for impinging the "good name" of their clients. Today [7th October 2016] Lin Wood announced a lawsuit against Werner Spitz.

From businessinder.com:

According to court papers…Burke is suing Spitz for stating that Burke killed his younger sister, JonBenét, during a radio interview with CBS Detroit — not for his participation in the televised CBS special. In the complaint — filed in the third circuit court for the County of Wayne, Michigan, on Thursday — Spitz is accused of being a "publicity seeker," who on the 20th anniversary of JonBenét's murder has "once again interjected himself into a high-profile case to make unsupported, false, and sensational statements and accusations."

Accusing Spitz of being a publicity seeker is a little rich coming from the Ramseys or any of their affiliates. The entire month of September 2016 has been a media blitz from the Ramseys and their attorney.

From businessinder.com:

[The complaint] details that during the radio interview, Spitz "claims Burke, age nine at the time of his sister's death, bludgeoned her to death. Defendant Spitz made this accusation without ever examining JonBenét's

body, without viewing the crime scene, and without consulting with the pathologist who performed the autopsy on JonBenét."

*The complaint calls for a jury trial and requests **no less than $150 million in damages**, a retraction, and no further defamatory accusations against Burke.*

If we consider <u>Burke's reputation – valued at $150 million</u> – against JonBenét's life, valued either by "real" kidnappers at $118 000 or the Ramsey's [in terms of a reward for finding her killers] at $100 000, the $150 million is interesting. We can see that there's a capitalistic sense that a reputation spun in the media is worth far more than a person's life. In this instance the implication is that JonBenét's death has spun a narrative franchise of some sort for the Ramsey family which is worth 1500 times the value of JonBenét's life.

From <u>businessinder.com</u>:

Last month, Burke's attorney said he would be suing CBS over the findings in its special, "The Case of: JonBenét Ramsey." The special's investigators landed on the theory that nine-year-old Burke Ramsey allegedly killed his younger sister by accident in a fit of anger. According to their theory, his parents, John and Patsy Ramsey, then allegedly created the scenario of an intruder who killed their daughter in order to protect their son.

Burke's attorney, L. Lin Wood, told Business Insider in an email that the "CBS complaint will be filed at end of October to allow statutory time for correction to expire."

In response to the proposed suit, a network representative previously told Business Insider, "CBS stands by the broadcast and will do so in court."

From the perspective of a litigator possibly defending suspects who may be guilty of the crimes they're suspected of, one can also see a profit motive based on transacting money [death] based on defending a narrative [life/innocence] for his clients. If successful and if his clients are guilty to begin with, the death destruction is magnified and even leveraged. If his clients are innocent, then the death destruction is magnified and leveraged anyway.

To casual observers *The Matrix*, the psychologies of comic book heroes, endless episodes of *Survivor* reality television and perhaps even Becker's spiritual insights may seem fanciful speculations. What do they have to do directly with JonBenét? What do they have to say whatsoever about Burke? Let's turn our eyes to the Christmas Tree in the Ramsey home on December 26th. Does it give off a merry light? What does it reveal, what is reflected in those gleaming gold baubles?

From empoweringparents.com:

Ideally, a family is supposed to be a safe place where everyone is loved and everyone is equal. Your children may feel jealous of each other, but again, jealousy is a normal human feeling; it's a perception. Normal sibling rivalry and jealousy will not be taken away by anything you, as a parent, can do. But what you can do is make sure that there's enough love, nurturance and positive regard to go around for everybody, while at the same time, setting limits on the amount of chaos that ensues from this bickering behavior.

The Grand Jury indictment papers essentially accused both Ramsey parents not of murder but child abuse. Had John and Patsy – individually and collectively – made sure there was enough nurturance for both their children? Had John and Patsy set limits on the chaos that ensued from the bickering that went on between JonBenét and Burke, not just during the crucial hours of Christmas Day, but for the many days, weeks and months leading up to it? Had they?

From empoweringparents.com:

If one of your children is envious of his sibling, I recommend that you try to downplay it. Don't make it a big deal. I think you ought to say something like, "Well, you know, that's natural, we all feel jealous sometimes. Ryan may have done well in soccer, but I watched you do your math homework and get it all done the other night, and I know it was hard." Always point out your children's good characteristics. **Mention concrete things you saw and heard them do, and let them know that you're valuing their efforts as much as their brother or sister's.**

At Christmas, concrete things are the prime message to let children know they're valued for who they are by their parents.

…money has been the single red line connecting the failed historical ideologies of immortality – from lupeto*…through Pompei, through the buying of Martin Luther's Catholic] indulgences, through Calvin* **and modern commercialism**. — Ernest Becker

Of course failure to deliver sends a counter-missive – that they're *not* valued, and worse, a sibling *is valued more.*

A perceived material failure to deliver *lupeto* in the form of a required or expected Christmas gift – something of the right size and heft, could be considered a fatal undermining of the sibling dynamic. Supremacy undermined in such a critical way on such a critical day had to be fundamentally addressed, didn't it?

One again we should note if Ramsey counsel value Burke's reputation at $150 million, the kidnapper(s) JonBenét's life at $118 000, the Ramsey's justice for their daughter at $100 000, then if Burke was guilty, did he value whatever was missing from Santa's sack as grounds for a bludgeoning? And what was missing? A bicycle or a box of Legos worth $200?

Was this, on that cold Christmas Day, a seriously big deal bugging an inadequate nine year old boy? Did Burke feel he was losing control, not only of JonBenét, but of his place in the family pecking order? If money/Life Force had been withheld, then a balance had to be re-established, didn't it? <u>If no material could be found to transact with,</u> then all that remained was a little girl's Life Force.

Back to Burke

"Has it ever occurred to you that your parents actually thought you did this...?" — Dr. Phil to Burke Ramsey

"I know people think I did it; that my parents did it. I know that we were suspects. [Chuckles]."
— <u>Burke Ramsey</u> on Dr. Phil

"I want to honor her memory by doing this interview. I don't want anyone to forget."
— Burke Ramsey

What if the star at the top of the Ramsey's Christmas Tree, rather than <u>a source of light</u>, was <u>a source of darkness instead</u>? If that is the case, we need to address that darkness. We believe the craven figure buried in the darkness of this story is Burke. We believe that rather than honoring JonBenét, that Burke may have been present when JonBenét died. Further, rather than honoring JonBenét by giving an interview, we think Burke was honoring himself, exonerating himself.

If this is true, what does the black star point to? If the bright Christmas star illuminates the birth of the savior of the world, what does the black star floating over a "Perfect Town" illuminate? The answer is that it illuminates what is *hidden*.

Hasn't Burke remained hidden – the most hidden, remained silent – the most silent, for the past twenty years?

From the <u>Bonita Papers</u>:

…when [JonBenét] had a bedwetting incident during the night, JonBenét would usually get up and change her own clothes. Sometimes she would go into her brother's bedroom and crawl into the extra bed to avoid going back to her own cold, wet one.

It's important to establish a precedent here, and we have one – habitual bedwetting, and then JonBenét's going to her brother's bedroom to sleep. Now we must ask the question – did she sleep in Burke's bedroom around Christmas? And who better to pose that question to – besides Burke – than his mother. Patsy should know, right?

From the <u>Bonita Papers</u>:

As in most households on Christmas morning, it was the anxious children who awoke their parents. **JonBenét had slept in Burke's room that night [Christmas Eve, Dec 24]** *so he could awaken her early – too early.*

"Too early" is an important point to emphasize. The Ramsey parents had had a number of back to back parties in the run up to Christmas:

From <u>pbworks.com</u>:

11-30 40th Birthday Celebration for Patsy.

In her newsletter a few weeks later Patsy described that party on the last day of November 1996 as *"the biggest, most outrageous 40th birthday bash I've ever had!"*

But Patsy's 40th birthday was actually a month later – on <u>December</u> 29th. The Ramseys probably figured on getting it out of the way, and not letting it get in the way of all the other pageants, Yuletide parties and Access Graphics-related celebrations. At the end of a month of feasting and partying, John and Patsy planned on a final birthday bash to cap the year and see in the next one.

In her newsletter penned sometime just prior to Christmas, Patsy gushed:

"We'll be spending my actual birthday on the Disney Big Red Boat over the new year!"

Through the rest of December, the Ramsey household ramped up for a rough-and-tumble bumper to bumper party-fest.

From <u>pbworks.com</u>:

*12-6 Lights of December Parade. **JonBenét** appeared on her own "Little Miss Colorado" float during the Lights of December Parade on the Boulder Mall; **Burke** also was in this parade.*

12-13 Church Party in Ramsey Home…attended by more than 150 friends from church.

12-16 Access Graphics…billion dollar sales celebration.

*12-17 **JonBenét** [wins] "Colorado's Little Miss Christmas"… [and] wins [a] "Santa Bear" in Denver-area pageant…*

In the first two weeks of that December, simply by looking at the timeline, we see JonBenét's name coming up at least twice as often as Burke's does. Significantly in the Parade of Lights JonBenét is vividly seen by the whole Boulder community as a burgeoning <u>princess on her own float</u>. Burke is at the same parade, but he's a spectator – he's with the rabble; he's just like everyone else.

On the same day as the parade, Patsy is in New York with John shopping and socializing with friends.

From pbworks.com:

12-20 Access Graphics Luncheon [attended by 300 employees] at the Boulderado Hotel

*12-20 **JonBenét** appears in Rock Around the Clock performance at High Peaks Elementary School*

12-21 Access Graphics…celebrates $1 billion mark

12-21 Camera Business Writer article on Access Graphics reaching $1 billion in sales

*12-22 **JonBenét** [appears] in beauty pageant at Southwest Plaza Mall*

Patsy Ramsey writes Christmas newsletter

12-23 Ramsey Christmas Party includes approximately 30 guests… [including] former journalism professor Bill McReynolds playing Santa Claus…

12-23 Mistaken 911 Call. At 6:47 p.m., someone attending the party placed a 911 call, which was answered by police dispatcher Therese Hilleary. The caller hung up without saying anything. Police call back only to get the Ramsey's answering machine. Officer "B.O. 266" goes to the home at 6:54 p.m. and leaves at 7:09 p.m., after being assured that there was no emergency…

12-24 Article appeared in the Boulder Daily Camera regarding the Ramsey Christmas party

*12-24 **JonBenét** played at her friend Megan Kostanick's house and told Megan's mother about a secret visit from Santa…*

12-24 Ramseys attend twilight service at St. John's Episcopal Church in Boulder…

*12-24 At 9:00 PM John Ramsey retrieves a brand new silver girl's bike stored in neighbor Joe Barnhill's garage and places it under the Christmas tree for **JonBenét**...*

12-24 Ramseys get stashed gifts from basement area

In the last week of her life, JonBenét appears in two beauty pageants and a dance festival. What does Burke do? He may or may not be the rhyme or the reason behind the December 23rd 911 crank call. It's possible the call was a genuine cry for help following an incident. Given that less than three days later a 911 call would be made from the same location, one has to wonder. If the second call was a crank call but actually masking a real emergency, wasn't the call on December 23rd precisely that as well?

Now we deal with the crucial sequence in the timeline as far as Christmas Eve and Christmas day, particularly in how it relates to Burke. In *The Craven Silence 3* we'll deal with another arguably more vital section of the timeline, the night of December 25th. In that narrative we'll interrogate precisely what Patsy has to say about Burke and JonBenét's sleeping arrangements on the fateful night in question.

To understand the fateful night we must focus our efforts first on the night before JonBenét's murder.

From acandyrose.com:

TRUJILLO: *[Speaking about Christmas Eve, December 24] Go home, got ready for bed um, where did everybody sleep that night?*

PATSY: *Well, **JonBenét was in her bed in her room**...*

TRUJILLO: *Okay.*

PATSY: *...and **Burke was in his bed** and we slept in our room.*

TRUJILLO: *Okay. **Do you have an idea if JonBenét moved over towards Burke's room at all that night? Slept in his room?***

PATSY: *Um,* **I can't remember,** *can't remember.*

TRUJILLO: *Okay. Is that something that she would normally do?*

PATSY: **No.**

Not?

From the Bonita Papers:

...when [JonBenét] had a bedwetting incident during the night, JonBenét would...sometimes...go into her brother's bedroom and crawl into the extra bed to avoid going back to her own cold, wet one. This is something John confirms.

From acandyrose.com, John's Police Interview 1998:

SMIT: *I just had a quick question. I just want to know if they had any problems with them... Did Patsy or yourself ever go down and help JonBenet? Did she ever cry or indicate that she had wet her bed or anything like that? Do you remember anything like that?*

JOHN: *No. No.* **I don't remember if it was Burke or JonBenet, but they would change beds if they had an accident. They would start doing that and usually if they were uncomfortable they'd just change beds.**

Patsy seems very iffy on this subject matter. One can speculate either way, but what's interesting is how certain John is on sleeping arrangements and how uncertain Patsy is. Just a reminder: the Grand Jury sought to indict both parents on child abuse, and on recklessly endangering their child. This assumes both parents knew JonBenét was imperiled and yet did nothing to protect her.

If Burke had acted out aggressively towards JonBenét in the past, then just how responsible could it be for JonBenét's parents – worn out from a month of bumper to bumper bashes – to allow the little girl to sleep in her brother's bedroom following yet another incident of bedwetting and associated sleeplessness.

Incidentally, that's another issue we'll be finalizing in *The Craven Silence 3* – the idea of JonBenét sleeping soundly. Was she? Did she? We have every reason to believe she did not, and especially not on the night of December 25th. Further, we believe the pillow on the kitchen counter is a misdirection to suggest JonBenét had been sleeping, and then came downstairs, carrying her pillow.

But we're getting ahead of ourselves.

From acandyrose.com:

TRUJILLO: *Sleep in Burke's room. I know everybody's got, you got, they both have two beds in their rooms.*

PATSY: *Yeah, right um,* **I don't think so. I just can't remember.**

THOMAS: **Do you recall on December 24th into the morning of December 25th, whether or not JonBenét slept in her bed or over in Burke's room?**

PATSY: *I,* **I just don't remember exactly,** *but it seems like she was in her bed, but I don't remember exactly.*

Next detective Steve Thomas asks Patsy about where JonBenét slept on Christmas night. We'll deal with Patsy's response in the next narrative. What's interesting though is while Patsy is reluctant to answer [and/or forgetful on this particular point], she boomerangs back to Christmas Eve and seemingly has a lot of extraneous information relating to December 24th.

From acandyrose.com:

PATSY: *The reason I can't remember whether they, where she slept* **on the 24th** *were, not cause it seemed like* they were conspiring *about what time they were going to get up in the morning and I can't remember whether they, it seems like there, that she did,* **they did talk about her sleeping in his room, but I can't remember whether that** *really happened or not, but I remember <u>they were conspiring</u> about what time to get up and...*

Patsy's double use of the word "conspiring" given the context of the accusations against her and John, and the mythos of this case is confounding. It's also classic Patsy.

Conspiring is a word that means:

- Colluding
- Contriving
- Devising
- Working together
- Uniting

And Patsy's explanation seems intended to show two mischievous children engaged in something supposedly innocent rather than two mischievous adults engaged in damage control. Many casual observers to this case point out that had Burke "accidentally" hit JonBenét over the head, it would have been entirely rational and reasonable for her parents to call it in. Would it? Well, how accidental is a series of accidents? How reasonable would it be to call in an "accident" leading to death, but not all the others that occurred prior to? An analogy – although not a very good one to this – are the nine 911 calls Nicole Brown Simpson made reporting O.J.'s abusiveness. Eventually what she feared would happen to her did happen – she was murdered and O.J. got away with it, just as he had on all the other 911 calls.

That's different to a child dying in one's care, but witnesses – friends, housekeepers, teachers perhaps – being aware of a pattern of underlying neglect. Was there a pattern? If there was, it would provide ample motive to cover-up a crime from Burke that was not merely an accident, but a serious accident waiting to happen.

Rumor Control

"I don't really know what was going through my head, but she was gone, so I didn't draw her." — Burke Ramsey on <u>why a sketch he drew of the Ramsey family</u> excluded JonBenét

Bruce Wayne: You're not brave... men are brave. You say that you want to help people, but you can't feel their pain... their mortality... — Batman V Superman: Dawn of Justice

Rumors are like ripples in a cornfield. They are ephemeral, but they do indicate which way the wind is blowing. — Susan J. Palmer, Aliens Adored

<u>Andrews</u>: *Once again, this is rumor control. Here are the facts. At 0800 hours, prisoner Murphy, through carelessness on his part, was found dead in vent shaft 17…We need to organize and send out a search party; volunteers will be appreciated. I think*

it's fair to say that our smoothly running facility has suddenly developed a few problems. I can only hope we are all able to pull together over the next few days until the rescue team arrives... — Alien 3

Are we done with bicycles? No, we're not done. Do we think bicycles are a major missing link to the psychology of this story? Yes we do, and further, we think everyone has missed it – the cops, the media, the investigators, the narrators.

Inexplicably twenty years after the fact, there's a lot of muddiness and misdirection around the question of bicycles at Christmas – who got what?

To address this murkiness under the dark star, we'll be retracing some of the steps we took on this topic in the previous narrative by conducting another *Who's who of Christmas Bicycles.*

We want this narrative to provide a sturdy bridge so we can pedal across to a brand new bicycle platform. We're trying to elevate the importance of this aspect to the narrative, and we do so by simply quoting each occasion when John, Patsy or Burke talk about it. Do they talk about it? More than many realize. Funnily enough, the media seemed to miss Burke waffle on about bicycles on Dr. Phil. Perhaps it seemed meaningless. When misdirection is being managed behind the scenes, each and every misdirection is gold.

We believe this is a big one.

Once we have the misdirection dismantled then the set up for *The Craven Silence 3* will address our final conclusions in how the bicycle sideshow lines up with the childhood psychology that unravelled on that day of all days. In this narrative we wish to continue that process of erecting a pedestal displaying and spotlighting what's been hidden from view.

On April 30, 1997 Patsy was interrogated at length by Boulder Police in the Boulder District Attorney's Office. But that interrogation – led by Detective Steve Thomas – didn't really cut it, if anything it sent the false flags flying.

14 months later on June 23rd, 1998 – a year and a half after JonBenét's death – detectives were able to get another shot at Patsy.

Detective Tom Haney eventually got this bicycle-related nugget from Patsy first-hand:

PATSY: *JonBenét got a bicycle that year. I got a university bicycle, and she got a twin doll which I mail ordered, and...*

Mid-way through the first of Dr. Phil's three episodes broadcast in September 2016 where Burke would exclusively "break his silence" for the first time, Dr. Phil asks Burke:

"Do you remember what you did that [Christmas] morning?"

BURKE [looking right down, smiling]: *"I remember [glances at camera, wide-eyed] peeking down [the spiral staircase]...and I remember seeing like a...electric train... [inaudible] a bike [said with emphasis]. And I was super-excited."*

DR. PHIL [Smiling]: *"Was JonBenét with you?"*

BURKE: [Playing the piano with the fingers of his left hand on the side of the sofa]: *"Yeaaah... [inaudible]. Yeah, I think so. Yeah."*

Clearly Burke was super-excited about what he was getting for Christmas. But he seems less sure of himself in this rosy [ruse-y?] version when it comes to his sister – where was she? Was she with him? What was going on regarding the discovery of the gifts? Isn't there a hint here of *The Craven Silence* all over again? Here, in this sense specifically.

DR. PHIL: *"Did you get what you asked for that year?"*

BURKE: *"Nintendo 64."*

Notice Burke doesn't actually answer the question. The question is 'Did you get what you asked for'. Burke may have asked for a Nintendo 64 and gotten it, but had he wanted more? What's also evident is Burke shows no hesitation when asked about what he got – he knows exactly what he got for Christmas 20 years ago. Would you remember what you got for Christmas as a kid?

DR. PHIL: *"And what did JonBenét get?"*

BURKE: *"I think she got a dollhouse. We both got bikes."*

Someone seems to be lying. Is Patsy lying or Burke? In all our research there's virtually no talk about Burke getting a bike – Patsy doesn't say so, when Lou Smit asks John, John pertinently notes "Burke was getting one next year". And then BOOM, on Dr Phil Burke drops bikes back into the narrative. We think it's suspicious not only based on the itinerant psychology, but also because it contradicts numerous other versions given by both Burke's parents.

That being said, at one point John also backtracked and threw a third bicycle into the works.

From shakedowntitle.com:

SMIT: *Okay. Did you go to the Barnhill's to pick up a bike?*

JOHN: *Yeah, Christmas Eve. We'd given JonBenét a bike; we got Patsy a bike.* **We were giving Burke a bike but not that year.**

This is a specific detail that John remembers and offers up without prompting – they had made a decision that Burke wasn't getting a bike that year.

SMIT: *And how would you do that? What would you do to organize Christmas?*

JOHN: *Well, we'd get up, haul the presents and put them under the tree. And **a lot of the things were not wrapped so the kids had the surprise when they came down**. And we put those out and we got the bike.*

SMIT: *Where would you keep these bikes?*

JOHN: *They were usually in the basement. That was Patsy's department. But I think she kept them in that cellar room. We usually kept all of Christmas stuff in there. Our Christmas trees and lights and that stuff, the trim.*

SMIT: *So you think that somebody would have gone down to get those? Did you go down there?*

JOHN: *I don't remember specifically. I mean —*

John doesn't want to go down there not even in theory. Smit is asking John whether he needed to go down into the basement – the ground zero [supposedly] – of the murder. Had John been at ground zero? Could he place himself at the scene? Well if he could he didn't want to…

From shakedowntitle.com:

SMIT: *Kind of think about that because that's kind of important.* **Who was in the basement close to the time of Christmas?**

JOHN: *Well certainly we both would have been because Patsy did most of her wrapping down there. And that's where all the present stuff was stored. So in the process of getting ready for Christmas that would certainly have been down there and been in there. The only thing I remember is going over to Joe's and getting the bike out of his garage. And* *then after Patsy went upstairs, **I had her bike in our garage** and I got that out and put it by the tree. And then I went upstairs.*

Notice how John switches from the basement being where all the present stuff was stored, to suddenly shifting the bicycle storage to the garage. If one wants to surreptitiously move Christmas gifts into the lounge late at night or early morning, it would be a dang lot easier just to get them up from the basement [which could be secured, and where all the other gifts were] than from the garage, where they were also far more visible.

From shakedowntitle.com:

John is still crystal clear with his memory of only two bikes. He remembers exactly where they hid JonBenét's, as well as Patsy's, prior to Christmas day. If they had gotten a bike for Burke, wouldn't they have hidden that at the Barnhill's too?

SMIT: So both bikes then were at the tree. You just took the one from Joe Barnhill and put it by the tree?

JOHN: And brought Patsy's in from the garage.

SMIT: I was just wondering, like when you brought the bikes back in and Patsy was already in bed and then —

JOHN: Yeah.

One of the cardinal virtues of misdirection is allowing the listener to go with the flow and not adding unnecessary information when it seems like they are going with the flow. This is why when Larry King asks John and Patsy about the crime both wake up the next morning. JonBenét's death is reported as Christmas day, in other words the night of December 25th, but all the information we get from the Ramsey parents is about the morning after. It's another subtle misdirection in our opinion, but an important one.

The more brazen misdirections are those where out of nowhere a new narrative is thrown into the mix. Burke did it with Dr. Phil, we think, and here's an instance – in our view – of John doing it out of the blue with Lou Smit.

From shakedowntitle.com:

From John Ramsey's Interview with police in 1998:

SMIT: *Do you remember kind of what the kids got? What she [JonBenét] got?*

JOHN: *Well JonBenét got a bike. I think Burke got a bike too. It seems like we had three bikes there.*

SMIT: *And can you think of anything else?*

JOHN: ***They always get so much stuff.*** *I guess I don't remember. It's always kind of a **little bit overloaded with so many things.** I remember she did a little (INAUDIBLE) that night and a little jewelry maker wrapped up in little strips of paper and little beads. **I remember specifically playing that with her that evening, Christmas day evening.***

Does it seem as though John's laying it on a little thick here:

They always get so much stuff.

It's always kind of a little bit overloaded with so many things.

I remember specifically playing that with her that evening, Christmas day evening.

Let's be ridiculously clear about what we're getting at here: Lou Smit has just asked John a perfectly simple and innocent question. JonBenét got a bike, Burke [we don't think] got a bike, and yet Smit is pressing

John for more. In this line of questioning – around the bicycles – we feel something carefully hidden has been revealed.

They always get so much stuff.

It's always kind of a little bit overloaded with so many things.

I remember specifically playing that with her that evening, Christmas day evening.

While we believe there's revelation in these words, there's also more layers of misdirection. If we peeled them away what would they say?

Burke always got so much stuff [but not the Christmas of '96]

He's always been overloaded with so many things.

I remember specifically playing with JonBenét that Christmas day evening [and Burke?]

If this line of interrogation seems iffy, let's see what John himself writes about this area of the narrative [because he does] in his own narrative. Are you ready for this?

From shakedowntitle.com:

John peppers his answers with the phrase, I don't remember, yet he seems to remember a fair amount of details about what JonBenét got for Christmas that year, as well as her reactions. He even wrote about it in their book The Death of Innocence.

From acandyrose:

"The kids screamed and cheered as they realized that Santa had brought just about everything in their lists. JonBenét wanted to take

her new bike outside for a spin, but Burke suggested, "Let's get all the other gifts opened first."

If Burke had also received a bike, surely both of them would have wanted to get riding at the same time, right from the get go? This, we feel, is a narrative slip from John. Just as the cover-up of the crime has too many layers of cover-up [we feel], there's saying too much to address too little. Do that and you have a booboo – you've exposed your carefully crafted misdirection. Is that what happened here? Does that make sense?

From acandyrose:

*Ah, the wise and experienced big brother. **JonBenét agreed.** They quickly busied themselves playing Santa's elves and distributing the beautifully wrapped gifts. JonBenét **asked for Burke's assistance** with the name tags since he could read and she couldn't. It was **the most fun in the world**, doling out the gifts and seeing whose pile would become the biggest."*

This feels like John laying on the yuletide harmony in the Ramsey home a bit thick, doesn't it? It's the same thing all over again – the siblings getting along like a house on fire, especially JonBenét. She agrees with Burke, she asks Burke to help her, they have the most fun in the world. And behind the scenes of this perfect Christmas portrait, and its blinding white Christmas star atop the Ramsey tree, is an invisible third bicycle, which Burke only now says he got for Christmas too. Yet John forgets to mention Burke's phantom bicycle [including in his book] then "seems to remember" Burke. John and Burke remember the third bicycle but Patsy never mentions it. Why?

Let's assume Burke didn't get a bicycle and that JonBenét did, and move on. Keep the phantom bicycle in the back of your mind as we pedal forward.

From acandyrose.com:

HANEY: *What special things would John do, say, with Burke, I guess they were both in the plan. What do they do together?*

PATSY: *They build models and trains and cars. And **Boy Scouts**. Homework. Yard, and they built a tree house, John built a tree house for Burke. And – climbing, you know, trail hiking in the (INAUDIBLE).*

HANEY: *How about John with JonBenét, did they do any special things together? Is there anything that she liked dad to take her to do?*

PATSY: *Well, she loved her dad to be around all the time. You know, she liked John to carry her up on his shoulders. And they liked to bike-ride. And he went to the pageants.*

This may seem like harmless waffle, but notice what Patsy reveals. John and Burke build things together, including a tree house. They have a mutual connection to boy scouts. And hiking? Do you see where this is going? Now let's take it a step further, and hoist our platform a little higher.

From acandyrose.com:

KANE: *Okay. Let me jump around a little bit here. The train room, you know what I mean when I say the train room, is that what you guys called it? There was a train set down there? What was that? I know you said that there was a lot of storage down there and from looking at it on the diagram, it was – actually looks like there was a little bit of a divider in there so it was two different rooms. Where was, you said there were a lot of things stored. Where were they stored?*

JOHN: *Well, we had, this used to be an elevator shaft and that was like the electronics for the elevator, so that's – we were kind of stuck with that when we bought the house, so we had stuff stored in those closets.*

Some of the stuff "stored" in the elevator shaft appears to be a tangle of junior golf clubs.

From acandyrose.com:

JOHN: *There was stuff, I think we had some shelving installed, here, here, stuff stacked on shelving. There was a little bookcase here. What's that is? Usually had junk in it.*

KANE: *Did the kids play there?*

JOHN: *They played, Burke of course played with the train off and on. Sometimes he would play back here. **Not a lot, but once in a while.***

KANE: *Was it primarily used for storage and–*

JOHN: *Yeah.*

KANE: *And did they play with the trains at all?*

JOHN: *Yeah, Burke did a lot.*

Here's another contradiction. According to John Burke wasn't down in the basement much…but then John seems to remember, well if he was playing with his trains he must have been down there a lot… and goes with the flow.

From acandyrose.com:

KANE: *Do you remember the day after this happened, being on the phone talking to someone about getting your **golf clubs**?*

JOHN: *No. Absolutely not.*

Having studied these folks in detail in many interviews, what I notice is when a particularly iffy question comes up, both father and son answer with a telling "absolute" denial. A simple yes or no will suffice. In *The Craven Silence 3* we'll deal with a small collection of "absolutely nots" and see what these may reveal.

From acandyrose.com:

KANE: *Okay. From what I have, JonBenét had an injury at one time to her face. What do you know about that?*

JOHN: *Burke was up at the lake and Burke was in the yard swinging a golf club, and she walked up either in front of him or behind him,* **I was not there***, and she got clobbered. It was* ***a pure accident.***

A pure accident? What's a "pure" accident compared to any other accident?

From acandyrose.com:

KANE: *Where did you hear about that?*

JOHN: *Oh, Patsy called me.*

KANE: *You were out of town?*

JOHN: *Yes, I was – she was at the lake, I might have been in Boulder, I don't remember.* **I was not there.**

KANE: *I guess this was another – Burke went to school after this. Had a black eye. Do you know anything about that?*

JOHN: *Um, he got – there's a picture of him in his baseball uniform with a real shiner and he had gotten a black eye playing baseball. He was a fielder and "I got1 it, I got, I got it", clunk.*

KANE: *Was it during a game?*

JOHN: *Yeah.*

KANE: *As part of – (MULTIPLE SPEAKERS.)*

JOHN: *Yes, it was part of the league he was in, a practice or a game.*

KANE: ***You weren't there?***

JOHN: *No.*

KANE: *Where did you hear about it?*

JOHN: *Patsy told me about it.*

KANE: *Okay.*

JOHN: *But he got conked by a... because [of the] ball. It should have been in the glove but he missed it.*

KANE: *You never heard it was **Patsy that threw the ball**?*

A theme that comes up again and again is John being away. In one of Patsy's Christmas videos inviting Boulder residents into the family home she also adds "John's away". But was he away enough for it to amount to neglect? And if so, was it a kind of benign neglect or... something other?

Linda Wilcox has asserted that Patsy's job was to prevent the kids from "disturbing" John. That suggests a form of neglect that's hardly benign, doesn't it? John's disappearance on Christmas Day for 3-4 hours while the kids played with friends at the house is noteworthy in this regard as well.

Let's turn our attention back to Patsy, and the night of December 25th.

From acandyrose.com:

PATSY: *And the children were going to eat at their own table and [Priscilla White] had several tables set up for the adults, and I remember her saying that she specifically held some out for JonBenét so JonBenét would get some of this crab. I don't think –*

HANEY: *Two?*

PATSY: *Well, my children both like seafood and she wanted to make sure that – my presumption was she didn't want us all to eat and the kids not get any. But why she said specifically JonBenét, and not Fleet and Burke, I don't know.*

Could it be that if some sought-after food was put out for JonBenét and Burke, Burke would take JonBenét's too? Had there been an underground battle raging between the siblings about food – about chocolates and helpings and pieces of pineapple? Was the bickering about food merely a symptom of much deeper stirrings of anger and outrage? Of being "materially" malnourished?

The Black Star in the Basement

'I come to you last who are not last in my thoughts.
For you I have prepared this.' She held up a small
crystal phial: it glittered as she moved it, and rays
of white light sprang from her hand. 'In this phial…
is caught the light of Eärendil's star…. It will shine…
when night is about you. May it be a light to you in
dark places, when all other lights go out.'
— J.R.R. Tolkien, The Two Towers

We're almost done. We're almost ready to deal with another reconstruction and see if we have what it takes to navigate our way to the golden thread. Can we use it to draw open the seal and break open *The Craven Silence* buried in the box beneath? We believe we can. We believe we're almost there.

From acandyrose.com:

HANEY: *Okay. Anything else on those photos, 41, 42?*

PATSY: *They made Burke's [16] bed, that's unusual.*

In crime scene photos what's obvious is the messiness of JonBenét's bedroom, and in particular her bed. Does that look like a bed someone recently slept in? Do you – does anyone – sleep in a bed covered in clothing and other detritus?

Burkes' bed by contrast is nicely made up – this despite the fact that he slept in it, and was [apparently] roused early in the morning.

What sort of moron went and made Burke's bed after he'd slept in it in the middle of a crisis? Well, if it wasn't a moron it was misdirection, wasn't it? Wasn't the bed made to get rid of evidence not just of Burke, but JonBenét? Were washed sheets and washed blankets used to replace sheets and blankets that might be covered in Burke's – and JonBenét's – DNA? Whatever is the case it's extremely sinister that Burke's bed should be made and JonBenét's undone.

We feel especially strongly on this point because we doubt whether JonBenét ever went to bed that night. We also think the pillow on the kitchen counter is a calculated aspect of this misdirection. What more than that?

From acandyrose.com:

HANEY: *And that's one of the things, we are trying to work some of this in as we go through the photos, obviously, but* **have you seen changes in Burke** *since the incident?*

PATSY: *Um, he's grown like a weed. I think he's a little more cautious...*

Well this is classic Patsy. After his sister's death Burke couldn't be better. Well whaddaya know! The little tyke is happier than ever. He's growing etc. etc.

But that's not what Haney's fishing at Patsy. Even if Burke is innocent, the question is how has the incident changed him? And implicit in this question isn't the idea how well Burke has bounced back now that JonBenét is out of the picture.

The other aspect of Patsy's answer does address the psychology, and as such is damning in our view.

I think he's a little more cautious...

If Burke did bludgeon his sister in a fit of pique, and not an isolated tantrum either, then it may seem like good, responsible parenting to observe that naughty Burke has learnt his lesson. He's become "more cautious"....

Now let's venture into the darkest of dark places, the euphemistically named "wine cellar". In fact it was little more than an unpainted tomb, a point of no return for JonBenét, and an extremity of the Ramsey home where a body might be dumped and it might not seem like its residents had anything to with it.

As we descend the stairs to the wine cellar we must ponder: if the Ramseys – all three of them – were responsible for JonBenét's death, it would explain why they didn't dump the child's corpse outside in the elements. It would certainly improve their appearances of culpability if JonBenét's body were found outside, even *just* outside.

In this we have a similar, and it must be added bizarre, conscientious effort across two dimensions:

First it is the brutal dispatching of a child, followed by the gentle covering in a blanket and protection and care of a temporary tomb.

Second is the carefully executed Ransom Note. The carefully crafted spelling mistakes in the beginning give way to an impressively neat and considerate missive [which no one ultimately pays much attention to].

Did the Ramseys count on the possibility of perhaps disposing of JonBenét's body later, once the crowds had left? Was this why there was an emphasis on the idea of there not being a body available for "proper burial".

And now we're ready to step into the wine cellar.

From acandyrose.com:

PATSY: *Okay. You know, it wasn't like a full-blown wine cellar, but we kept a couple boxes of wine in there. And I want to say that – I don't remember whether it was the night of the 23rd, that party or some party we had, I remember somebody saying we are out of red wine. And I said please (inaudible) to or something. But at some time, please go to the basement to get some more red wine, but he would know where that was.*

HANEY: *Okay.*

PATSY: *This guy named Bob Ballis (phonetic) who did some Christmas decorations, he made these things, you know, a year or more before when we had the Christmas open house. He would know about that.*

DEMUTH: *My question is: Who had been in that room prior to Christmas of '96, Bob Ballis, was he the Christmas of '95?*

PATSY: *Yeah. Right.*

DEMUTH: *Okay. In the months prior to Christmas of 1996 Fleet would have gone in there?*

PATSY: *I would say Fleet, the cleaning lady[49] and –*

DEMUTH: *Maybe the husband?*

PATSY: *Maybe the husband and maybe the daughter.*

DEMUTH: *How about yourself?*

PATSY: *Me, taking hiding.*

It's a cryptic trio of words isn't it, given what we're dealing with? Again this is classic Patsy referring to herself going into the basement, the room in which her daughter was found murdered and she uses the

---

49 Linda Hoffman-Pugh.

words "taking" and "hiding" to describe her own actions. DeMuth alas seems to miss this slip. He could misdirect her misdirection by simply suggesting: "Taking JonBenét? Hiding JonBenét?"

From acandyrose.com:

DEMUTH: *Would the children go in there?*

PATSY: *No.* **If I had presents in there** **I would have** **locked it up.**

DEMUTH: *They couldn't reach that?*

PATSY: *No.*

HANEY: *What else was stored there?*

PATSY: *That is what I was trying to think of. I had a little bicycle of Burke's, a little Batman, the first bicycle with little tiny wheels. I couldn't bear to part with that. Part of it was broken, I think.*

HANEY: *The last time you were in the wine cellar was Christmas Eve, Christmas day.*

PATSY: *Probably Christmas Eve bringing packages out.*

HANEY: *Would there have been any reason for you to go back in there on Christmas day or did you go back in there?*

PATSY: *No, I don't believe I did. No.*

HANEY: *Okay. And on Christmas Eve, when you went in there –*

PATSY: *No.*

HANEY: *–this [JonBenét in a blanket] wasn't there?*

PATSY: *No.*

HANEY: *How about the blanket?*

PATSY: *No.*

DEMUTH: *If we could go back, [we] kind of skipped over a couple of pictures here, 145.*

PATSY: *There is the bicycle.*

DEMUTH: *I have a question for you, 148 here.*

PATSY: *These were **gifts I think I was holding back for Burke's birthday**.*

DEMUTH: *They are in the red and white and yellow FAO Schwartz wrapping?*

PATSY: *Right.*

DEMUTH: *Now in 148 there is also this white pocket, do you know what that is?*

PATSY: *Huh-uh, it looks like cotton. I don't know.*

DEMUTH: *Okay. It is hard to sort of figure out where all of these pictures are taken, but **there is another package over here.***

PATSY: *Uh-huh.*

DEMUTH: *Does that look out of place or in the proper place?*

PATSY: *Well, I had – you know, I stacked up some packages along there (inaudible). Kicked (inaudible) or something. I kind of have it backed up here.*

DEMUTH: *Okay. So the packages in 146, it looks like it is out of place to you?*

PATSY: *Uh-huh. Yeah. See, that looks – the door would be here.*

DEMUTH: *It is hard.*

PATSY: So *that would be back in here somewhere. I was right in front of the door.*

DEMUTH: *No. Here are the screens. You see* <u>the screens over here</u>, *the small screens, so it is more back in this.*

PATSY: *Yeah. I would tuck them there.*

DEMUTH: *I guess the point is, there wasn't one that was off by itself. They should have all been together. The location in picture 148 is the correct place for all of the packages to have been?*

PATSY: *Right.*

HANEY: *Before we go on, could we just talk briefly about the packages, these were presents for whom, the ones that were left in there?*

PATSY: *I believe for, you know, I held some back for Burke's birthday which is in January.*

DEMUTH: *Okay.*

HANEY: *So that could have been that.*

PATSY: *Yeah. I don't remember what was in them.*

HANEY: *Would any of these packages be opened?*

PATSY: *Probably. Well, see, these came up, I was at FAO Schwartz in New York when JonBenét and I were up there for a trip, and I had them sent back to Boulder **and they wrapped them, free gift wrapping.** So like right here it looks like **I kind of peeled a little back to see what was in it because I couldn't remember what was in them.***

DEMUTH: *If the wrapping has been undone partially, that was –*

PATSY: *I probably would have done that to peek to see what was in there.*

DEMUTH: *Okay.*

Okay? If we're on the right track, if Burke peeled away the wrapping on his gift and got into trouble, we may have stumbled on aggravating circumstances if not a motive for murder.

The Scream and the Silence

Starry, starry night
Portraits hung in empty halls
Frame-less heads on nameless walls
With eyes that watch the world and can't forget —
Vincent/Starry Starry Night by Don McLean

Three Two small unopened boxes are piled on top of each other. One is red, the bottom box is green. We only have time left to pick one and open it. But which do we pick, and what do the colors mean?

I reach for the green box and open it. There's a dead twig inside. When I reach for it the whole room seems to dissolve into dark matter. The grainy darkness of the room fizzles into swirling flurries laden with history and meaning. The black snow beneath the dark star of the Christmas Tree swirls…

There is a town set against high mountains filled with bicycle paths.

A boy's life is baseball, basketball and golf.

A very fine snow is falling.

A boy starts to eat pineapple from a bowl. His mother sips tea from a glass.

"JonBenét it's time for bed," the mother says. When everyone is upstairs, the mischievous boy abandons his bowl and sneaks downstairs into the basement. He's not supposed to be here, he's been expressly forbidden, but no one will catch him.

There are more presents stashed there, _presents meant for him_. He'd thought he'd get them for Christmas, but whatever's left will be his in three weeks because his birthday is January 20th.

He can't resist a peek. He wants to see what they are.

"I kind of peeled a little back to see what was in it..."

"BOOO!"

He starts violently. But it's only her! He sees _the little girl has been spying on him_, catching him red handed. _She loves to play pranks_, and she's succeeded in this one: her appearance shocks him and makes her chuckle with delight. In a flash the boy's shock turns to anger.

He's not supposed to be here, but neither is she.

He's fuming at this intrusion, yet another, and sensing his rising ire, the little blonde girl makes a hasty retreat, teasing, "I'm going to tell on you..."

She doesn't run upstairs. Though she's supposed to be in bed, she giggles instead. She thinks _it's a game_ and she's played it before.

He will chase her _around the train room_, but she's fast enough now to elude him. If she can't escape, a scream will alert her parents. Either way she'll beat him at his own game.

And she does.

The boy feels bile building in his throat. He can't catch her. He runs one way, she darts the other. His chest burns. He needs _something to put_ *a stop to this humiliation, and as the thought rises his eyes catch on his golf clubs against the basement wall, right beside his father's.*

The girl, seeing the club being drawn out of the bag like a sword, becomes afraid and stumbles against the carefully crafted train structure – breaking it.

She's been hit with a club like that before…[50]

Rattled by the appearance of the same weapon, JonBenét stumbles and screams, a piercing yell.

"YYYYIIIIIIIIIIIEEEEEEEEEEEEEEEEEEEE………………"

To silence her, to silence his own demons the boy wallops her – a mighty blow for a boy.

The meaty noise is a satisfying sound in the boy's ears as the club splits her skull.

Although she lies motionless on the basement floor the little girl seems uninjured; she seems to be sleeping…

She's silent.

His ears are still ringing.

She lies on the basement floor like a giant doll.

She doesn't move.

He smiles as he prods her, thinking this is another prank. But then fear takes over. Worried he might be in trouble, he prods her back hard, agitated, with a piece of broken railway track.

---

50 While staying at their home the exclusive resort community of Charlevoix, Michigan, Burke hit JonBenét in the face with a golf club. This occurred within a day or two of her fourth birthday in August 1994. The blow to her cheek required stitches and two months later, plastic surgery.

"JonnieB! JonnieB!"

His heart starts beating a mile a minute. He <u>pokes her again</u>, harder, <u>against her neck</u> believing she's bluffing, but she still doesn't move, doesn't seem to breathe.

Suddenly <u>Patsy is there</u>. Suddenly there's slow motion. <u>Golf clubs</u> are <u>stashed</u> in the <u>elevator shaft</u>. The one in Burke's hand is plucked away. Patsy's lips move but he can't hear anything. He gathers he must go to his room and stay there.

For the rest of the night he hears muffled noises. There's soft sobbing mingled with earnest whispering and chatter.

He slips into and out of sleep, a mixture of excitement and terror swimming through his veins. Beneath his feet a throne seems to rise out of the ether. It brings a wry smile to his face. He pulls out his Nintendo64, and presses START. At least there is no one to interrupt him now...

That is the green box. It's closer to where we mean to be, but is it quite there?

Something like a song drifts through the silent night...

<u>*The ragged men*</u> *in ragged clothes*

The silver thorn of bloody rose

Lie crushed and broken on the virgin snow...

I close the lid. We're back in the dark, in the basement with <u>a lifeless doll</u> and a barely visible black star. It swivels in the dark. It swivels over the red box. The red square appears dull and grey in the half light of the basement.

My shoe touches the edge of the towel, dirtying it. I pull it back, my foot, the shoe. I look to the red box but I dare not open it yet.

Suddenly a colossal darkness descends upon everything, envelopes her body, envelopes me. Like a vast wave of death it swims over me and then swallows <u>the little girl</u> and the house and the town whole in the maw of that maelstrom. Then it withdraws. Like a black wave on a volcanic beach, the wave washes back making the Earth slip beneath my feet, or me slip across the Earth – I'm not sure which.

Which direction is which? Where is up, where is down, which way is this, which way is that? Like Alice tumbling up through the rabbit hole, my arms and legs spider outwards, fingers spider even more in search of something to grab onto.

A silver thread, as though spun from fishing reel unravels out of the green box. Like a strand of moonlight the strand beckons. Like the tiniest of hands with the slimmest of fingers it cajoles. Do we choose to take this silver thread?

We do not.

I spin end over end through dark oblivion, through silent whorls of snow. I become a swimmer, stuck in the black ooze of a Van Gogh piece of art. But somewhere in that ooze I spy a golden vein. Does the final answer brood in the last unopened box, somewhere in the suburban murk far below? Do we dare to open it? We must. Because though it is closed slim veins prickle with fairy dust. Then gradually <u>the surface begins to burn everywhere with stars.</u>

Acknowledgements

In order to piece together this narrative, we've cast a wide net. We've drawn on information from a number of forums, documentaries and online resources which have been cited. We gratefully acknowledge the suggestions and support we've received from our readers while on this journey towards justice. Please report errors, omissions or corrections directly to @lisawJ13.

About the Authors

Lisa Wilson (aka Juror13) *is a trial blogger who resides in California, USA. She's a marketer by day and true crime maestro by night.*

After years of discussing cases online with fellow armchair detectives and trial watchers, Lisa started her own blog in 2013. Since then, she and Nick van der Leek have formed a True Crime-themed partnership. Under the #Shakedown banner they have begun conducting deep investigations into the narratives of Oscar Pistorius, Jodi Arias, O.J. Simpson and Amanda Knox cases, and have co-authored several books on these criminals, with many more in the works.

Follow Lisa on Twitter at @lisawJ13

Please follow #Shakedown @Shakedowntitle and at https://www.facebook.com/shakedowntitle/

Nick van der Leek *is the author of over 100 narratives including the 13-part true crime series on the Oscar Pistorius Trial and co-author of a series of six books interrogating the Jodi Arias trial.*

Besides books and freelance photojournalism Nick is a professional photographer and passionate sportsman. In another life he climbed Mount Kilimanjaro, rafted the Zambezi and completed the Ironman.

If you've found The Craven Silence a worthwhile read, look out for <u>The Craven Silence 2</u>.

Join Nick van der Leek and the True Crime Rocket Science community on Patreon at www.patreon.com/TCRS.

Printed in Great Britain
by Amazon

58284356R00175